★ THE ★
RENEGADE
SPORTSMAN

★ THE ★

RENEGADE
SPORTSMAN

Drunken Runners, Bike Polo Superstars,

Roller Derby Rebels, Killer Birds, and Other Uncommon

Thrills on the Wild Frontier of Sports

ZACH DUNDAS

RIVERHEAD BOOKS

New York

RIVERHEAD BOOKS
Published by the Penguin Group
Penguin Group (USA) Inc.
375 Hudson Street, New York, New York 10014, USA
Penguin Group (Canada), 90 Eglinton Avenue East, Suite 700, Toronto, Ontario M4P 2Y3, Canada (a division of Pearson Penguin Canada Inc.)
Penguin Books Ltd., 80 Strand, London WC2R 0RL, England
Penguin Group Ireland, 25 St. Stephen's Green, Dublin 2, Ireland
(a division of Penguin Books Ltd.)
Penguin Group (Australia), 250 Camberwell Road, Camberwell, Victoria 3124, Australia
(a division of Pearson Australia Group Pty. Ltd.)
Penguin Books India Pvt. Ltd., 11 Community Centre, Panchsheel Park, New Delhi—110 017, India
Penguin Group (NZ), 67 Apollo Drive, Rosedale, North Shore 0632, New Zealand
(a division of Pearson New Zealand Ltd.)
Penguin Books (South Africa) (Pty.) Ltd., 24 Sturdee Avenue, Rosebank, Johannesburg 2196, South Africa

Penguin Books Ltd., Registered Offices: 80 Strand, London WC2R 0RL, England

Copyright © 2010 Zach Dundas
Cover design by Benjamin Gibson
Book design by Tiffany Estreicher

First Riverhead trade paperback edition: June 2010

Library of Congress Cataloging-in-Publication Data

Dundas, Zach.
The renegade sportsman : drunken runners, bike polo superstars, roller derby rebels, killer birds, and other uncommon thrills on the wild frontier of sports / Zach Dundas.
        p.   cm.
Includes bibliographical references.
ISBN 978-1-59448-456-8
1. Sports—United States—Anecdotes. 2. Sports—United States—Miscellanea. I. Title.
GV583. D8 2010
796.0973—dc22   2009050489

PRINTED IN THE UNITED STATES OF AMERICA

10 9 8 7 6 5 4 3 2 1

For Christina and Cash

INTRODUCTION

RENEGADEWORLD

Not long ago, I attended one of my favorite sporting events ever. In a boggy patch of forest outside my home city of Portland, Oregon, filthy bicyclists splashed through mires and up muddy hillsides. A few hundred fans, bundled against a damp autumn afternoon, crowded along a serpentine race-course, screaming like asylum inmates and devouring free beer. Grimy but friendly dogs scampered around. A foreboding figure called El Diablo, a man wearing a blue cape and four one-foot-long blue foam spikes on his head, brandished a plastic trident as he stumbled on and off the course, menacing the riders at the crest of the steepest hill.

Somehow, *SportsCenter*, Jim Rome, Stephen A. Smith, Bob Costas, Deadspin, CBS SportsLine, all major newspaper sports pages, and every other recognized sports-media outlet missed the World Single-Speed Cyclocross Championship. Cyclocross, a rustic form of bike racing that combines grueling obstacles, hellacious ascents and descents, a fetish for bad weather, athletic masochism, and rabid beer consumption, lives on a very distant orbit of the American sporting cosmos. 'Cross races take place all over the U.S., but the sport's spiritual heartland is—well, Belgium, or somewhere like that. More Americans probably get arrested on drunk-and-disorderly charges during a weekend's worth of NFL games than have ever heard of cyclocross. Too bad; a good 'cross race makes other spectator experiences seem bland. On the other hand, the fact that the World Single-Speed Championship played to an exclusive crowd just meant more free beer to go around.

The championship wrapped up a long day of competition called the Cross Crusade, which calls itself the world's largest participatory cyclocross series. The day's races involved kids, men, women, complete novices, and some of the country's best pro cyclocross riders (they do exist). At the start line of the World Single-Speed Championship, a race for both men and women, riders copped swigs from fans' bottles. Female spectators in all-black cheerleader-cum-dominatrix outfits shrieked and waved pom-poms. By the middle of the race, El Diablo achieved top form, bellowing at the juncture of the course that attracted the densest knot of fans. We fans jostled about eighteen inches from passing cyclists. We also served as an aid station. At first, an assembly line ferried little waxed cups of beer to the front row, where riders grabbed them as they passed. Soon, that system collapsed, and someone just jammed a line of full, open bottles of MacTarnahan's Ale into the mud. Racers swooped down and grabbed bottles as they rode past—except for the guy who decided to drop his bike and sit down in the mud while he guzzled one.

Gratis microbrew aside, I trekked out to this grubby patch of timber to follow a hunch: I sensed that the World Single-Speed Cyclocross Championship, despite (because of, actually) its off-the-cuff air, just might embody a certain kind of sporting excellence. A couple days before, I'd talked to the Cross Crusade race director, Brad Ross. "A few of us were sitting around drinking beer, and someone commented that, for all of the world championship events out there, there's no single-speed 'cross championship," he said. Given the mysterious popularity of one-gear bikes among the pain-loving cyclocross demographic, Ross and friends decided to fill the gap. "Some ideas are just too brilliant to be stopped, man. We put it out there, and some of the websites that are kind of the custodians of single-speed objected a little bit, but pretty soon I think we reached some consensus. If this isn't the world championship, there isn't one."

What's not to love? Yes, some prefer their competitive athletes sober, aerodynamically shaved, and honed to a pitiless muscular edge. They prefer their events "organized." As a blast of foam from a botched fan-to-rider beer handoff sprayed across my face, I decided this thinking is distressingly narrow, and that the cyclocrossers had discovered a better way. No billionaire team owners prowled the sidelines making spectacles of themselves. No middle-aged rock stars played during intermission. No athletes brought their posses, their agents, or their personal masseurs. Instead of pricey concessions and midseason-NBA-style apathy, the Cross Crusade offered mud, rain, S&M cheerleaders, mutts everywhere, fans and athletes thrown into the same near chaos, pros tossed in against amateurs, girls against boys, drunks indistinguishable from heroes. It was raw and alive in a way no major-league arena experience ever could be. From this hillside, I could see a new, free sports world—a world I'd been searching out for quite some time.

For much of my life, my relationship with sports was fraught and unrequited, like a romance in an enormous, weepy, excruciatingly detailed novel about nineteenth-century repression in which the heroine, deprived of her life's love by Society's cruel strictures, flings herself off a cliff or beneath moving iron wheels on page 572. Some people are natural athletes. Others achieve sporting greatness through hard work. And some people spend most of their childhood and early adolescence in their bedrooms, reading Sherlock Holmes stories and memorizing lists of early Olympic champions, then find themselves unable to make the middle school basketball team.

Not like I'm bitter or ashamed or anything. Still, my personal athletic career began with almost-total failure to develop any physical abilities whatsoever. To make matters worse, I grew up in Montana, a paradise of muscular fun, where it requires active effort *not* to learn to shoot deer, navigate Class V rapids, ski black diamond runs, haul in creels stuffed with rainbow trout, or survive in the wild off lichen and huckleberries. My hometown, Missoula, also harbors a mid-major university and the sports mania that goes with it. None of this prevented me from reaching young adulthood in a frail and "artistic" condition.

Personal failings aside, however, I was always interested in sports—a huge fan, in fact, willing, at a tender age, to spend hours in subarctic conditions watching our beloved University of Montana Grizzlies lose football games. I just managed to miss every single cultural cue that might have turned me into an athlete myself. Instead, I became a standard-issue teenage dissident, writing snotty columns for the school paper, cranking out would-be subversive zines, playing in a punk band, and wearing flannel. I remained a fan, but it often seemed an awkward fit.

A herd of boorish talk-radio louts dominated sports media. Even as the demographics of some major leagues became more interesting, with Latinos taking over baseball and Euros colonizing the NBA, American sports fandom still seemed resolutely provincial. Football, the least foreigner-corrupted team game, came to rule American sports to such a degree that baseball sometimes seemed like a cast-off TV replacement series, biding time between the Super Bowl and NFL preseason. NASCAR harked back to baseball's golden age . . . at least in the sense that it featured many, many white dudes. If I closed my eyes and envisioned the American sports nation at the turn of the century, I saw an unappetizing picture: a bunch of dudes obsessing over fantasy football and calling their local sports-talk shows— every one, coast to coast, exactly the same—to make fun of the WNBA, tennis, or soccer. These were not my people . . . and yet I still wanted to belong. Somehow.

As for the athletes, owners, coaches, agents, and other clowns in the circus—well, what can you say? Indicting American sports for gross misbehavior and moral bankruptcy is so easy, it pretty much amounts to cheating. Any sports columnist, pundit, or blogger starved for copy can always tap the nation's nostalgia for the mythical days when They Played for the Love of the Game. And what? You say the owners are venal plutocrats? That no rule is sacred when money's at stake? That amateurism is a bleak joke when twelve-year-old baseball phenoms are forbidden to skateboard, lest they damage the merchandise? I am *shocked*, sir. Most fans realize, about the time they hit puberty, that serious competitive sports constitute a completely amoral realm. Major-league wrongdoing bothers us in the abstract, but not in practice.

My problem with sports didn't have much to do with Barry Bonds's mysterious late-career cranial development, the comportment of Pacman Jones, the New England Patriots' industrial espionage, or any other of the innumerable offenses against common decency committed in sports' name. After the age of eighteen, I no longer actively feared being pummeled by jocks. (Usually.) My problem was with the whole thing, the entire vast situation, the all-too-predictable dynamics of the sports-industrial complex itself. I was bored. Sports and I needed to renegotiate, and I suspected that in that feeling, I was not alone.

Amazing, what you learn with your head jammed between two rugby players' thighs. It was a dank October evening, and I was at work on a story about the Oregon Jesters women's rugby team. They invited me out to a practice, and at the coach's suggestion, I brought my soccer cleats. I soon found myself ordered to crouch on the scummy turf, then to wedge my head between the legs of two players in front of me. These women—a "prop" and a "hooker," and please feel free to make up your own jokes—applied a stubbly vise grip to my skull, pressing from each side in an apparent effort to reduce my ears to pulp. Then, I reached up between my new friends' legs to grab the waistbands of their grit-spackled shorts.

I heard the hooker growl. "Grab crotch, not hair," she said. "It sucks when that happens."

Okay.

Intimate arrangements complete, we formed a compact human battering ram, or "scrum." We smashed full-force into an iron sled called the Dominator. The Dominator looked like something that would be useful in taking out a Frankish castle. My face was about a foot above the ground, and I could only hear barnyard squelching as we hurled ourselves against this torture device.

Thirty seconds later, I wobbled to my feet.

"Well done, rookie," the prop said. "Well done." I nodded my head, now smaller, in gratitude.

The Jesters practiced on a sprawling complex of unkempt fields bordered by strip malls and industrial parks. In keeping with these rough environs, the squad was a mix 'n' match band of sports outsiders: thirty-something moms, butch tough girls, young professionals with braided pigtails. "Most of these girls don't come from the jock crowd," a veteran told me later. "They never fit in. And then they find this incredibly accepting sport, where size doesn't matter, athletic ability doesn't necessarily matter, and a lot of factors that might keep you down socially are actually cherished."

The Jesters' turf, once grass, was now reduced to oozy, foul-smelling black muck. From here, I could see the outermost edge of the sports world. Lacrosse players bellowed on the next field over. Just over the rugby field's boundary, two guys were exercising attack dogs. A few street lamps, orange and hazy in the perpetual Portland mist, provided the only light. I felt like I was in the right place, even though I hadn't expected near decapitation.

I guess Dominator-related damage fell into the category of occupational hazard.

I was writing about my newfound rugby friends for Portland's weekly newspaper, which drafted me out of Montana to edit its music section in 1999. Not long after I arrived in Portland—perhaps feeling that an endless diet of underfed, emotionally bereft indie-rock bands threatened to sap the zest from life—I started badgering my employer to assign me sports stories. My editors agreed to let me cover this self-declared beat, under the mistaken impression that I would generate actual news about sports of interest to the public at large. I planned to do the opposite. I went to soccer bars at five a.m. to watch games from Europe, in the company of large and very intoxicated gentlemen painted the colors of the Scottish flag. I covered bike messenger races and an adult soapbox derby. I profiled the best amateur female boxer I could find. I dug up the city's most insane/intrepid "adventure" racer, a man fresh off the Centers for Disease Control's watch list after contracting one of the more exotic tropical fevers while swimming a Borneo river infested with nine-foot cobras. While this direction didn't exactly fit my editors' definition of breaking news, I felt I had pierced the polished surface of mainstream sports. And that was before the thing with the rugby players' thighs.

Meanwhile, I was also assembling my own gawky, late-bloomer athletic career. I humiliated myself at indoor soccer arenas across the Portland metro area. The young woman who worked in the next cubicle over—a sporty type, a veteran of the NCAA Division III field hockey Final Four—inveigled me into running the annual Hood to Coast Relay, a brutal mass self-flagellation that involves pounding down remote mountain roads, by foot, at three o'clock in the morning. As my body protested every step and the icy, high-altitude air of the Coast Range caused a variety of unpleasant shivers and contractions, I wondered why the hell I was doing this. Then it occurred to me that I might be in love. Before long, I found myself following that same girl onto a blazing AstroTurf field, carrying an odd stick. Portland's field hockey scene proved quite a demographic discovery. Besides my future wife, my teammates included devout (and very male) Pakistani Muslims, brawny South Africans (both genders), Smith College-y jockettes, one very polite Anglo-Icelandic fellow (an ethnicity of one!), and a few other wayward American guys. It was almost a perfect society, but any moment I found myself distracted by our potential to solve the clash of civilizations, the rock-hard ball ricocheted off my shin.

What did it mean, all this fumbling around the margins of sports? I thought I detected faint but definite tremors, something stirring underground. Yes, the major leagues now achieved new frontiers in hype and pomp every season. But what if, at the same time, a secret revolution was taking shape? What if a whole alternative sporting nation—a more perfect union of independent athletes, nonconformist fans, wildcat leagues, and guerrilla clubs scattered across the country—could rise up to challenge the mainstream? I began to dream big, imagining that a total inversion of the sports power structure was occuring just out of sight, somewhere near the rugby practice field.

Instead of gawping at highlights on the nearest high-def screen, my sports revolutionaries and I would form our own leagues, inventing new games or hijacking old ones for our own amusement. Instead of following corporate franchises owned by billionaires and staffed by millionaires, we would form our own clubs, which would emphasize the joys of hanging out as much as the thrill of competition. Instead of consulting our liability lawyers before setting foot outside, we would swagger through life, staging recreational sword fights and plunging down toboggan hills. Rather than worshipping distant, media-created superstars, we would take sports into our own hands.

I admit that it sounds a little far-fetched and dreamy, but I knew vaguely similar upheavals happened before. If you think about it, major-league sports could be the athletic equivalent of stadium rock—the production values are awesome, but the scale is alienating, the egos enormous. The bitchy psychodramas of the Kobe/Shaq Lakers recalled Fleetwood Mac in full wife-swapping meltdown mode. Tiger Woods once reminded me of James Taylor in his brand excellence; now we know he's more like a less interesting one-man Mötley Crüe. The Beijing Olympics' over-the-top grandiosity not only recalled the ten-minute drum solo in *The Song Remains the Same*—Zeppelin actually played the closing ceremony. The excesses of stadium rock, of course, inspired the punk-rock reaction, a stripped-down rebuke that insisted that anyone who could play three chords could—and should—form a band. Now, I thought, the same thing could happen in sports! The renegade sportsmen and women of America would come together to create a DIY insurgency, a spiky home-brewed antidote to the macroblandness of the Show. I pictured a future in which every city would celebrate the tattooed women of its hometown roller derby team at least as much as the tattooed mercenaries on its NBA squad. Just about every other sector of what you might call the "culture industry" is in the midst of a radical decentralization. Sports still operate on the old twentieth-century model, run by a few closed cartels. My fantasy rebellion would change that.

I also imagined the rebirth of a sporting tradition different from our standard-issue model. Strangely (and nerdily) enough, I thought of my old pal Sherlock Holmes—the prototypical independent oddball, whose portfolio included not only the ability to identify different brands of cigarette by their ash, but fencing, a distinguished amateur boxing career, a combat pursuit called "single-stick," and "baritsu, the Japanese system of wrestling." (Guy Ritchie's recent Hollywood makeover of the character emphasized these muscular traits.) In real life, Sir Arthur Conan Doyle, Sherlock's creator, played competitive rugby, soccer, and cricket, and allegedly introduced skiing to Switzerland. Now that is living. Those old Victorians may have been a stuffy bunch of imperialists with unfortunate views on most social issues, but they knew how to play. Could that same freewheeling spirit thrive today? I thought so—that a new, bold, renegade sportsman's ethic could arise.

How great it would be—if I wasn't simply crazy. I thought the raw ingredients for a renegade sports movement existed, but obviously had yet to emerge as an identifiable cultural force, unless you count self-aware urban twenty-somethings' tendency to form dodgeball teams. Perhaps I was engaged in wishful thinking. So I decided to go exploring beyond the boundaries defined by newspaper sports pages, talk radio, and twenty-four-hour cable. I wanted to see if the sports counterculture I hoped for really existed, or if it could. As I stood on the rugby field that night, checking my spinal column, I began to think I was getting somewhere. If I survived, it would be fun.

At first, my motives were more or less completely selfish. Living through others and pontificating on issues of which we may or may not know anything—that's what we journalists call a good time. As I went deeper into the sporting unknown, however, I realized issues of moment might be in play. Americans long ago placed sports at the center of our national life. Sports now serve as a load-bearing pillar of our culture, one of precious few commonalities that hold together our diverse and sometimes fractured body politic. And I think that's a significant problem—but not because of the usual objections advanced by effete cultural elitists (like me). I don't think sports make the People dumber, or necessarily serve as some malign bread-and-circuses distraction to keep the masses from asking tough questions about national health-care policy. But I do think that something is seriously wrong with our relationship with sports, and I think that matters.

Are sports keeping us in shape? No. We're all familiar with our nation's achievements in the morbid obesity field. Does our sports obsession help us build camaraderie, team spirit, the kind of deep social bonds that make for enduring communities and heart-stirring cinematic moments between Tom Cruise and Cuba Gooding, Jr.? Not well enough. A well-publicized 2006 Duke University study showed that Americans report having one-third fewer close friends than they did twenty years ago. (If that phenomenon seems to transcend sports, consider that sociologist Robert Putnam used the decline of participatory, sociable, grassroots sports as the centerpiece of *Bowling Alone*, his landmark book on the "collapse . . . of American community.") Maybe we've just forgotten how to have fun, or at least fun not deliverable by flat screen. A 2007 study found a 25 percent drop in visits to national parks and other outdoor rec areas since the 1980s; researchers attributed the trend, seen across the Western world, to "videophilia." According to one set of federal statistics, the average American day includes 2.6 hours of television, as opposed to seventeen minutes of sports, exercise, or other recreation. ("Socializing and communicating" get forty-six minutes; "relaxing and thinking," nineteen.) Meanwhile, since the 1970s American workers somehow stuffed an extra forty-hour workweek into the average month. Anyone who's seen *The Shining* knows where all work and no play leads.

I'm not going to argue that sports might somehow fix our social problems, cure global warming, reverse economic collapse, and ensure that no child ever spends three straight hours watching Hannah Montana DVDs while the sun shines bright. But the state of our cultural union—including our relationship with sports—could use a makeover. Bowling alleys, kickball fields, cyclocross tracks, skateparks, hiking trails, basketball courts, sledding hills—they seem fine places to start.

I decided to see what's out there, on the wild frontier of American sports. I sought out places on the American sports landscape where a spirit of adventure—the renegade spirit—still reigns. What, exactly, did that mean? Like a man once said about pornography, I knew it when I saw it. Still, as the journey commenced, a few characteristics came into focus. If I believed Americans were too fat and too bored—in danger of becoming a nation of rotund sedan pilots, driving from home to office park to shopping center—I needed to find hands-on, participatory sports. If I objected to big-business dominance and corporate slickness in the majors, I needed to find sports that operated on a true grassroots level, without monied owners or huge sponsors, where players and fans controlled the action. Given that I found mainstream sports narrow and stale, I would seek out the weird. To the extent I found the big time predictable, I would plunge into the smallest of the small time, where people make it up as they go along. With fandom itself turning into a form of choreographed herd behavior, I would try to figure out how we could reclaim the grandstands in the name of rowdiness and spontaneity. If sports now failed to bring people together, I would track down athletes who valued sociability—in other words, who used sports as an excuse to drink cocktails and sing songs—as much as competition. You may remember these qualities as "fun."

I like to think that I started this quest not because there's something wrong with sports, but because there's something right about sports. Sports can be reinvented as a pop-cultural force; they can be a repository of weird knowledge and a vehicle for self-discovery as well as a source of good times. I hoped my expedition would lead me to the characters who would prove my case. If all else failed, I figured drinking would be involved.

So I conducted an expedition into sports' terra incognita, where the tigers and dragons and drunk cyclocrossers and skull-crushing rugby players dwell. The results follow. Grab your pith helmets. We hunt the mighty Renegade.

ONE

LOST, DRUNK, AND ON THE RUN

O n a crisp autumn day, I found myself just off a winding
road through the foothill parks above downtown Portland,
a plush complex of century-old forest reserves and mani-
cured rose gardens with killer views of downtown and miles
of looping hiking trails. Every weekend, Subaru Outbacks
decorated with politically upright bumper stickers ("Live Simply So Others May Simply Live") swarm into these hills and
disgorge Gore-Tex–clad nuclear families, eager to savor Portland at its most hale and hearty. On this particular afternoon,
I stood in the middle of this civilized wonderland, wearing a
tight red dress and a massive blond mullet wig, drinking from
a twenty-two-ounce bottle of Kentucky Ale. I listened as a man
known as Stinkfinger sang a song glorifying a full menu of sexual acts.

"Today is Monday!" Stinkfinger bellowed. The large crowd
around him, composed of other people, of both sexes, also

wearing red dresses, also drinking beer, screamed back: *"Today is Monday!"*

Stinkfinger brandished an extended index finger in a manner somehow unspeakably obscene. *"Monday,"* Stinkfinger shouted, *". . . is a finger day!"* Stinkfinger's chiseled face and gray curls lent him a distinct resemblance to a pre-*Godfather* Marlon Brando, except that at the moment he wore flapjack-thick layers of foundation makeup, mascara, lipstick, and a scarlet negligee. The crowd echoed him again, and Stinkfinger continued. *"Are we gonna have a good time? You bet your ass we will!"* On this cue, people in the crowd held plastic beer mugs or Kentucky Ales directly above their heads and performed a counterclockwise pirouette, warbling something like *"Doodle-doodle-doodle-oooooooo!"* As I did likewise, I glanced toward the opposite side of the narrow road. A mother and father were hustling their three children into a Chevy Tahoe, moving with some urgency.

"Today is Tuesday!"

Another family emerged from the woods.

"Tuesday is a wanking *day!"* Stinkfinger accompanied this declaration with a universally recognized hand gesture.

"Monday is a finger day! Are we gonna have a good time? You bet your ass we will! Doodle-doodle-doodle-ooooo!"

Now small bands of ordinary people—decent citizens, taxpayers, frightened townsfolk, call them what you will—huddled on both sides of the road. Mothers clutched their children. Fathers folded their arms and furrowed their brows as though pondering decisive courses of action. The children, I noticed, looked . . . curious. No doubt we made an intriguing sight: about seventy-five people, men and women, all wearing bright red cocktail dresses, pajamas, lingerie, or other boudoir garments, many in

wigs, all in sturdy, dirty running shoes. Hey, we were just out
for a little fresh air and exercise, same as them.

I had come to join the Hash House Harriers—or at least Portland's local chapter, for the HHH exist worldwide—for their
annual Red Dress Run. After living most of my life in blind
ignorance of their existence, I now knew the Hash House Harriers as a self-proclaimed "drinking club with a running problem," a global confederacy of loudmouthed drunkards with a
taste for rigorous improvised cross-country runs and sizable
quantities of fermented beverage. The "hash"—both a noun and
a verb—isn't so much a club as an open-source concept. Running several miles, usually over difficult terrain, and simultaneously drinking beer may be a good idea or it may be a bad idea,
but it is a highly adaptable idea. In my brief introduction to the
HHH, I discovered that it's possible to hash in Rwanda, Andorra,
Uzbekistan—anywhere, in fact, where one of the approximately
two thousand hasher "kennels" has taken root. A truly hard-
core hasher might travel to the biennial Interhash, a worldwide
convention/binge that tends to happen in places like Sarawak,
Borneo. ("Like all Interhash," the Borneo-based hasher Josh John
wrote me, "beer drinking will be a must and we plan to have a
free flow of these available." Right you are, sir.) Brave souls even
hash in Baghdad and Kabul. In Portland, the strong of body and
oblivious of liver could theoretically hash four or five evenings
a week. If I wanted to meet some of the sporting fringe-world's
most gregarious and arguably obnoxious "athletes," the Hash
House Harriers seemed ideal candidates. I also suspected that
hashing would provide the ultimate antidote to fitness-club
culture, which encourages every American consumer to think
of him- or herself as a pricey Thoroughbred horse, in need of

special training and expensive potions. Judging by the scene at the Red Dress Run, the average Hash House Harrier looks more like a hard-luck drag queen with a very dirty mouth. I could get into that.

In the parking lot, we continued to sway to the dulcet tones of Stinkfinger. He suggested that Wednesday is a day best devoted to a nonverbal, lip-smacking tongue trill intended, I believe, to dramatize the provision of oral pleasure to a female recipient. Another man, a man known as Farticus, turned to me. "I think it will probably take the cops about six minutes to respond," he said. "If we get out of here as soon as he's done, we should be fine." The plan was to leave the lot en masse, in hot pursuit of two individuals, one in a top hat, the other in a giant pink rabbit costume.

"Today is Thursday! Thursday is a fucking *day!"* Stinkfinger really knew how to throw body and soul into an Anglo-Saxon gerund.

About ten minutes earlier, the man in the top hat and the man in the giant pink rabbit costume—Mary Lou Rectum and Pabst Smear, respectively—sprinted off into the woods, each carrying a large bag of white flour. They would use that flour to create a series of cryptic symbols (arrows, crosses, crude renderings of human anatomy) on the ground, "laying trail" for the rest of us to follow. They were the hares. We were the pack.

"Today is Friday! Friday is a drinking *day!"*

As the prospect of running loomed, I considered my attire. I wore a tubular smock made of cheap maroon felt with some impressive heat-trapping properties, purchased at a Goodwill store a couple days before. From a distance, it looked like a red dress, but closer examination revealed a pseudo-medieval tunic, something an ambitious costumer for a high school drama department might whip up for a production of *Two Gentlemen of Verona*. I had accessorized with a beastly blond wig that made me look like one of the dewy-eyed Teuton-trash kids waving sparklers in the Scorpions' classic "Winds of Change" video. Unfortunately, the wig, perched on my head like a dead rodent, also had an intense thermal thing going on. Itchy sweat already pooled where hairnet met scalp. I would probably have to shave my head and report to a delousing facility the next day.

"*Today is Saturday,*" Stinkfinger cried.

"*Today! Is! Saturday!*"

"*And Saturday . . . is a* hashing *day!*"

The crowd shrieked and hollered, and then someone yelled, "*On-on!*" and the mob trundled out of the parking lot, across the road, past the mortified witnesses, up a hill, and into the fog-bound woods. I still had about half my Kentucky Ale, so I took the bottle with me. Fortunately, I had a whole flotilla of red-dress-wearing lunatics to provide cover. And I could take comfort in the thought that somewhere else, maybe in the next time zone or maybe on the other side of the world, another pack of Hash House Harriers was doing much the same thing. Like us, they would run miles and miles over rough terrain—"shiggy," in hasherspeak—with many, many pauses for beer, while calling each other disgusting nicknames, chanting obscene verses, and performing sophomoric rituals. It was a hashing day, but then again, for thousands of dedicated Hash House Harriers the world over, every day is a hashing day. Were we gonna have a good time?

As I lumbered down the first half mile of trail, roasting inside the red tunic, Kentucky Ale seething within, I recognized that

my exposure to the Hash House Harriers would be both a physical and a social experiment. None of these people knew me,
and I didn't know them. Nor could I give my attorney their real
names should an actionable tort occur, as seemed very possible
as I ran full-tilt along a precipitous drop into a deep green gully.
Still, so far, so good. My decision to take a half-full beer onto
city-owned trails seemed to curry considerable favor among my
new comrades. A towering, bearded man in a red evening dress
blew past me at a wide spot in the trail. "A roadie!" he yelled.
"Sweet move, man, sweet move. *On-on!*" *

I first heard of the Hash House Harriers through odd scraps of
urban legend. A friend of a friend was part of this semicultish
running and drinking club. Some guy who worked in account-
ing went out and got loaded while he was *jogging*. "Dude, we
were in Hong Kong and ran into these crazy people . . ." That
sort of thing. When I made actual contact, I received an e-mail
from Mary Lou Rectum, a.k.a. Tyler Lynch, a twenty-five-year-
old employee of a major sportswear manufacturing firm and
one of the grand wizards of Portland's HHH world. The e-mail
was to the point. If I wanted to learn about the HHH, he wrote,
I had to come out on a run. There was no other way.

So about a week before the Red Dress Run, I turned out for
my first hash. Hashers save elaborate, gender-bending costumes
for special occasions. For this more standard outing, Mary Lou
told me to bring old shoes and a flashlight, and not to wear any

---

*A hasher shouts "on, on!" when he or she spies a mark, rendered in chalk or flour,
indicating the correct path for the pack. Or just whenever.

item of clothing that made explicit reference to the sport of running. This was a foretaste of the HHH's somewhat involved internal etiquette, which among other taboos bans all discussion or even acknowledgment of the very sport the club engages in. I met Mary Lou at a bar, and he led me out into the twilight. We soon left the sidewalk and headed up a mangy hillside, one of those gnarly human-made wildernesses that take over neglected urban space, its slope crisscrossed with hobo trails and peppered with empty bottles. This, Mary Lou informed me, was perfect shiggy. Hashers love shiggy in all its forms. Shiggy can consist of virgin rain forest or posturban industrial decay, trackless rural meadows or a urine-marinated freeway underpass littered with discarded hypodermic needles. Doesn't matter, as long as the terrain poses some sort of challenge to the mildly intoxicated runner. In its purest form, shiggy is an environment in which running does *not* ordinarily occur—a hotel lobby, say.

"You want something secluded," Mary Lou explained as we bushwhacked. "If you're laying trail on a given night, you pride yourself on getting the pack out somewhere where most of the people have never been. And you pride yourself on finding serious shiggy. We're lucky in Portland, because there's lots of good shiggy not far out of town. In Phoenix, they have problems because there's just not a lot of natural shiggy. You have to go way out to get out of the sprawl. Las Vegas, on the other hand, has some of the best urban shiggy in the world, but it's hard to exploit it because of the security situation. If you want to hash through a casino, you have to be really on top of it. Besides the guards, the cleaning crews are so efficient that any flour the hares use to mark trail is liable to be gone before the pack can even show up. So everywhere's a little different."

At the top of the hill, we reached the parking lot that served as that evening's take-off point. In short order, Mary Lou introduced me to a few of the three dozen or so assembled hashers. I met Pavlov's Bitch, Farticus, I Blow, Hydro Licks (a rather winsome early-twenties young lady with a small-liberal-arts-college aura), Fertilize Her (ditto), Gang Bang (Mary Lou's wife), Wet Spots, Twatsicle, He Shoots but Does Not Score, Red Light Special, and several others. I believed I grasped the theme. Mary Lou then ordered me to present myself to an imposing, bespectacled blond woman who held a dog-eared notebook. This logbook contained the complete pseudonymous rosters for hundreds of hash runs, and I was supposed to sign in. Mary Lou told me that as a "virgin," as yet unnamed, I would sign in as "Just Zach."

"Who the fuck are you?" the woman with the book asked.

"I'm . . . Just Zach, I guess."

She stuck out her hand. "Pleased to meet you, Just Zach," she said. "I'm Hairy Crotchna. Sign in. That'll be five dollars hash cash."

At this point, I made the unhappy discovery that I had neglected to bring the nominal fee for the evening, which would pay for beer and postrun food. I confessed to Mary Lou, who started yelling. "Does anyone have five dollars to lend this fucking virgin who doesn't know how to bring five fucking dollars— *five fucking dollars*—to the hash?" Someone came through, but I had a feeling that Just Zach wouldn't be receiving a lovable pornographic nickname anytime soon. Soon after this faux pas, we headed into the night for a fun, flash-lit excursion up and down twisty woodland trails. About a mile into the run, as the fifty-strong pack strung out a bit, Mary Lou began to sing. *"My girlfriend is a vegetable! She lives in the hospital!"*

The other hashers near us on the trail instantly took up the chorus. *"I'd do most anything to keep her alive!"*

"She has no arms or legs! She looks like a pony keg! I'd do most anything to keep her alive! She's got a new TV! They call it an EKG! Her EKG does not rise! But still she spreads her thighs! My girl lives in an iron lung! But she can still give good tongue! My girl has leprosy! Parts are always landing on top of me! She had a tracheotomy! That's just another hole for me!"

"I'd do most anything to keep her alive!"

Not to be outdone, Hairy Crotchna launched a little ditty to the tune of the *Bonanza* theme:

"Get it up, get it in, get it out, don't mess my hairdo!!"

And so forth. I soon gave up keeping track of the innuendos, double entendres, foul suggestions, versified descriptions of intimate acts, insults, and other statements, usually made at the top of the lungs to the melody of a 1950s show tune. I enjoy a rhyming couplet about masturbation set to the tune of "Finiculì, Finiculà" as much as the next seasoned man of the world, but the nonstop verbal smut begin to pall before long. Have you ever noticed that pornography is always better in concept than in consumption? I began to worry the Hash House Harriers might fall into the same category. And I wondered, as I considered the probability that one particularly steep, off-trail section of the course might provide ideal poison ivy habitat, why anyone would take this up as a lifestyle-defining hobby.

Kuala Lumpur, 1938: the Malaysian capital, under British imperial rule, wasn't far removed from its Wild, Wild East days as a triad-governed, tin-mining outpost rife with gambling dens, licensed brothels, and casinos. It seems strange that a young buck needed to make his own fun in such a place, but a Catalan-British accountant named A. S. Gispert apparently found time on his hands. Like many expatriate bachelors, he lived at the Royal Selangor Club, a hostel so infamous for its loathsome food that everyone called it the Hash House. Gispert, provoked by both boredom and, maybe, the brain-softening effects of tropical heat, began wrangling informal running expeditions around the colonial city. His outings attracted a handful of military men and other imperial wayfarers.

The "paper chase," in which a "hare" attempts to baffle a pack of "hounds" by laying an improvised course across open country, is a traditional fixture of British running. (Students at the Rugby School conducted a chase in 1837; in 1868, the Thames Hare and Hounds, today considered the world's oldest cross-country club, inaugurated its own version on Wimbledon Common.) Gispert & Co. adopted the format, but added copious booze consumption to the program. Their outings soon caught the eye of local authorities, who informed the group that if they wanted to keep up their antics, they needed to register as a formal organization. (The Brits—gotta love 'em.) Thus were the Hash House Harriers duly established, under a club constitution that laid out a few simple, admirable missions:

> To promote physical fitness among our members.
> To get rid of weekend hangovers.
> To acquire a good thirst and to satisfy it in beer.

And so on. "Hashing" became a popular diversion among Gispert's crowd of gone-troppo slackers. In a brief reminiscence, penned in 1973, an original hasher recalled: "Gispert was not an athlete, and stress was laid as much on the subsequent refreshment etc. as on the pure and austere running. It was non-competitive, and abounded in slow-packs . . . we prided ourselves on being rather disorganized." Even so, hashing proved resilient. The Japanese invasion of Malaysia put an abrupt end to the original HHH's well-lubricated golden age—Gispert himself died in the unsuccessful British defense of Singapore—but the few semiofficial hash histories more or less dismiss the global conflagration as a mere nuisance. The Kuala Lumpur "kennel" resumed operations soon after V-J Day—in fact, the club filed an official war damages claim for "one tin bath . . . two dozen mugs and possibly two old bags (not members)." Gispert's followers persisted again during the nasty proto-Vietnam waged by British forces and Malay rebels in the 1950s. "The Emergency cramped our style but did not diminish our activities," wrote that primordial hasher in his memoir. "We were even called in for information on various by-ways in Selangor . . . our usefulness to MI-5 was brief, and our information probably otiose. But the hares ran into two bandits at Cheras, who were later copped."

All very charming and dotty and what-ho-Jeeves British, no doubt: the Drones Club on the run. What interested me, though, as I ventured into the scrub-choked canyons outside Portland in a bright red schmatte, beer in hand, was what happened in the decades that followed. A Singapore division of the HHH began in the 1960s. By the early '70s, there were a few dozen hasher kennels sprinkled around the globe. Two historical developments then converged to unleash Gispert's brilliant union of two of humankind's signature activities: the first-world fitness boom, a somewhat ironic catalyst, broadened the pool of potential hashers; the Internet's expansion allowed these runners to transform a few pioneer kennels in Southeast Asia into a huge worldwide cabal. Today, no one really knows how many Hash House Harriers might be out there—one estimate, circa 2002, counted about two thousand separate kennels in 180 countries, with hundreds in the United States alone. A strong (or, at least, pungent) case could be made that the HHH is one of the world's most successful sporting institutions.

"We're everywhere, man," the Portland hasher who goes by the relatively benign alias Pabst Smear told me not long after the Red Dress Run. "There are eight different hashes just in San Diego. They even had to make a rule that if you came to the Saturday hash, you couldn't come to the Sunday hash—there were just too many goddamn people. They're getting two hundred runners at some of these things. Washington, D.C., has so many hashers, they bought a van so they could have mobile beer. If you're a hasher, you basically have a brotherhood in any city you can name. When you go to another city's hash, it's like you walk into your favorite bar, but the guy sitting next to you isn't Norm, it's some dude you've never seen before in your life. And now you're best friends."

How many "legitimate" sports would love to have thousands of adherents, and representation in about as many countries as hold United Nations membership? Hashing achieved this with no owners, no budget, no bureaucracy, and only the sketchiest outline of a global structure—as far as I could tell, hashing operated on a scaffolding of poorly designed websites and e-mail groups. Perhaps the enduring appeal of beer is even more powerful than the vaunted Internet. Even so, as I received my sweaty, ale-soaked induction into Hasher-world, I wondered if it really amounted to anything besides an extremely inconvenient way to get blasted.

Every Hash House Harriers run ends with something called "Religion." The night of my virgin outing, the pack arrived at a large park picnic shelter. The night's hares—both members of a women-only hasher subsect called the Dead Whores—had somehow managed to finish the convoluted trail in the hills above in time to arrange a potluck feast on six picnic tables. A keg of beer appeared, and Religion began.

Religion has two purposes: to enforce punitive, compulsory beer guzzlings, known as "down-downs"; and to bestow hasher names. The former practice is just good clean fun. The latter cuts right to the heart of the hasher culture. When a "Just" commits an act of notable stupidity during a run, says something moronic, lets slip an incriminating personal detail, or otherwise distinguishes him- or herself, a hash name could be born. For example, Gang Bang, Mary Lou's wife, was named in honor of her heritage. "Shitty Kitty asked me what I was," Gang Bang later explained. "And I said I was Mexican-Filipina-Japanese-German-black. And she was, like, you're a one-person melting pot . . . how about 'Melting Twat'? And then Village Idiot said, well, it sounds like it took a gang-bang to get her here. . . ."

Not just anyone warrants this treatment. You have to earn it. Full-fledged virgins never get names, and many hashers find themselves waiting, and running and drinking, for a long time before their magic moment arrives. "We're stingy with the names, for sure," Mary Lou said. "One thing I've learned in my time is that of any forty or fifty people who come out as virgins, only five stick around. It's like throwing Play-Doh at the wall. If you blow a good name on someone who then never shows up again, that sucks. And then, it's just a practical thing: people who come to their first or second hashes are going to tend to be wallflowers. They're not boisterous or outgoing enough to get named. There are people who've been coming for two years who still don't have names, because they never speak up or stand out. They never do anything stupid. They never say anything obscene. How are you supposed to name that person?"

Fair question. As a virgin myself, I saw why neophytes tended to hang back. I had, however, nowhere to hide. A hasher can be sentenced to a down-down for any offense, but the worst crime of all is, of course, being a hash virgin. Along with a few other first-timers, I mustered to the front of the crowd, full beer in hand. After a brief preamble—I introduced myself, and everyone yelled "Hi, Zach—how'd you *come*?"—we all commenced to drink, to the great amusement of the assembly. Somewhere between my college commencement and that moment, I lost my power-guzzling touch, and failed to finish the mug. So, in accordance with hash tradition, I dumped the rest of the beer over my own head.

The night of the Red Dress Run . . . listen, it went on for quite a while, alright? Descending out of the hills into the city, the pack hit about seven bars, stopped at a hasher's house for beers, stopped in parks for beers, then arrived at yet another picnic shelter for more beer. By the end, I was a glazed donut indeed.

The world now bore an amber-ale hue. I stumbled off into the surrounding bramble to relieve myself. At this point, I realized I had lost my wallet.

I was overcome with what a prominent politician would later describe as the fierce urgency of now. I pictured any one of the innumerable afternoon drunkards, at any one of the greasy-floored bars the pack had visited, clutching my ID and bank card. I imagined funding said drunkard's next trip to Cabo. I imagined six consecutive down-downs. The internal hydraulic churn created by jiggling about a gallon of beer over five or six miles of varied terrain began to take on volcanic qualities. Peristaltic emergency loomed. As the jolly beginnings of Religion resounded from the picnic shelter, I slunk into the night. With alcohol as my infallible guide, I mounted an investigation straight out of *The Pink Panther*: me, still looking like a reject from America's scariest Renaissance Faire, still very drunk, retracing the pack's circuitous route, eyes locked on the ground, looking for the missing key to my identity and financial existence. Yeah, I was in a bit of a state. Only after I gave up and began the humiliating mass-transit journey home—no collegiate "walk of shame" could top this—did it occur to me to call all the bars and ask if they'd found the thing.

The next day, I e-mailed Mary Lou a shamed confession about my disappearance. His reply, while a relief, also made me feel worse by highlighting just how dumb I'd been. "Not only do I have your wallet," he wrote, "but you are a douchebag two times over. First, for not trusting yourself to a group of people who make bad drunken decisions on a nightly basis and live to tell about it. Second, and even worse, you missed Religion! It was a good one, too."

*   *   *

I had disgraced myself—not by losing my wallet, which is exactly the kind of exuberantly idiotic act that hashers celebrate, but by violating the unspoken core of the hasher credo. Which is, roughly, if I can put it into words: Who Gives a Fuck? Earlier in the Red Dress Run, I saw a lumbering, six-foot-plus man in a wisp of bargain-hooker red lace wipe out on a wet patch of grass, blow his knee, and earn an immediate trip to the emergency room. The people who took him to the ER rejoined the run within an hour or two—not because they were callous, but because the injured hasher wouldn't have wanted it any other way. I had inadvertently stumbled on one of the last bastions of stiff-upper-lip, merely-a-flesh-wound thinking in our increasingly lawyered-up world. You're a hasher. You drink. You run. You get hurt. Some meth addict ends up with your wallet and cleans out your bank account and commits a series of blunt-force bank robberies under your name. Get over it. Have a beer.

A few nights after the Red Dress Run—a rare nonhashing night—I met up with Mary Lou Rectum, Gang Bang, and Pabst Smear. A lot of people drift in and out of the Hash House Harriers' world. Only a select few discover something of a vocation in hashing's steady diet of booze and misadventure. Mary Lou and Pabst, lifelong friends, first stumbled upon hashing in the midst of a long night of barroom shenanigans that somehow led to Mary Lou wearing the skirt of a woman he'd never met before. Someone with a keen eye for talent told them about the HHH. Two years later, both had attained positions of power, of a sort, within Portland's hasher scene, joining the inner circle responsible for buying kegs, choosing hares, scouting drinking facilities, and conducting Religion ceremonies. In a relatively short period of time, they had amassed a lifetime's worth of very hazy memories of near-catastrophic experiences.

"I remember this one time, we were running across a railroad bridge, with a train staring straight at us," Pabst Smear recalled.

"The fear of death was strong at that point," Mary Lou threw in.

"Then, the cops were waiting for us at the other end. You always remember the ones where the cops show up."

"One time," Mary Lou continued, "we ran to a spot down on the riverbanks, and then had to get in these inflatable rafts and paddle down to the spot where we had Religion. Our boat was sinking the whole time. Gang Bang was trying to bail the thing out with her plastic beer mug. I was trying to paddle with an oar that broke about halfway through. And Pabst was just lying in the back, drinking."

"That was the one where I realized that I actually liked hashing," Gang Bang said. But the drunkenness! The profanity! The sexual innuendo! How did she stand it all, this willful rejection of feminism, not to say the Enlightenment in general? She shrugged. "I know it probably wouldn't be for everyone," she said, "but the women who go and keep going are into it. I think you're celebrated as a woman on the hash. Who wouldn't want to hang around with a bunch of guys who constantly tell you how hot you are? It's fun."

I could buy that. After trying to run many miles with a small wading pool's worth of beer in my internals, I recognized that hashing was not for the weak. "Yeah, you first think, man, if I go out running with beer in my stomach, I'm going to feel awful,"

Pabst said. "But now I feel weird if I run *without* beer in my stomach."

"When I tell people about hashing," Gang Bang said, "they always ask me how many people pass out. And I'm, like, pass out? Maybe if someone breaks their leg."

"People don't understand that there are different kinds of drinking," Mary Lou added. "I think a lot of people are deterred by the drinking thing—they think they have to get wasted and then go running. But there are hashers who don't drink at all, and they're totally welcomed. You don't have to drink any more than you want to. It's not about getting all trashed. Well, not exactly."

So, uh—what, then?

"Well, I've been going out just about every week for over two years, and I still get really excited when I think about the hash," Pabst said. The other two nodded vigorously over their pints. "You get excited when you run somewhere that you've lived your entire life, and you run down trails and paths that you had no idea were even there. The first time we went out, we were on trails less than a mile from our house, and I was completely lost. You see more of your own city when you're hashing than you've ever seen before. You meet people you would never meet, go to bars you would never go to—and you take them over."

Then they told me about the Shirt. This garment showed up in Portland hashing circles some time before. The Shirt had traveled around the world, passed from hasher to hasher. Runners in cities around the globe had worn it on the trail, signed it in black permanent marker, and passed it on—without washing it. The thing was now an almost unreadable palimpsest of signatures, rude slogans, and uncouth drawings from five continents.

The lucky Portland hasher who took custody of the thing constructed an improvised biohazard containment system in his closet, until a visitor from Washington, D.C., just happened to show up on a Portland run. The Shirt then continued its unhygienic but strangely touching relay voyage—bound, pending the intervention of hazard-sniffing dogs at Customs, for parts unknown.

"God, it smelled so bad," Gang Bang said, "but it was the coolest thing to see. The thing had been in countries I had never heard of."

"That's the thing," Mary Lou said. "The hash may seem dumb, but it makes you a part of a community that's just everywhere. There are times when you trust these people with your life. You're running across slippery rocks, across farmers' fields, or just across the goddamn highway. There's definitely an element of danger. And that just makes it better."

On a rainy, dark Wednesday evening, the hash pack gathered at a small side-street tavern. Everyone looked a little haggard, except a few excited virgins. This was the fifth HHH event in seven days. The veterans drained warm-up pitchers along the bar. Just before seven o'clock, Mary Lou called all virgins out to the sidewalk for a primer. With a bag of flour in hand, he explained the various symbols the night's hares would use to mark our trail.

"If you see a dot, like this, that means you're on the right track," he said, dumping a round little white pile onto the pavement. "You let your fellow hounds know by yelling 'on-on.' If you're following someone and you don't know if they're on the true trail, you yell, 'Are you?' As in, 'Are you on-on?' Got it? If you see a cross, like this, that's called a check: it means the true trail could be in any direction, so you have to check it out. Sometimes a check leads to a false trail. If you're following what you think is the trail and you come to a giant *F*, that means you're fucked, basically. If you see the letters *BN*, that means 'beer near.' Get excited. If you see *BC*, that stands for 'beer check,' and that means you've arrived at a spot where we're going to stop and drink. All this stuff is designed to slow the pack down and keep it together, so obey the checks if you can. Any questions? No? Good."

Someone raised the "on-on" and the pack tramped off into the gathering night. We sprinted through quiet residential streets like an unsubtle ninja dojo, making for a huge stretch of darkened parkland. The trail circled stagnant ponds; plunged down crumbling stone stairs; looped through Victorian neighborhoods transformed into goth Charles Addams wonderlands by the autumnal gloom and decay. We shouted and chanted, bombed through heavy traffic with minimal regard for our own safety, and amid dense urbanity, sought out the nappiest weeds and thickets we could find. At the first beer check, the pack passed around a garbage sack full of Tecate cans and wedges of lime. The second beer check featured tequila-infused Jell-O shots. The run ended in a rough-beamed, unfinished basement, at a table piled with tacos. Steam rose from our sweaty bodies under a bare 60-watt lightbulb.

I was beginning to understand. The black halo of profanity wasn't the point, at least not in and of itself. Freemasons have their exclusive lingo and behavioral codes, and the Hash House

Harriers have theirs. Of all the HHH's many peculiarities, my
favorite is the ban on all discussion of one other topic besides
running: work. Hashers do not reveal, much less discuss, their
jobs—if they have to refer to work at all, they call it "the W."
(As in: "Oh, yeah, I know that guy from the W.") The ban, combined with the fact that everyone on a hash—costume events
aside—tends to dress like an unusually sporty vagrant, deepens
the anonymity of people who mostly know each other by aliases
in any case. Looking around the basement, I couldn't tell the
lawyers from the carpenters, the social workers from the graphic
designers. And with the most banal cocktail party conversation
starter—"So, what do you do?"—forbidden, it was impossible to
do the category-sort we all use to navigate rooms full of unfamiliar people. And because of the rule prohibiting any and all
talk about running, no one could use athleticism as a stand-in
status marker. Among hashers, to talk of work would be vulgar
and pointless. To acknowledge interest in running would violate
an all-important conceit: that running is pretty stupid, and so
are hashers. (Some hashers mock competitive runners, calling
them "race-ists." Pabst Smear explained, "The attitude is sort of,
you pay twenty-five dollars for a race and don't even get beer at
the end? Ridiculous.")

In other words, people actually had to talk. "We have elite
athletes in the hash," Pabst Smear would explain later. "But they
keep it to themselves. We also have hashers who weigh over
three hundred pounds. We have hashers who are over seventy
years old. The only relevant qualifications are, Can you drink
a beer? Can you run a quarter mile at any pace without dying?
You're in."

* * *

In the end, my Hash House Harriers career was short. I endorse running and I endorse drinking (both in moderation), and I suppose even chanting profanity in public might have occasional uses. In the end, though, I just couldn't see myself as a weekly hasher, as someone who would ever earn a revolting anatomical nickname. I came to respect the hash too much to make a halfhearted commitment. This is some people's lives we're talking about. (There's also the matter of my declining constitution: I used to take perverse pleasure in midweek hangovers, but now they leave me feeling as though something very hard, with serrated surfaces, punched a ragged hole in the fabric of my consciousness.)

Still, I admire the hashers' beery vim—in many ways, they embody the kind of parallel-universe, renegade sports culture I set out to find. My inner armchair anarchist loves their global, cellular, leaderless-resistance structure, and the idea that anyone can start a new HHH kennel and plug into the worldwide network of other drunken runners. When one thinks of sports "globalization," it tends to be in terms of the freaky *Neuromancer*–meets–Thomas Friedman developments that cause the words *international expansion* to glow on the inside eyelids of every sports executive or team owner in the world as they drift off to Sleepyland. The NFL sells out games in London; Manchester United sells replica shirts in Cleveland; the NBA wants an international division; baseball holds opening day in Japan. All this is a great boon to those of us who enjoy a good barstool rant about the World Trade Organization, capitalism's assault on cultural identities, et cetera. Meanwhile, the Hash House Harriers' example points to a completely different kind of sports globalization—and suggests that the whole process could be a lot more fun if we all had a buzz on.

By sidelining competition and imposing an outright ban on office gossip and résumé comparison, the Hash House Harriers have invented a new sports-club ethic—or maybe reinvented one. Before the good Lord gave us Twitter, sports clubs based on neighborhoods, churches, fraternal organizations, and, I suppose, street-fighting gangs formed an important social nexus. When the first baseball clubs emerged in New York before and after the Civil War, postgame feasting and tavern drinking matches were as much the point as the hardball itself. To look at a sepia-toned photo of an outfit like Atlantic of Brooklyn, baseball's first dynasty (circa 1859), is to glimpse an era—with its villainous facial hair and hardened pre-Gettysburg stares— when sports clubs were more like touring heavy-metal bands than carefully constructed marketing vehicles. Those clubs gave their members a chance to express themselves. In his 1998 book *A Clever Base-Ballist*, writer Bryan Di Salvatore assembled a tasty list of antique club names: Live Oaks; Dauntless; Swift Foot; Bum Stingers; Hell Busters; Pill-Garlics; Ne Plus Ultra; Redemptor; High Boys; Young America; Asteroid; the Nine Orphans. Imagine being a member of the Pill-Garlics—or Redemptor! I envision a smoky away-gray jersey stitched with six-inch-tall letters in that scary AC/DC font. We need to bring back that spirit. We need to stop thinking of sports as a pathway to rock hard abs and start thinking of them as an excuse to get together and raise some hell. If anyone asks, we'll call it civic engagement.

*   *   *

If I ever sign into an HHH logbook again, I'll be Just Zach. Still, my brief hasher experience lingers in odd ways, as though the benevolent ghost of A. S. Gispert, a man who knew how to live at a time when the world lost its mind, watches over me. I often look down to find mysterious, fading symbols, sketched in white on the city pavement, like signs of the world's most drunken conspiracy. I think of Mary Lou, Pabst Smear, Gang Bang, and Stinkfinger cruising past wherever I'm standing under cover of darkness, having their weekly time of their lives.

One winter night, I stood in my kitchen peeling carrots. Then I heard it: a top-of-the-lungs cry of "on-on!" thundering just outside my window. And then a herd of feet pounded past, and voices shouted and catcalled. Whistles blew and flashlight beams zigzagged through the inky dark. As I went about my domestic chores, the secret life of the Hash House Harriers continued about twenty feet away. It was a cold, wet night, and I must say I was glad not to be half wasted and trying to keep up with crafty hares and a thirsty pack. I was, however, also glad to know they were out there.

TWO

ALLEY CAT NOTES

After my Hash House Harriers "fieldwork"—as my internal organs and moral compass slowly healed—I kept watch for other signs of the renegade sporting life. Winter in Portland is not prime time for outdoor activity. Yes, the mountains outside the city crawl with rosy-cheeked skiers, snowboarders, snowshoers, and ice-cave architects, but in town everyone just wants to roast squash, taste-test their grotty homemade cider, and read *The Hobbit* for the 254th time. As I migrated through monsoon season, however, I did notice one group of people untroubled by the muck and sodden piles of dead leaves—who, for reasons of stubborn professional pride and personal fortitude, seemed to revel in the slime.

Bike messengers: I knew them, of course, at least to the extent that most city dwellers know them, as a skinny tribe of half-admirable, half-annoying daredevils. Even when ones and zeros can allegedly be trusted with anything, messengers seemed to hold their own as the last remnant of the streetwise city proletariat. (A little research revealed that someone, somewhere writes an article foretelling the Death of the Bike Messenger about every eighteen months, and has for years.) I saw messengers every day downtown and thought the courier life looked enviable in many ways. They lounged around in coffee shops drinking espresso, reading newspapers, projecting a standoffish cool that was no less impressive for being an obvious pose. Occasionally, a radio would crackle and one would go careening off.

I also knew, from my newspaper alterna-sports days, that messengers maintained an elaborate self-created competitive world. So-called alley cat races, a flexible form of quasi-legal speed scavenger hunt, took place all the time. A little digging on the Portland United Messenger Association website clued me in to national and international meets—there was, in fact, an alley cat racing world championship, plus North American and European titles. Of most interest to me, messenger racing existed outside the framework of "official" competitive cycling. The Union Cycliste Internationale had nothing to do with it, and neither did Lance Armstrong. YouTube footage of alley cats in Toronto, New York, Boston, London, San Francisco—just about anywhere with the right combination of population density, sensitive-information-based business, and loose-cannon cyclist nut jobs—suggested that, in this world, "performance-enhancing drugs" meant coffee, Red Bull, beer, and, sometimes, mandatory hard-liquor shots between race stages. Races took place in live traffic, with no street closures, and police forces tended to take a jaundiced view of the practice. Here was a sports microcosmos of its own, created by and for its competitors with little regard for the outside world. I wanted to know more.

On a drizzly day, just as the weather began its damp break toward spring, I met a man named Joel Metz at a coffee shop. I'd seen Joel around, a tall, stout-shouldered guy in his late thirties, with his hair pulled into a ponytail, biking through the center-city traffic maelstrom with a seen-it-all expression. Joel helped run the Magpie Messenger Collective, a small worker-owned courier outfit. He was also an amateur historian with an admirable streak of monomania. Digging through old French newspapers, he had compiled a fascinating record of cycle-messenger racing in Paris, back to 1895. Through the 1960s, Parisian newspapers employed cycle-borne *porteurs* to deliver their multiple daily editions, and those *porteurs* waged regular battles over twisting, cobblestoned racecourses—which Metz, of course, retraced and photographed himself, the better to document on his info-dense personal website. As I sat down next to Metz, I noticed the tattoos running up his arms, a mosaic of interlocking cycle cogs. Committed? I reckoned so.

In fact, Metz told me, he'd been involved in the upper echelons of the International Federation of Bike Messenger Associations for years, at least to the extent that an organization of people who tend to hate all forms of authority has upper echelons. "Officially, IFBMA consists of every working bike messenger in the world who wants to participate," Metz said. "That's so wide open, not even all messengers can wrap their heads around it. In practice, people who say they're willing to make decisions end up making the decisions. Of course, we have an open meeting every year at the Cycle Messenger World Championships, and every one of those decisions can be voted down. I've been a facilitator at those meetings, which makes it easy for people to mistake me for the president. The idea that there has to be an all-powerful leader is so ingrained, it's hard to break, even for a bunch of people who think they're anarchists or whatever."

This rather fluid entity managed to put together a series of major competitive events every year. The old Parisian races died out as the city's newspapers dropped editions and switched to motorized delivery. The first modern alley cat race, according to Metz, took place in Toronto in 1987. After an ad hoc event in Berlin, the first "official" Cycle Messenger World Championships took place in London in 1994. The federation took shape and the CMWC moved from one host city to another, typically attracting hundreds of competitors and hangers-on to a global festival of messenger culture. (The 2008 event took place in Toronto, while Tokyo hosted in 2009.) North American, European, and Australian championships arose to create a de facto world circuit. All this activity continued in the face of the perennial deathwatch on couriering as a business, despite subshoestring budgets and an organizational and financial paradigm that might be called chaotic. "Organizing the Worlds has left people in debt for a decade," Metz said. "But we didn't want this to be run by messenger companies, and we sure as hell didn't want it run by the UCI. It's still a completely grassroots thing. The Worlds and the Nationals have to be almost completely reorganized, from the ground up, every single time."

People did this, I gathered, for a couple of reasons. First, cycle messengers enjoy an unusual degree of professional solidarity, based on shared danger, bike geekery, lowbrow cosmopolitanism (bike messengers often score under-the-table work in foreign lands), wages that amount to a voluntary vow of poverty, and beer consumption. This palpable esprit de corps—accompanied, of course, by a look that defines urban/

apocalyptic/extreme fitness chic—inspires loyalty to the trade. Second, alley cat racing sounded very fun.

"There's a near-infinite variety of formats," Metz said. "The most basic race is a point-to-point, but even within that there are a lot of variations. You'll get to a checkpoint and find that the next checkpoint is changed. You come to the address for a checkpoint, and it doesn't exist. You have to carry things. You have to drop things off. You have to carry your bike up five flights of stairs. Personally, I'm not the fastest rider, so I tend to prefer problem solving, and when I organize races, that's the emphasis. I send people to streets that don't exist. People build in all kinds of game-play and strategy. I've seen races based on Monopoly. I've seen Choose Your Own Adventure races. Basically, a good alley cat is just a heightened version of the decision making a messenger has to engage in every day. It's an odd and almost unique thing. You don't find a lot of occupations where people will mimic what they do for work for fun."

Of course, he added, if I really wanted to understand the appeal, I would have to check out a race.

The 420 Alley Cat began in an austere, brick-walled, high-ceilinged room on the sixth floor of a scruffy old downtown office building. The place looked like an artist's studio—bedsheets over windows, random scraps of salvaged décor—and maybe it was one. When I showed up, at about seven o'clock on one of the first warm evenings of the year, the scene looked like a kegger hosted by a bicycle-mounted partisan unit. Dozens of messengers, with short-cropped pants and huge courier bags slung over their shoulders, milled around, drinking prerace beers and smoking cigarettes out on the fire escape. In one corner, the race organizer, a bearded young messenger named Drew Kinney, scrambled to hand out course directions and explain his race's complex, thematic rules. I made my way over.

"Okay, so—we're simulating drug dealing," Kinney said. At his feet sat dozens of little plastic baggies full of a substance that I was able to identify, thanks to my wide forensic experience, as oregano. Kinney's race would riff on the fact that the date was, of course, April 20—4/20—which enjoys a puzzling degree of cachet within the fuzzy-minded world of cannabis enthusiasts. Tonight's competitors would each receive a little payload of fake weed, which they would transport to a designated checkpoint and "sell" to a race official there. They would then either receive more "marijuana" or some make-believe cash—in addition to the mock stash, piles of Monopoly currency lay everywhere—which they would transport to the next checkpoint, and then . . . honestly, I was a little unclear. Kinney jumped up on his chair and shouted directions to the assembled racers. I wasn't too confident that any of them could explain the nuances either. It seemed some combination of speed and "money" earned would determine a winner, but racers wanted to hit the road rather than parse the thing. Soon we were all sprinting down the multiple flights to the street, where a fleet of rides entombed the sidewalk bike racks. When Drew screamed *"Go!"* dozens of messengers sprinted across the street to their bikes, mounted up, and rocketed westward, whether they understood the race rules or not.

I hopped in my car and headed for a midrace checkpoint, namely a bench in the middle of a park in a quiet, quasi-suburban neighborhood. Two amiable dudes sat on the bench, drinking beer, with a bag full of Monopoly money and oregano eighths at their feet: the race officials. They gave me one of their Newcastle Brown Ales. A few minutes later, the first racers began hauling ass up a grassy slope, and complicated, semicoherent transactions took place. Some riders shaved every possible second off their stops, while others lingered, drank beer, shot the breeze, exchanged notes on parties later in the week, and ambled off at their leisure.

A vestigial winter chill crept into the air as the light faded. Cyclists' wheels squelched on the wet grass and rasped against the pebble pathways through the park. The race required riders to perform an ambitious, cockeyed-star-shaped crisscross of Portland's densest neighborhoods and to locate checkpoints in parks and under bridges. I liked the thought of this roving detachment of clandestine athletes. As far as my renegade thesis was concerned, it was perfect: a grassroots, DIY event, made up on the fly and essentially organized by the same people who participated in it. The beer drinking and urban orienteering created a certain philosophical overlap with the Hash House Harriers, and the knowledge that the alley cat racers were out there, combating the forces of nature in the form of automobile traffic, infused the cityscape with romance and a sense of adventure. The competitive edge (even if—no pun intended—blunted by a smart-alecky theme) also anchored Drew's alley cat in the broader tradition of cycle racing, evoking the sport's 150 years of history while simultaneously hijacking it. The alley cat wasn't mocking the art and science of cycling, a sport usually practiced in artificial conditions, on closed roads or banked tracks. It celebrated cycle racing by thrusting bikes deep into the environment in which they have the most practical application: the bustling, traffic-swarmed city. On streets engineered (at huge expense, in just about every sense) for cars, the alley cat racers struck a little blow for low-tech individualism, not to mention fun.

At the same time, the race made me slightly uncomfortable. It's not illegal to ride bikes on city streets, but coordinating a high-speed pursuit through traffic might just push the point. Cops tend to think so. As much as I admire a touch of benign anarchy here and there, at heart I am a bourgeois fan of the rule of law. (I mean, of course I am: I appreciate fancy coffee, Campari and soda, hot and cold running water, habeas corpus, and other by-products of well-ordered, well-protected civilization.) As a commuter cyclist myself, I am acutely aware that my life depends on the tenuous social contract between riders and drivers. I signal. Then again, maybe the alley cat's value lies precisely in the way it probes legality's edges and stretches the definition of urban cycling in libertarian directions. Or perhaps two Newcastle Brown Ales were enough for me.

I decided it would be good to drive back to the start/finish line before my thinking became any more conflicted. I found Drew, Herr Kommissar, in the lobby of the old office building. His cell phone kept ringing. Racers appeared out of the gathering darkness with unanswerable questions about the rules. Drew seemed too distracted by the prospect of his imminent arrest to answer—cop cars now circled the block in ominous fashion. Johnny Law was obviously wise to the 420 Alley Cat, and I could tell that the race's theme made Drew even less excited to discuss the event with a uniformed officer than might normally be the case. He decided to pull the plug on the secret headquarters upstairs and began frantically trying to spread word about a change of venue. He now planned to head for a bar on the other side of town, await whatever riders could make it over there, and figure out a winner and distribute prizes after everyone had a chance to have a beer and settle down. The 420 Alley Cat had descended into chaos. In other words, as far as I could tell, things had pretty much gone according to plan.

I loved the idea of a sporting event so effervescent that it threatened to disintegrate at any moment. The experimental sketchiness marked a stark contrast from the clockwork predictability of big-time sports. (What, you mean they're doing the Super Bowl *again* this year? Dreary.) Even so, I couldn't discount the messenger-racing scene's larger achievement. The couriers pull together major championships every year, despite an "organization" that consists of whoever decides to show up. One inclined to overblown political analysis about everything (ahem) could point to the bike messenger racing scene as a fascinating example of natural democracy. As a model for sports revolution, I thought it worked pretty well, in that—absent owners, pro athletes, cash-spinning sponsors, public recognition, a discernible bureaucratic framework, or the blessing of most local authorities—it somehow worked at all.

And the bike, the iron stallion of past, present, and post-peak-oil future self-propulsion, now seemed like the ideal mechanical symbol of the hands-on sports ethos I was looking for. After the 420 Alley Cat, I developed sort of a fatal attraction to bikes. Where others saw lanes full of cars, I saw the solitary cyclist making his or her intrepid way through a thicket of mobile danger. I found myself thinking romanticized thoughts whenever I took one of my bikes out on the road. I envisioned the cyclists of Portland as an order of freedom-loving gauchos, natural aristocrats amid bovine motorists and the poor serfs on the bus. I took to staring at cycle manufacturers' websites, lost in product lust.

At the time, I was involved in a series of doomed affairs with cheap, clunky, fourth-hand bikes that seemed like good ideas when I found them, but proved to be doomsday machines in use. First, I owned something called a Physio Fit, a brand of no known provenance and North Korea–esque engineering standards, which weighed about as much as I do. After an enterprising but misguided thief snatched the Physio Fit, I bought a beautiful, copper-painted 1983 Schwinn Traveler. In a fit of irrational cornering exuberance, I smashed it and myself into a sidewalk, damaging the Schwinn beyond repair and earning myself a round of minor physical therapy. At this rate, I wasn't going to survive the spring. If I planned to commune with the renegade soul of bicycling, I needed a bike that wouldn't try to kill me.

Even though I continued to admire bike messenger machismo, I also recognized that I couldn't hack one of their preferred combat-stripped single-gears. I plunked down about nine hundred dollars for a Bianchi Volpe, a machine I dubbed the Wolf. I liked the Wolf's utilitarian blend of road bike agility and mountain bike toughness, and I loved its Italian pedigree: Edoardo Bianchi built his first frame at 7 Via Narone, Milan, back in 1895. (Of course, the Wolf itself, like most consumer bikes sold in America, was made in Taiwan.) I started inventing reasons to extend my slow six-mile daily commute into rangier expeditions. I rediscovered cycling's zen-poetic character, grasped on an intuitive level by every kid but stripped from our minds when the state issues us our precious driver's licenses. I was reading a lot of Tom Hodgkinson, the English editor of *The Idler*, who once described biking's "exhilarating sense of freedom and self-mastery," words I took as a personal manifesto every time I rode.

Yes, I was mutating into a hopeless bike nerd, carried away

with the idea of the parallel, two-wheeled society I'd glimpsed during the alley cat. Still, one isolated instance of successful amateur mayhem does not a revolution make, any more than a bunch of boozed-up runners can redefine physical fitness in a single keg stand. I needed to delve deeper into the free-living velo underground, to see other ways this superb vehicle could change the sporting paradigm. And so, not long after the 420 Alley Cat Race, I ended up in Iowa, a little more than halfway out of my mind, standing on the side of a road in my underwear at two o'clock in the morning.

THREE

IRA VS. IOWA

Hawkeye, Iowa, population 489. At Trinity Lutheran Church, the sign announces that at eight a.m. (just six hours from now!) Pastor Mike Horn will deliver a sermon entitled "Safe in God's Hands." A spooky moon shines down through the skeletal lattice of an old cottonwood. I am not wearing pants. Leaning into the passenger-side door, I rummage around inside the Red Pretender, my rented Pontiac pseudo sports car, fighting the entropic storm of granola bar wrappers, empty soda cans, suppurating gas station coffee cups, crumpled clothes, and dried yellow-tan mud. I find my thermal long johns, hop around on the cold gravel as I pull them on, then step into Carhartt cargo pants and hiking boots crusty with grime. The good people of Hawkeye can rest easy—not that local sensibilities seem too delicate. Ten minutes before, a pickup truck lumbered around the corner at the telltale pace of a DUI dodger and bumbled over the curb and into the middle of the lawn across the street. A woman jumped out and sprinted inside the house. She left the driver-side door open. She left the country radio station on. Blaring. The latest Nashville hits now pound through Hawkeye's half dozen comatose streets, a twangy and tinny surrealist performance-art installation in the making. First I expect the cops to come. Then I realize there probably aren't any.

Ten yards away, a man called Guitar Ted leans against his car, a blue, beat-to-shit Honda. He is drinking Red Bull, talking. Since four o'clock the previous morning, I have followed Guitar Ted down hundreds of miles of dirt roads and two-lane highways, with long, frequent stops. He has been drinking Red Bull and talking pretty much the entire time. "Man, some of these people in these small Iowa towns," he continues, pointing over at the pickup truck between pulls at his little aluminum can, "they're bad—I mean, they can get *wild*. You think these farm towns would be all nice and quiet and traditional, small-town America, and I guess in a sense they are, but when the bars close . . ."

I can't really follow it. I like Guitar Ted a lot. Caravan with a man for twenty-two straight hours, and he either becomes your temporary brother or an enemy for life—but Jesus Christ, like I say, *twenty-two hours*. He shows no sign of weakness, exhaustion, or imminent silence. Right now I could strangle Guitar Ted through his Wolf Man beard, curl up on Trinity's porch, and beg Pastor Mike for forgiveness and sanctuary. Safe in God's hands! This whole thing—this pogoing around pantless in some forsaken hamlet on a diet of PowerBars and gas station coffee, waiting in the deep freeze for a pack of *bicyclists*, for the love of God—right now, I blame Guitar Ted. We are tracking the

Trans Iowa, a three-hundred-plus-mile nonstop endurance bike race through some of Iowa's most beautiful and least vehicle-hospitable quadrants. A race entirely the product of Guitar Ted's febrile mind. He is the race commissioner, course designer, referee, timekeeper, logistician, and prize committee. I guess that makes me the press corps.

The Trans Iowa enjoys no sanction from any cycling organization, no status within any kind of recognized competitive framework. It charges no entry fee and offers no prize of cash value greater than the price of a bottle of whiskey. It provides no support, no course marking aside from Guitar Ted (and, in this case, me) standing roadside every fifty miles or so, and operates on a strict every-man-for-himself basis as far as health and safety go. It traverses roads that Iowa transportation authorities see fit to post with "Enter at Your Own Risk" signs; the previous year, rain turned the course into a mud sluice and not a single contestant finished. Still, about sixty riders started Trans Iowa Version 3 at four o'clock yesterday morning. At least a few of them are still alive and on course. In Hawkeye, Guitar Ted and I hope to catch sight of the leader, a rider named Ira Ryan.

". . . you're pretty much guaranteed a bar fight at two a.m. in any one of—ooh, light!"

Guitar Ted points down the deserted road, past the pickup truck. A tiny blinking white speck wobbles just beyond the weak penumbra of one of Hawkeye's few streetlights. Ira Ryan, a bony shard of a man in a red windbreaker and Lycra tights, takes shape out of the gloom, canted forward over the handlebars of a gunmetal gray bike he welded together himself. Ira is a thirty-year-old native Iowan, a professional custom bike-frame builder, a cycling zealot, and, by virtue of winning the first and only completed Trans Iowa, back in 2005, the event's defending champion.

As he blows past us, Ira crushes his pedals with an automatic remorselessness, steering by glazed stare. Later he doesn't remember much about this scene. Hawkeye itself he recalls as a smudge in the periphery, indistinguishable amid visual hallucinations (phantom cows, ghostly rival cyclists) and split seconds of lost consciousness. At this point, he has ridden over two hundred miles with no sleep. The brain chemistry gets a little dicey. As Ira's flashing taillight fades into the darkness at Hawkeye's far end, I likewise feel delirium setting in. Of course, delirium is the Trans Iowa's bloody point.

I first learned of Ira Ryan and the Trans Iowa while I was checking out Portland's bike messenger racing scene. Ira was a former messenger, an ex-partner in Joel Metz's Magpie Messenger Collective, and, in fact, Joel's old roommate. Ira quit the courier game to open a one-man workshop, where he built bikes inspired by the very same French newspaper delivery cycles Metz researched, sturdy but sleek steeds that now enjoyed a cult following. Ira himself, I discovered, was a rider of demi-legendary fortitude. He used his own rides to haul huge pumpkins into town from farms fifteen miles out. Besides an extensive alley cat career, he seemed to participate in just about every form of bike racing known to man. Most intriguing to me, he competed in this torturous road race back in his home state, an . . . undertaking, called Trans Iowa, quickly acquiring sinister repute among endurance cycling enthusiasts. I looked up the official Trans Iowa blog and saw a photo of three cyclists on a dirt road, silhouetted against a sunset's blaze. The site promised "one big-ass loop." Another photo showed a rutted bog that may once have been a country lane. The caption read, "Racers have been known to mentally break down and cry alongside of the road."

I saw several angles. Big-time bike racing, never exactly the toast of America, was snared in an endless series of doping scandals that would soon culminate with the midrace disqual-ification of numerous leading Tour de France riders. It looked like a sport facing the End; the '07 Tour soured even some of the sport's longtime boosters. *New York Times* columnist George Vecsey, a big cycling fan, would write: "When do sports fans everywhere start waving their wooden pitchforks and picking up paving stones and blocking the roads to these fakes?" At the same time, though, cycling itself seemed to be on the verge of a new populist golden age, brought on by expensive gas, global warming, and other signs of looming, SUV-related apocalypse. The Trans Iowa—or so I suspected—promised a perfect rene-gade prototype: an independent (and preposterous) event, com-ing out of nowhere to breathe fresh life into a troubled sport. I knew I had to meet Ira Ryan without delay.

Ira Ryan builds bikes in the basement of Portland's oldest cycle shop. The day I visited for the first time, the big, chilly, fluorescent-lit space was mostly empty, except for scattered old bike parts and a giant taxidermied elk head lying in the dust. In a back corner, Ira stood at a worktable wearing gray-blue coveralls, rasping a shank of steel. He looked like the protago-nist of a Woody Guthrie song: short, compact, skinny, a blond cowlick going every which way, stubble, a face sharpened by plenty of time outside, rough knuckles, oily fingernails. The shop itself also possessed a retro-industrial charm. A jumble of bike wheels leaned against a tank that held some chemical-green scum. Unfinished bike frames hung from ceiling hooks. A battleship-gray hydraulic drill stood in the middle, like a Jules Verne butler-robot awaiting cocktail orders. In short, I thought Ira's place was extremely cool.

Ira started racing at about sixteen in his native Iowa City, moved to Portland, and spent his midtwenties couriering. He apprenticed with a local custom-bike builder, then struck out on his own. "I would say this is a dying art," he said, "except there seems to be all kinds of demand." His waiting list was now up to seven or eight months, but he had no plans to hire help. "This isn't really an industry," he said. "It's an artisanal craft that for the most part consists of a bunch of people who much prefer working for themselves."

After a half hour of talking with Ira about bikes, racing, bikes, racing, life philosophy, bikes, cycling history, and bikes, I realized I was in the presence of a serious romantic, a man who pined for a lost age. Above Ira's workbench, stubs of black electrical tape fixed a handful of old posters and photos to the wall. The largest showed Eddy "the Cannibal" Merckx, the Belgian phenom of the '60s and '70s European race circuit, in a kamikaze tuck, jet-black hair swept back. In another shot, two other '70s cyclists pounded down a filthy cobblestone track, bare legs bathed in mud. "That's from the Paris-Roubaix, one of the Spring Classics," Ira said. "They call it 'the Hell of the North,' because it uses all these old cow tracks and farm roads."

Ira's own riding regime, as he described it, struck me as an attempt to achieve a level of misery worthy of his vintage heroes. While he competed in conventional amateur and semi-pro races around Portland, he specialized in self-designed feats of endurance. In 2003, he rode from San Francisco to Portland in four days. That works out to about 160 miles a day. He slept in roadside ditches, wrapped in plastic. The ride was part of a project called the Rapha Continental, a half dozen riders' effort to document their most ambitious and/or psychotic long-range bike exploits. Rapha, a cycling apparel company, describes the idea on its website: "The Continental is our commitment to the lost art of cycling and the glory of suffering."

All this made a race across his home state—on gravel roads and worse, outside support forbidden, completely outside official cycling—perfect for Ira. I could tell the Trans Iowa's low-fi dynamics appealed to him. The first race, two years before, drew just a couple dozen endurance nuts and mountain bike fiends, mostly on word of mouth. "There wasn't even a finish line," Ira recalled. "I just rolled in, and there was a dude standing next to a pickup truck. I asked him, am I done? And he said, yep, you're done. I found my van and cracked open a beer. That was it."

The Trans Iowa was part of an emerging circuit of similar races, like Kansas's Dirty Kanza 200 and Manitoba's Red ASSiniboine 300, united by lack of sanction, brutal distances, and the Internet. "If it weren't for the Internet, this would be confined to a very small and probably very strange group of people," Ira said, perhaps not recognizing that the group in question was still very small and arguably very strange. "The Web is just such a sensitive amplifier. It takes something tiny and can make it national, at least to an extent. Without the Internet, the Trans Iowa is just a group of guys flogging themselves. With the Internet, it becomes the *Trans Iowa*, y'know? Things develop this aura—you hear about the crazy shit some guy did, or this weird new race someone's putting on in . . . wherever. It generates larger-than-life personalities. Someone does Canada to Mexico in eight days and you're like, what the hell? You catch wind of these mythic figures who do insane things."

In addition to long hours in the shop, Ira now logged huge prerace mileage. He had given up beer and placed an order for "superconcentrated" three-hundred- to four-hundred-calorie ration bars custom-made at a local bakery. Beyond those preparations, his race strategy was simple. "There's a huge amount of information in all the Web forums, a huge amount of discussion," he said. "I try not to get drawn into all that. In the end, it's just elemental. Travel light, freeze at night. That's about it."

Yes. The glory of suffering awaited.

At some point on the drive south from Minneapolis to Decorah, Iowa, the Pontiac and I crossed an invisible but definite boundary between the bland Twin Cities exurbs and deep bucolic America. Midspring sunshine lent a fresh-cut snap to the rolling fields and budding cottonwoods. Broken-up two-lane highways took me through a succession of little farm towns—Chatfield, Minnesota, "the Home of Trophy-Class Turkey Hunting"; Prosper, Iowa, which hadn't. In a two-street Iowa village called Burr Oak, I pulled off the Laura Ingalls Wilder Historic Highway to visit the Laura Ingalls Wilder Museum and Visitor Center. Once back on the road, I witnessed an impressive (to me and, I suspect, the cow involved) display of masculine vitality on the part of a huge black bull. Road signs warning of Amish wagons on the roadway began to appear.

Decorah popped up out of this idyllic spread, compact as a European walled town. Eight thousand or so people and a Lutheran-affiliated college made Decorah the area's decadent metropolis, its brick downtown a minor masterpiece of small-scale urbanity. A few dense blocks of graceful nineteenth-century buildings harbored gamy old taverns, a '50s-vintage pizza parlor, and Hotel Winneshiek, a restored *dame* so *grande* it boasted an opera house on its third floor. At one end of the main drag, the Fareway Grocery sold "squirrel corn" and seed potatoes, and all the clerks, male and female, wore crisp white short-sleeved shirts and black ties. I saw a Mennonite couple, dressed for the Oregon Trail, buying pallets of wood for a buck apiece. Meanwhile, at the other end of the strip, cute granola-lite girls from Luther College staffed a Berkeley-issue organic grocery. The poultry supply store was across the street; the espresso bar, a couple of blocks away.

That evening, the Trans Iowa racers gathered at T-Bock's, a tavern housed in a former Odd Fellows Lodge, for a prerace meeting. On ground level, T-Bock's was a college-town sports bar. Upstairs, it looked more like a bootleggers' retreat. A chipped, scarred antique bar occupied one side of one unfurnished room, dispensing dark brown beer in plastic cups for two dollars. Cyclists tromped upstairs in twos and threes, creating a fashion tableau of little brimmed caps, Lycra, race T-shirts, and old-fashioned, high-necked wool jerseys. Ira showed up in a powder blue and white cap adorned with his workshop's logo, a blackbird in flight. The fellow seemed to be experiencing some mild front-runner paranoia. "It's like I can feel the eyeballs on me," he said, more to himself than to me. "I'm just going on a bike ride, man. Just going on a bike ride."

The other riders ranged in age from early twenties to late forties, a mix of thick-trunked manly-man mountain bikers and scrawnier urban types with cuffed pant legs. I saw only one female rider. Some Trans Iowans looked decidedly tougher than others—for instance, Team Polska, three guys from Wisconsin with the iron-wire musculature of Tour racers. ("Those guys made me nervous immediately," Ira later recalled. "They looked all Euro hard-core.") Most would not turn a head on the street. Perhaps the Trans Iowa required a particular mindset more than any physical toolkit. As the beery preliminaries commenced, I tracked down a rider from Duluth named Tim Ek, whom I'd spoken with on the phone a couple weeks before. Tim didn't strike me as a "glory of suffering" guy; he was more in tune with the tao of the thing, an introspective approach. Like Ira, Tim looked a little edgy. Unlike Ira, he seemed less worried about what the competition thought of him than about his own impending misery.

"For me, this isn't about trying to win or place or anything," he said, in an affable and stereotypical accent. "There's always someone at these things that makes you look silly. But the real stuff all happens internally. There's a point at which you're beyond tired, when it's really a gut-check moment. I believe your body is capable of a lot more than you think, and those are the moments when you find out if that's really true. Can you keep going when everyone else is dropping out? That's the value of this race."

To train for this, ah, inquiry, Tim put in uncounted trail miles during the winter, in the dark, in the snow, in Duluth. His race kit consisted of a compartmentalized ten-pound pack containing spare clothes, food, tools, rain gear, an iPod, a one-hundred-ounce water sleeve, a rehydration product called Accelerade, assorted nutrition gels and PowerBars, peanut butter and jelly sandwiches and ham sandwiches, salt, and caffeine tablets. He packed Mace after discussion of Iowa farm dogs' antisocial bent filled the Trans Iowa Web forums. He would stock up on Mountain Dew at the convenience stores, the route's only resupply options. Batteries worried him—lights out in the dead of night? He hoped his backup headlamp would suffice. "I really, really hope people are prepared for that," Tim said. "These expensive batteries people buy, they don't last that long." He trailed off. "I don't plan on being last, but beyond that, just finishing will be fine with me. This is a huge beast. It's just an incomprehensible distance."

Social hour ended. The racers filed into the next room for a briefing delivered by a man named Mark Stevenson. Trans Iowans rarely called Mark Stevenson by name, and when they did it just confused me. This was the man everyone called Guitar Ted. (He received the nickname in high school, due to his love for guitarist Ted "Wang Dang Doodle" Nugent.) A husky, pale-faced man of indeterminate middle age and noteworthy facial hair, Guitar Ted worked at a bike repair shop in Iowa City. When, that is, he wasn't slow-driving hundreds of miles down gravel back roads to plot the Trans Iowa course. I'd met up with Guitar Ted earlier that afternoon; he told me he considered this year's race his most diabolical yet. Now, standing under fluorescent lights and next to a battered old piano, he called racers up one by one to receive their "cue sheets," a sequence of directions and distances printed on stubby half sheets, to the first half of

the race. To compete in the second half, riders needed to reach
a checkpoint before a specified cutoff time. This was just one of
several inflexible rules Guitar Ted now spelled out.

Rule: Riders could receive no outside assistance of any kind.
They could help each other, if they so chose.

Rule: Lost? Tough. Off-course riders must reenter the route at
the point they left it or be disqualified.

Rule: Dropping out? Better have someone you can call to pick
you up in the isolated township or cornfield where you give up,
because Guitar Ted sure as hell wasn't going to.

Rule: Ride any kind of bike you damn well please. A separate
prize category would go to riders on single-speed or fixed-gear
bikes. The idea that some of these guys would forgo an elementary mechanical advantage seemed rather brazen. That some
would ride fixed-gear, a neo-Luddite configuration that does not
allow a rider to *coast* let alone adjust gear ratios, struck me as
madness. Several riders attempted the first Trans Iowa on fixed
gears. None finished.

Rule: Guitar Ted held no permit from any governmental
entity, no event insurance, nothing. In fact, the Trans Iowa did
not exist.

All of this boiled down to what Guitar Ted called the Trans
Iowa's Golden Rule, which was You Are Responsible for You. As
he passed out the cue sheets, I thought of something Guitar Ted
had told me earlier: "I don't want to overstate my own race, but
this is real. This is raw. It's dangerous, man—potentially really
dangerous. Guys are going to get dehydrated. Guys are gonna
bonk."

Outside, the sunny day gave way to a delicate, clear evening. Downtown's old brick buildings glowed; so did a cobalt

and white '50s Ford Fairlane at the curb, the Dwight Eisenhower
to my rented Pontiac's Dan Quayle. Bikes clogged the sidewalk
racks in front of T-Bock's, and after the meeting, riders lingered
to check out each other's steeds. I particularly admired Minneapolis rider Ken Yokanovich's orange-Creamsicle-colored Quickbeam, outfitted with roomy, old-fashioned olive drab pannier
bags and a custom cylindrical handlebar clip that held a tube of
Blistex. Yokanovich would ride fixed-gear. Other Trans Iowans
tended to greet that decision with studied nods of approval, as if
spurning one hundred years of bicycle evolution was indeed the
most honorable course of action.

Everyone soon saddled up and rode off, bound for rooms at
various cheap motels on Decorah's outskirts, to try to snatch a
few hours' sleep before the Trans Iowa's start, at four a.m.

I arrived at the intersection of Quarry Hill and Ice Cave Road
before anyone else, and parked along the creek that bounds
downtown Decorah, next to a lone darkened car that reminded
me of several serial-killer movies. A fat moon hung above. After a
few minutes, Guitar Ted's Honda growled around the corner. He
climbed out, chipper-eyed, clutching a foam coffee cup, a tight
black stocking cap pulled over his graying mop. Then a column of
headlights—cars and a few bikes—came across the short bridge
out of town. Soon the wee-hours silence gave way to mechanical clanking and occasional profanity as riders unracked their
bikes, snapped wheels into place, and tried to wake up, with the
assistance of friends, wives, and girlfriends.

I found Ira standing with a few other guys, already strad-
dling his bike. This was the same machine that conquered the

first Trans Iowa, though since then it had undergone extensive transplants after getting T-boned by a car during a Portland-to-Seattle ride. He had two water bottles in brackets below the frame's crossbar, and the back pockets of his red Magpie Messenger Collective jersey bulged with rations. About twenty yards up the road, the three uniformed Team Polska dudes seemed to have gathered a small group of other riders, all bare-legged in the cold. Most of the rest of the pack dressed like polar explorers.

As Guitar Ted bellowed his final instructions, I clambered up a hillside about one hundred yards down the road. Guitar Ted would lead the pack out in a controlled start, everyone behind the Honda's bumper for the first mile or so. (The first mile, of course, climbed a daunting hill.) From above, the Trans Iowa field looked like a more or less organized swarm of lightning bugs. Guitar Ted hit the gas and swung up the hill and a ragged cheer rose from the riders. As the cyclists turned into the uphill grind, some bystander rang a cheerful cowbell. It would be the last outside moral support until the finish.

I ran back down the hill and jumped in the Pontiac. I could already tell that this particular example of Detroit engineering hadn't been designed with gravel roads in mind—the car swanned all over the place as I gave chase. Within a quarter mile, I started passing cyclists already laboring and wobbling in the dust. I found Guitar Ted where he'd turned off, about a mile up the hill. "Ira's already off the front," he reported. "He and Brian Hannon were on my bumper from the beginning, and as soon as I pulled over, they just hit it." Hannon, from Colorado, finished second in the first Trans Iowa. "A bunch of other guys took off after them. They're all just hammering it." We watched the stragglers pass, then jumped in our cars and rolled into the night.

The previous day, Guitar Ted and I had taken a leisurely drive over the opening miles of his course, so I could both get a daylight feel for the landscape and admire the man's cruelty. Despite the moonlight, the absence of electric lighting meant that riders could not see the caved-in old barns, moldering pickup trucks, and ruined brick homesteads along the road. More to the point, they would have to navigate a vertiginous network of river-bottom valleys and ascending ridges in pitch-darkness. Contrary to state stereotype, northeastern Iowa is anything but flat. Guitar Ted figured this geological roller coaster could produce downhill speeds of thirty miles per hour, meaning riders would run into any obstacle before their little bubbles of artificial light gave them time to register it.

"The lights most of these guys are using are no different than what you'd use to commute with," Guitar Ted said during our tour. "Under twenty miles an hour, they're fine. Above twenty miles per hour, they can't really show you what's coming." He told me this worried him, which seemed a bit of a paradox. Why design a course that seemed to me to promise maximum brutality? Guitar Ted admitted that the imp of the perverse played a significant role in the Trans Iowa. "As the organizer of something like this, you have this weird yin-and-yang thing going all the time," he said. "You design a course that's dangerous and awful, then you hope no one gets it."

An Iowa native, Guitar Ted came to his taste for OSHA-unapproved fun by blood: his parents loved dirt-track drag racing and hauled him around the rural hot-rod circuit as a kid. He dodged his fate as a grease-stained pit rat, however, when a stint as an auto mechanic radicalized him. "Everyone should be forced to spend six months of their lives working on cars to understand just how stupid and evil they are," he said. "The brake fluid alone can kill you, easy." It would be bikes, then. Guitar Ted fixed them. He rode them on tours of insalubrious parts of the Heartland. He traveled to bike races of all kinds, all over the place. And in recent years he had devoted a huge chunk of whatever spare time his job, wife, and two kids left him to the torment of other cyclists, in the form of the Trans Iowa. As we cruised the opening miles—sweeping downhill turns through cattle pastures, long straightaways disciplined by sine-wave hills—I told him that the Trans Iowa concept reminded me of what I'd read about early Tours de France. *Le Tour*, a garrulous history by British journalist Geoffrey Wheatcroft, recounts that the first stage of the very first Tour in 1903 ran a Trans Iowa–esque 291 miles; the stage winner finished in twenty-seven hours. Tour pioneers collided with wandering drunks, fought off wild dogs, and faced attack from hayseed mobs armed with broken bottles and stones. Like the Trans Iowa racers, they usually had no idea where they were going, and no one expected them to be there. This comparison excited Guitar Ted.

"All the big European cycling events have their roots in things like this," he said. "The difference is, they've been totally transformed by money and TV. They've been sanitized for mass consumption to the point where they're no longer recognizable as what they were. I'm not saying the Tour isn't a great athletic event and a spectacle, because it obviously is. But c'mon—it's kind of become a sick joke, hasn't it? Even if you ride, you can barely relate to it because it's become so detached from reality."

I murmured my general agreement.

"But that's all of sports," Guitar Ted continued. "I ask people sometimes if they remember watching football in the '70s. It even sounded different. Louder. Crazier. You could bring airhorns. You could throw confetti and crap all over the field. That was part of what football was, but now it's not. It's like all of sports have become packaged for TV. I guess the Trans Iowa is consciously the opposite of all that."

I had another antimodernist romantic on my hands. Insofar as Guitar Ted wanted to explore the rustic boundaries of sanity and safety, he seemed thus far successful. I slammed the Pontiac's gas in an effort to keep the Honda's taillights, two red dots in utter Apollo mission blackness, in sight. We took a shortcut to head off the pack at a lonely white crossroads church, 9.8 miles into the race. Guitar Ted had warned me that native Iowans tended to drive their home back roads "totally NASCAR style." Now I saw what he meant.

We stopped at the church, which belonged to some Germanic Protestant sect of which I'd never heard. Urbanites forget how dark the dark can be, how silent the silence, and just how damn many stars the Milky Way contains. Maybe it was sleep deprivation, but I felt awed. Guitar Ted pulled out his cell phone to file the first of a series of audio reports for a mountain biking website, which at least a few Trans Iowa "fans" would follow throughout the day. Guitar Ted had just started talking when the sandpapery noise of tires on gravel and two white lights heralded the leaders. "We've got two guys for sure," Guitar Ted announced, Murrow-in-London style. "I suspect it's Ira Ryan and Brian Hannon." I could hear Ira's voice; the two were— chatting? As they shot through the intersection, they sounded like a couple of khaki-clad office jockeys killing time around the Culligan cooler. The rest of the field was nowhere to be seen. Guitar Ted whistled after he finished his bulletin.

"Man, they are killing this thing," he said. "There's no way they can maintain that pace. No way." Brian and Ira collaborated throughout the first Trans Iowa, riding as a de facto two-man team. Guitar Ted speculated that they now planned to mount a preemptive attack so devastating as to either eliminate or exhaust any potential competition. (Most of the sixty or so riders just wanted to finish. Only a select few amounted to serious first-place contenders.) Ten miles down in less than half an hour put them—temporarily at least—on pace to finish the race in less than twenty hours.

"It's not possible," Guitar Ted said after doing this math. "They're going to hit stuff later on that you just physically can't ride that fast. Still, they're—"

More cyclists burst out of the darkness, about a half dozen riders almost matching the leaders' speed. To stand on a dark country lane and see six bicycles rip out of the void at twenty-five miles per hour is a disconcerting experience. This group included the Team Polska trio and the other riders I'd seen them with at the start. If Brian and Ira thought they would make a decisive escape, Team Polska had other ideas. Behind them, the remainder of the pack appeared, a thin rivulet of headlights streaming down toward the church.

* * *

The impact of two-hundred-plus pounds of accelerated human, metal, rubber, and gear against jagged asphalt produces a frightful sound. Riders must have felt relief when they hit the paved stretch of road past the Sattre Store, an isolated little grocery about twenty miles into the race—at last, a reprieve from mushy gravel. Unfortunately, a moon-crater pothole about two feet wide and six inches deep lay in the dead center of the lane. Just about every Trans Iowan hit it squarely as they came off the meandering hillside to the west. Wheels smashed into and out of the hole with successive *chunk-chunk-crack-thwacks*. Riders cursed and wobbled onward. By some intervention of the Patron Saint of Reckless Fools, no one crashed.

"It's a bad one," Guitar Ted observed placidly after one dozen near wipeouts. So it was.

Ira, Brian, and the Team Polksa pursuit squadron had evidently passed before we arrived at the Sattre Store. A single spotlight cast a weird green-yellow glow over the Wild West–style building, and an old Pepsi machine buzzed on its porch. The pack fragmented now, and we could hear little bands of riders off in the hills long before they zoomed through to encounter the crater. In between groups, the morning began to fill with crowing roosters and melancholic moos from waking cows. An erotic-pink band of sunrise cracked the eastern horizon. Guitar Ted leaned against the Honda and offered a few encouraging words to passing riders. "Lookin' good! Straight ahead! One hour down, thirty to go!"

Our next stretch of driving involved a hectic shortcut through twisty creek bottoms and plateaus dominated by plowed-over cornfields, all oozing silver haze into the gathering daylight. Outside the town of Waukon, we stopped on one of the course's rare overlaps with four-lane automotive civilization, across the road from a heavy-equipment lot. I saw Tim Ek, latched on to a small group in the front half of the pack, a look of adamantine determination on his face. We had once again missed the leaders, however, so we soon ducked back out into the country. This did not take much: Allamakee County, squeezed up against the Mississippi and the Minnesota border, is one of many Middle American places experiencing the demographic equivalent of a slow-motion plague. Its population was greater in 1900 than in 2000, and even a relatively major burg like Waukon—four thousand people and the standard ugly rack of gas stations and convenience stores—surrenders to deep countryside a few hundred yards off the main highway.

My ability to stay on Guitar Ted's tail improved. I could now devote half my attention to the scenery and half to searching in vain for half-decent radio. In a howling desert of bad modern country and generic pop, I found Willie Nelson warbling "Blue Eyes Crying in the Rain." Meanwhile, the ridgeline parallel to my left transformed from grayish black to bright green in a split second, as the sun cleared the trees off to my right. It was just after six a.m.

Guitar Ted stopped at a spot where an uphill gravel bend called Hickory Creek Road put an end to another of the Trans Iowa's short paved sections. I estimated Hickory Creek's incline at about 20 percent, and the few scattered midpack cyclists we saw tackle it groaned through the effort. Guitar Ted told me he had designed the course around two sizable complexes of hills: one at the beginning of the race, one at the end. "It flattens out quite a bit through the middle," he said. "The roads also get a lot nastier."

We glimpsed Ira Ryan and Brian Hannon at about seven thirty a.m., as they darted through a town called Postville, a two-thousand-human blip at the intersection of four of northeast Iowa's obsessive-compulsively rectangular counties. The two leaders still gave the impression of people taking a leisurely weekend morning spin, albeit a spin that, by a rough equation based on my limited sports medicine knowledge and their average speed, probably meant each had burned at least fifteen hundred calories already. They blitzed down Postville's humble main street and passed the convenience store without stopping.

I needed to check out for a bit. I told Guitar Ted I would see him down the road, and parked the Red Pretender next to the convenience store. I hauled my dazed ass into the store to buy—something, I didn't really care what, anything mass-produced and packed with meaningless commodity-corn-based calories. (Eat local, right?) As I stood at the counter, Team Polska showed up. Team Polska consisted of two scrawny Polish brothers, Marcin and Macjei Nowak, their American-born comrade, Doug Pietz, and, for the moment at least, three or four other riders equal to their pace through the opening hill sections. I liked the Nowak boys immediately. "We are very obnoxious," Marcin told me when we talked on the phone a few weeks after the race. "Some people would say we are *very, very* obnoxious. We are noisy. We ride our bikes. We drink beer. We basically just want to have a good time."

The Nowaks developed their rather singular idea of a good

time when they were kids in Poznan, the city where some of Poland's medieval rulers are buried. (Marcin summarized his youth thus: "Let's go up into the mountains and see what kind of crazy stuff you can ride.") After they moved to Wisconsin in 1995, they got involved in the local mountain bike and cyclo-cross scenes and hooked up with Pietz, a Milwaukee firefighter willing to wear Team Polska's patriotic red-and-white and even pick up some Polish cycling nomenclature; together they built Polska into a strong force on the upper Midwestern race circuits. They had not mellowed with age. "We did this one century [i.e., a hundred-mile ride] when it was, like, fourteen degrees," Marcin told me. "We have some weird pictures of Doug where he has this icicle hanging off his face."

The Trans Iowa, though, was something else again. Marcin attempted the unfinished second Trans Iowa alone. "I rode my mountain bike. The weather was so bad, the mud was so thick, my disc brake broke about thirty-five miles in, and I called my brother and was like, man, come pick me up," he recalled. "I still made it farther than about half the guys. On the way home I was saying, let's get some 'cross bikes and do this." Now he was back, in the style of a legendary gunfighter in a western flick, with his posse.

At the convenience store, Doug Pietz sought intelligence. I told them Ira and Brian had hit Postville about fifteen minutes before.

"They stop here?" he asked.

I told him no.

He shot me a look of puzzled dismay. "Have they stopped at all?"

I responded that it didn't seem like it.

"Well, they gotta stop sometime." He walked off to his bike, clutching some candy bars, muttering.

As I watched Team Polska wander the snack aisles and Big Gulp dispensaries, I realized that to stop or not to stop would become the race's key strategic decision. Trans Iowans needed to think of these no-frills Podunk gas stations, with their vats of foul coffee and grease-sheened hot dogs from the Reagan administration, as their personal caravansareis. A well-timed stop could sustain a rider for the next hundred miles, but each break meant a good twenty minutes off the road. I knew Ira, at least, wanted to win. He would stop only when necessary. The question would be, did anyone else want to win?

I crashed in the Red Pretender's backseat for forty-five minutes in Postville, awaking to a highly surreal scene of scores of Orthodox Jewish men strolling the small town's streets. (Postville, I learned, is home to America's largest kosher meat-processing plant.) I hit the road and caught up with Guitar Ted outside an ornate old train station a few miles away. The building itself now served as a local Chamber of Commerce, while the parking lot hosted an informal flea market. An old guy in a replica Confederate Army cap sat behind a folding table stocked with *Girls Gone Crazy* videos—not the brand-name *Girls Gone Wild*, mind you, but an underappreciated alternative. A sign on his van said, "Driver Carries Only $20 in Ammunition." We didn't chat.

Guitar Ted reported that Ira and Brian still held a respectable lead. The Team Polska gang appeared to be breaking up as a few accomplices dropped out and others fell behind. The Nowak brothers and Doug Pietz remained together and within

a few minutes of the leaders, and a couple of other riders hung
on as well. The rest of the pack was in pure survival mode. We
got back on the road and headed for the checkpoint, the almost-
halfway mark where riders would receive the cue sheets to the
remainder of the course. I knew riders tended to linger at this
particular checkpoint—during the first race, Ira called ahead to
order a pizza delivery—and that it would provide one of the best
opportunities to assess how they now fared, after more than one
hundred miles of gravel and hills.

Aside from booking the upstairs hall at T-Bock's for the prerace meeting and postrace festivities, Guitar Ted relied on vigorous use of squatters' rights. (As for the roads themselves—well,
bikes are street legal, aren't they?) The checkpoint consisted
of a covered picnic table in a sweet little creekside park, by far
the highlight of a dusty hamlet of unpaved streets and barking
curs. From here, the course would briefly follow an official public cycling/horse/hiking trail through a riparian area, into the
Trans Iowa's flatter and even more remote middle sections.

A couple of Guitar Ted's bike buddies awaited us at the table,
where we cracked Wisconsin-brewed Leinenkugels and lounged
in the grass and dandelions. After half an hour or so, two riders turned down the long dirt lane leading to the park: Ira and
Brian, still partnered up. The two of them set their bikes against
a wall and stepped around gingerly, fiddling with bags and their
computerized odometers. Ira then sat down at the table and
began to pull the old cue sheets out of the booklet of plastic
sleeves he kept clipped to his handlebars. "I don't know, dude,"
he said. "I'm really not feeling it. Brian is doing all the work right
now. I'm having a hard time even pulling through when it's my
turn to go in front. I don't know if this is happening. I just don't

know. The fact that there's still a double century ahead of me feels pretty daunting right now." The man did look authentically awful, with little blue hollows under his eyes and a microfine layer of grit all over. Brian Hannon, by comparison, looked like a gent enjoying some light and healthful roughhouse in the Great Outdoors—an extra in a J. Crew catalog photo shoot maybe. But I also had to allow for the possibility that Ira was engaging in some crafty psyops. He might intend to seed Guitar Ted and me with misbegotten intelligence he wanted to filter out to his competition.

Ira said he wanted rid of his custom-made ration bars, big brown clods made with every grain known to civilized man and flavored with ground espresso. He plunked them in my hand. "Take 'em," he said. "They were great last time, but this time they're just weighing me down. It's like ingesting a fucking neutron star." As I contemplated the digestive implications of eating a fucking neutron star while far removed from indoor plumbing, Ira and Brian conferred and decided upon a course I viewed as equally rash: they would ride back up the road to a small crossroads café, sit down, and grab a burger. They confirmed with Guitar Ted that this would not constitute an illegal deviation from the course—they would just retrace territory, no shortcuts—finished readjusting their bikes, and set off.

Just as they reached the turn, Team Polska whipped past them. A fourth rider, an implacable single-speeder from Kalamazoo named Joe Kucharski, rode in with Nowaks and Pietz. As they cruised toward us, I saw Ira and Brian pause, stand on their pedals, and look back at the group that had just heisted their lead. They then slowly turned and disappeared into town— reluctantly giving in to the siren song of beef, I guessed. Team

Polska gave a cheer as they pulled into the checkpoint. "Hello, guys, how's it going?" Marcin yelled. They grabbed their cue sheets and then they took off, wheeling out single file toward the rank of cottonwoods along the creek and trail. Total stop time: three minutes, max.

"No break," Guitar Ted said, nodding. "Gotta love it. And yep—here they come."

Ira and Brian reappeared at the end of the road, riding full-out, burgers forgotten. They slowed as they came up on us, Ira scanning around, confused. "Where are they?" he asked. "They didn't stop?"

No, we said, they didn't stop.

Ira smiled with rueful approval. "Those Polish bastards," he said. The two then shot away—"Tour de France time-trial style," Ira later said—in pursuit.

CAUTION

MINIMUM MAINTENANCE ROAD

LEVEL B SERVICE

ENTER AT YOUR OWN RISK

The yellow highway department sign stood on the grassy embankment above the trench. The trench, supposed to be a road, was more a sunken scar between barbed-wire fences. The strip of clay-colored muck stretched out to a horizon about two miles away. A spate of warm weather had dried the dirt—not gravel, dirt—at the road's center to a spongy cake. Sticky mud humus five inches deep sloughed off either edge of the lane. A Roman legion wouldn't deign to march down this thing.

" 'B Service'?" I asked Guitar Ted. "What's 'B Service'?"

"It basically means no service at all," he said. "They just plow these roads out to the farms, then leave 'em to sink into the earth."

B Service roads killed the second Trans Iowa. After a rainstorm left them impassable, riders resorted to hacking through the long, ribbonlike roadside grass. That didn't get them far. Today, conditions couldn't be better. The occasional gentle breeze ruffled perfect presummer warmth, and the light just now began to hint at evening. I felt more relaxed and pleasantly empty-headed than I had in months—I'd taken a forty-five-minute nap with both the Red Pretender's back doors flung open, my bare feet hanging out into space. Songbirds flitted around. Guitar Ted and I drank sodas, lounged against his car, and talked about kids and wives and bikes and stuff; I went on a few little walks along the bright green fields; a farmer wandered out to see what we were up to and chat for a bit. The only thing missing: cyclists. We hadn't seen any in over two hours.

"Huh," Guitar Ted said at one point. "This surface must be really givin' 'em fits." I kicked at the capillary pattern of cracks in the dirt and wondered what setup would best handle these conditions. Relatively narrow, cyclocross-style tires like those favored by Ira, Brian Hannon, and the Polska boys? Or fatter mountain bike tires? I asked Guitar Ted, and he responded with a shrug.

"I guess it depends," he said.

I guess so.

Time . . . continued. Guitar Ted and I kept thinking we saw cyclists crest the hill, and kept being wrong, so Ira and Brian's eventual appearance provoked a short but lively debate about whether they did, in fact, exist. From a distance, their pace looked deliberate. When they reached us, I realized they were still moving at a good clip, riding side by side with matching forward leans. Ira now wore a short-sleeved jersey patterned on the Italian flag. He flipped us his middle finger as they powered by.

Ten minutes later, a surprise: instead of Team Polska, single-speeder Joe Kucharski, accompanied by Aaron Millberger, an early-twenties beanpole in a Luther College jersey. Millberger made the checkpoint just a few minutes after Team Polska's getaway attempt. I'd watched in sick fascination as he mixed up some concoction of colored powders and fluids, unknown to nature, in his water bottles. He and Kucharski looked strong, both faces locked on the road. They barely acknowledged us. What happened to the Polska triplets? Ah, there—five or ten minutes later, three red and white blips lumbered down the road. The Nowaks and Pietz rode in a tight little column, trading the lead at regular intervals. Jerseys hung open, half unzipped, and the three labored up the gentle incline where Guitar Ted and I stood. Thirteen hours into the race, it seemed as though Team Polska's tag-team act might be nearing its end.

That made seven bikes in about three hours. While Guitar Ted received periodic calls from riders as they quit, most of the pack was still out there. Somewhere. The B Service section of the route wound around for miles after the checkpoint, pulling riders through lush but desolate scenery without so much as a chance to buy a Snickers bar. As we talked over our next move, Guitar Ted explained that now, as evening descended, stop choice became crucial.

"After this stuff," he said, nodding down at the dirt, "they're all going to need to stop at the next opportunity. Then there are

two more convenience stores after that. But here's the thing: that
third store closes at ten o'clock at night, and I purposely didn't
tell these guys that. After that, there's pretty much nothing open.
You got 110 miles to go, with no provisions. Ira and Brian seem
like they're far enough ahead that anyone who wants to catch
them will need to skip a stop. But then—"

I saw his point. Skip a stop, and you might make up time. But
if you skipped one stop and then showed up at that final store
after closing time—

"Oh, yeah," Guitar Ted said, "*then* you are totally screwed."

The B Service goo gave way to big hunks of gravel—I wondered
whether Iowans, à la the cliché about Eskimos and snow, had
developed a rich vocabulary to describe their variable road
granularity. I gassed the Red Pretender to keep up with Guitar
Ted, past hog farms and water towers. We found Team Polska
on a long straightaway, moving much more slowly than before.
We came up behind them, and Guitar Ted rolled down his
window to yell, *"Allez, allez, allez!"* At first the sight of the trio's
droopy shoulders made me a little sad, but Macjei Nowak gave
me a defiant raised-fist salute as I passed them. I was starting to
love these guys. Less than a mile later, we passed Kucharski and
Millberger, who looked better than the Polska boys.

The road crossed a couple of one-lane bridges over creeks,
and passed more endless, black-earth fields. We rounded onto yet
another arrow-straight stretch to find Brian Hannon, Ira's partner since the first seconds of the race at four a.m., wobbling at a
near stop in the center of the road. As we pulled up to him, he let

his feet drop to the ground and stood over his frame. Guitar Ted and I both parked in the middle of the road and climbed out.

To me, Brian didn't look any the worse for wear, but he announced that he was finished. "Yeah, at about 190 miles, I started to develop this unbearable and unrelenting pain in my knees," he said. He stood next to his bike and grinned, almost sheepish, and added that he blamed his brand-new custom bike, or more specifically his own failure to dial it in properly. "I've only ridden it one other time, and I guess I didn't have my saddle height quite perfect. It was good, it was fine. But for the Trans Iowa, everything has to be perfect." He was trying to call in a ride via cell phone, but couldn't find a signal. Guitar Ted advised him to head—unbearable and unrelenting pain notwithstanding—to a little town a couple miles behind us. We asked about Ira.

"He is feeling . . . not so great," Brian said. "I've been doing most of the pulling, and he's having a hard time just staying on my wheel. He didn't seem too sure about how he was going to knock off the rest of this thing." I believed him, of course. Sure. In this brief conversation, Brian struck me as the essence of a gentleman. Still, I couldn't shake the idea that Guitar Ted and I might be unwitting conduits for disinformation—especially if Ira wanted to tempt riders behind him into making dumb decisions at those critical gas stations. There was probably nothing to it.

We talked to Brian for a good ten minutes, with no sign of the nearest pursuit and no clear idea of how far ahead Ira might be. As he started back the way he came—gently, gently—Guitar Ted and I took off after the Trans Iowa's leader, now on his own for the first time.

* * *

By this point, I thought I'd detected a strange but persistent subtext: Guitar Ted didn't really trust Ira Ryan. It seemed that in the first Trans Iowa, Ira made a minor deviation from the designated course. "I could have DQ'ed him for that," Guitar Ted said, "but I didn't want to be *that* guy." When we first met up in Decorah, he told me that I could follow the race however I wanted, but that his own plan was to trail the leaders. He wanted to keep an eye on "them."

I considered this as we drove through miles of fields and saw not one sign of Ira. We stopped and waited at the entrance to a hog farm—no Ira. We kept going—no Ira. We now moved into hillier, more varied territory similar to the race's early landscape, though I had long since given up trying to track the route in the detailed road atlas Guitar Ted had lent me. The oh so very rational layout of Iowa roads meant that we reached the intersection of a north-south road and an east-west road just about every mile. Every intersection looked like every other intersection, and the roads often lacked proper names, labeled instead with an impenetrable system of numbers and letters: V-23, C-51, and the like. I felt the landscape would swallow me if I didn't stick to Guitar Ted's bumper.

We reached the next (and second-to-last) convenience store, one of many outlets of an omnipresent chain called Kwik Star. In one sense, the Trans Iowa was just a race between Kwik Stars. As we set up shop at a greasy little picnic table outside this one, I told Guitar Ted that he should hit the company up for a sponsorship. "Man, I wrote to their headquarters the first year," he said. "I never heard back. Guess they probably stuck it in the crank letters file." He added that he also sent press releases to all the small-town papers he could think of, generating exactly zero coverage.

Guitar Ted didn't say much about it, beyond muttering, "Huh. That's weird." Yet I could tell that our failure to spot Ira on that long stretch of road—he *must* have been out there somewhere—disturbed him. The notion that Ira could figure out where he was in the maze of identical crossroads, infinite cornfields, and spiraling cue-sheet directions; pick a tactically advantageous destination; and plot a shortcut struck me as logistically impossible. Plus, there was the matter of Ira himself: a fierce and possibly Machiavellian competitor, sure, but also bound by a somewhat fanatical sense of honor. Still, Guitar Ted was on alert. About a quarter hour after we pulled in, Ira turned down the residential street leading to the Kwik Star.

"Ah," Guitar Ted said.

Ira rode up. Guitar Ted narrowed his eyes. "Hey, man," he said. "What happened to you back there? We thought we'd see ya."

"Oh, dude," Ira said. "I got fucked up at one intersection and rode about three miles the wrong way. Am I still in the lead?" We told him that he seemed to be in good shape. I could sense Guitar Ted's relief—to a certain extent, he intended riders to get lost. Ira made a quick transaction with Kwik Star and pedaled across the four-lane arterial fronting the station, into the twilight. The dwindling sun washed everything in a golden varnish, lending the prosaic gas station a kind of *American Graffiti* charm. Kucharski and Millberger arrived maybe fifteen minutes after Ira left. Millberger squatted on the pavement and performed

more nauseating alchemy with various water bottles and wonder powders. I examined the tiny sprocket on Kucharski's minimalist single-speed, a lonely disc about three inches wide. On
my own totally domesticated little errands, the slightest incline
makes me click like mad to find the cushiest possible gear ratio.
I guess Kucharski's approach—pedaling (y) times wheel spins
(z) equals all you get, tough guy, for over three hundred miles—
had the charm of simplicity.

"I think I got it geared just about right," Kucharski said, sto-
ically, when he noticed me. I could only hope so.

Kucharski and Millberger were still futzing with equipment and supplies when Team Polska glided into the lot. These
three now looked ravaged, but maintained a daffy, cheerfully
demented spirit. Sunburns made Macjei Nowak's arms match
his red and white jersey, and he announced that he was finished.
"My knees, man," he said, grinning with only minor signs of
derangement as he stripped off cycling wear to stand half
naked at the Kwik Star's door. "I just can't go another mile." A
fat, balding guy in an orange polo shirt exited the store, clutching two frozen pizzas and a rental DVD. He looked at Macjei,
a scrawny wraith with militaristic cropped hair, a black bloom
of chest fur, and nothing much on except a pair of anatomically
definitive Lycra shorts. "Hi, there!" Macjei chirped. Maybe the
poor man wanted to run, but I don't think he was physically
capable.

"Man, it's just second nature to us to get naked as soon as
we're done," Marcin Nowak said. "It's almost like we're naked
on the bikes anyway."

The riders now made quite a spectacle indeed: five road-
battered, aerodynamic humanoids, somewhere between fit and

superfit, scattered bikes, and an astonishing array of provisions that seemed to have exploded out of their tiny packs. The Kwik Star's chunky regulars didn't quite know what to make of it. An eight-ball-shaped man in a Harley-Davidson T-shirt stopped to size up the bikes.

"How far you guys goin'?"

"Like about three hundred miles or something," Marcin answered.

Harley Dude scratched his stubbly head.

"Shiiiiiii-it. Three hundred miles on the bike and *I* get saddle sore. You know what you need, boy? A got-damned motor, that's what."

It came to pass, the thing I feared. It was dark—which does not begin to describe the mouth-of-the-abyss depths through which I drove. And I was lost.

Guitar Ted and I had parted company at the final convenience store, well after nightfall. He wanted to wait to see how many riders made it to this last supply depot before its ten p.m. closure. I somehow convinced myself of a plan. . . . To be honest, I don't know what I thought I was doing. I believe I concocted some vision of a peaceable meadow or Norman Rockwell–ish country store somewhere along the final miles of the route where I could bivouac until dawn. That might have worked, had any and all sense of the detailed oral directions Guitar Ted gave me not evaporated out of my mind about fifteen seconds after I left him. I drove thirty miles in one direction, then realized I was headed *away* from Decorah, the finish line of Guitar Ted's "big-ass loop." I executed a three-point turn in some farmer's driveway—waiting for the twelve-gauge blast—then took an aimless shot toward what I hoped was the correct yawning blackness.

I kept trying Guitar Ted's cell phone number, but it seemed my mobile-service provider did not account for clients bombing around the Iowan outback in desperate need of contact with bearded, aliased bike race organizers. After about an hour, I came to grips with the idea that I would be forced to wait for sunup, ask directions, and limp into Decorah long after the race finale. Meanwhile, I knew the lead riders were out there somewhere, engaged in the climactic battle against Guitar Ted's course.

Ira had stopped at the last Kwik Star and consumed two foil-wrapped one-dollar hamburgers, one after another, in a couple of bites each. "Man, such a bargain," he said between mouthfuls. "Who could pass it up?" As he sat on the curb, Aaron Millberger materialized. He looked at Ira and pointed, openmouthed, like he'd finally spotted the Loch Ness Monster after years of search. Ira gave him a friendly nod and finished his second burger. He then did vague things with his cue sheets until Millberger went into the store.

"Out of sight, out of mind," Ira said. He saddled up and disappeared.

Kucharski wasn't far behind Millberger and still carried himself as if another three hundred or four hundred miles would be no big deal. The two of them soon left, maybe ten minutes behind Ira. The surviving Team Polska duo rolled in. Doug Pietz hauled himself off his bike, looked at Guitar Ted, and made the silent gesture of slitting his own throat. His knees would go no further. After a few minutes of cell phone back-and-forth to determine just how long Pietz would have to wait for a ride to Decorah (quite a while), Marcin Nowak ventured out into the night alone, the last survivor of the group that first gave chase to Ira and Brian Hannon.

Then I stupidly took off, too. Now I had to accept that I might miss all the exciting—or really, really, really excruciating—stuff. I turned around again, in the middle of another dirt road, and picked my way back to a paved highway, where I hoped I might find a cell phone signal. Aha! Through a scrim of crackly interference, Guitar Ted gave me his new coordinates. I drove on to a town I could find on my map, then traced the right angles of the rural Iowa road grid to figure out how to get to him. After that— except for the part where I ran into a "Road Closed" barricade and continued anyway only to find the lane flooded by a miniature lake thirty feet across, then backtracked to yet another clone crossroads and devised a different route—it was easy. I found Guitar Ted outside Trinity Lutheran Church at the edge of Hawkeye, Iowa.

The Trans Iowa took up two days of my life, give or take, but sticks in my mind even now, almost three years later: gravel; fields and woods; wild turkeys, deer, and fox; tiny brick-mainstreet towns; utter blackout after dusk; the strange bond I developed with Guitar Ted. Rural Iowa, arguably synonymous with boredom in the popular consciousness, became beautiful and even exotic at the fine-grained level of detail perceived at Ira Ryan speed. I felt like I understood why Ira and his fellow masochists called their ride documentation project "the Continental." The Trans Iowa opened my eyes to their kind of slow/fast travel, an aggressive and exhausting trek to nowhere in particular that made America's enormity manifest.

Like all pro sports, elite cycling belongs to a microfraction of humanity; you must be a cardiovascular freak of nature to begin with, before the first injection, to even think about competing at the top level. Most people, however, can ride a bike, and bikes' accessibility makes possible all kinds of low-key explorations even if you have no interest in Trans Iowa–style punishment. A bike turns the trip to work into a daily barometer of weather and road conditions, risks and opportunities, construction and change and culture: an adventure. A bike race like the Trans Iowa also harbors a just-below-the-surface political agenda of sorts. In America, for some reason, riding a bike remains a kind of radical-chic statement—even though, with oil prices soaring, the globe heating up like a sauté pan, and alleged evildoers everywhere suckling at the crude, the feds should be urging all of us to take daily Victory Rides. To my mind, cycling could be the ultimate bipartisan activity for twenty-first-century America, tailored to core concerns of both liberals (environmentalism, self-righteousness; looking good in tight pants) and conservatives (rugged individualism; self-righteousness; looking good in tight pants). And yet the federal government, which invests something like $50 billion per year in highways, traditionally spends almost nothing on cycling. (That didn't stop our former transportation secretary, in the wake of the 2007 bridge collapse that killed thirteen people in Minneapolis, from blaming excessive spending on "bike paths" for the nation's infrastructure problems.) The recent change in administrations so far seems to portend good things for cyclists, but it will be a long time before any part of America resembles bike paradises like Amsterdam or Copenhagen.

And so the Trans Iowa, as it shared (or invaded) Iowa's public thoroughfares, was political by default. Guitar Ted told me stories of his run-ins with pickup-driving thugs who try to knock him over on his daily ride to work. "Some people think bikes are just toys and don't belong on the road," he said. "At least in Iowa, everyone who rides a bike has to deal with that attitude on a daily basis." Even (or maybe especially) at this unknown amateur race, the decision to ride constituted a statement, like it or not, about how to experience the world, even a theory of how a different world could be.

Hawkeye. About ten minutes after Ira Ryan passes through, the drunken woman stumbles out of her house, turns off the country radio, slams her truck's door, and somehow manages to wobble back inside. Then another lone headlight appears at the end of the road.

"Just one, huh?" Guitar Ted observes.

Marcin Nowak slows as he approaches us. (So what happened to Joe Kucharski and Aaron Millberger, who departed the last convenience store well before Team Polska's last man standing?) He looks wrung dry. "Is there a convenience store around here?"

"Sorry, man—no," Guitar Ted says.

"Is there a convenience store up the road or something?"

"Uh, I think they're all closed."

Marcin shakes his head. "Oh, boy, oh, boy," he says. He

stomps a pedal down, pulls himself up out of the saddle, and pushes himself into the chill and darkness.

"Once it got dark, I felt like I got a second wind," Marcin told me later. "Or maybe it was more like the third or fourth." He claimed that up until evening—and given how they devoured the rest of the field, I found this a little unnerving—Team Polska played it pretty cool, reaching a group decision not to challenge for the lead. "We were having this nice experience, you know," Marcin said. "It's something different from all the races we do. And we were in fourth place, something like that, which felt pretty good. We saw the pace Ira and Brian were setting, and then Joe and Aaron took off, and we kind of looked at each other and were like, we are not chasing them." Both Doug and Macjei had knees going out, and the group had to contend with heat and sun and wind and the consciousness-erasing sameness of Iowa. "We thought, why stress and push it to the red?"

After dark, things changed. Marcin now rode alone and felt good. The wind died, and he began to hit twenty miles per hour on flats and thirty miles per hour on downhills. In between the final convenience store and Hawkeye, he realized that Kuchar-ski and Millberger had disappeared. "They missed a turn some-where," he said, "and I think I know the place, because I almost missed it, too. I stopped and circled around, trying to figure out from the cue sheet, like, what the hell do I do now? I went maybe a hundred yards and it was that thing: I could tell this was not right. I turned around and I was fine." Once he hit Hawkeye, he sensed that Ira might be in his grasp.

"It developed into a race situation," he said.

Marcin, however, did have a couple of problems. He was down to a few ounces of water and a couple handfuls of food. At this point, the Trans Iowa became a matter of metabolism as much as anything. ("After that many miles, you just gotta keep the fire lit," Tim Ek had told me.) With no opportunity to restock, Marcin ran the risk of dehydration or a simple caloric meltdown in the wilds between Hawkeye and Decorah.

All the same, he wasn't long out of Hawkeye before he saw a red flashing taillight out in front of him: Ira.

Tapping. Something. Tapping. What the fuck is this tapping noise? Oh, yeah—"Dude!"

Guitar Ted yells through the Pontiac's rolled-up window, enthusiasm undimmed. "It's, like, almost four a.m. We gotta roll."

Guitar Ted pulls away from Trinity Lutheran Church. I fire the ignition. At the final convenience store stop, I purchased two little canisters of Starbucks Doubleshot, "a convenient, bold, authentic Starbucks coffee experience." As we blast out of Hawkeye, I crack one open, guzzle it, crack the other, guzzle it, and very nearly vomit. In fairness, this is probably not recommended usage. I gag back the DoubleDoubleshot as we hit a two-lane highway, one of Guitar Ted's route cut-throughs. My head wobbles and the white lines look porous and fuzzy-edged, like the backstage recreational buffet at a 1988 Guns n' Roses show. I turn the radio on and flick through stations, a new one every fifteen seconds, just to stay awake.

In the moment, I allow myself to think I have it pretty rough.

Later, both Ira and Marcin describe their experiences, at and around the time I dozed in the car and almost erupted mass-gourmet coffee. Aside from the pervasive neurological strangeness they endured, brought on by exhaustion and starvation, the road occasionally disappeared into vast black sinkholes filled with rainwater, lapping right up against impassable roadside berms.

"I don't know how deep this thing is, and I can't see how wide," Marcin later recalls thinking. "I can't walk around it and I can't walk through it. I thought, if I ride across this thing and lose my balance and fall, I'll be in the water. I'm going to get hypothermia and die. Four o'clock in the morning in Iowa—there is no one around. I took off my booties and socks and rode across them, with the water coming up over my feet. It sort of sucked."

After about forty extremely sketchy miles, Guitar Ted and I pull up to a little pop-up awning pitched against a grassy embankment, atop a formidable hill (of course) just outside Decorah. We find a bleary volunteer, another of Guitar Ted's friends, setting up a table and folding chairs. Here we are: the Trans Iowa finish line. In the darkness beyond, I can make out chalky white blocks and cubes, an ornate iron gate, a stone crucifix, an obelisk like a miniature Washington Monument.

A cemetery. Guitar Ted's race ends at a cemetery.

"I thought that would be kinda funny," he says.

Marcin caught Ira not far from Hawkeye, just when he felt on the verge of getting lost. He drew up alongside Ira and asked him if he understood what was going on with the cue sheet. While almost all the Trans Iowa riders used computerized odometers to track the distances between turns, the digital readings sometimes differed from reality by slight but potentially disastrous tenths of miles.

"He wanted to know how confident I was about where we were going," Ira told me later. "I said I was pretty sure we were on the right track. Then he asked me if we were out in front, and I think I said, 'I dunno, dude, I think there might be a couple of guys . . . I dunno.'"

After about three hundred miles, the Trans Iowa was down to two guys, the one determined to win all along and the one who only realized he could win in the last stages of the race. As the route edged back toward Decorah, Guitar Ted's beloved big rollers kicked in again: pell-mell blind descents followed by inquisitorial climbs, including, as Ira later put it, "A bunch of total bullshit up on some fucking ridge." Both riders hit the downhills hard and felt fine doing so. Marcin, however, was out of food and water.

Ira: "Okay, so . . . this is where Ira the Dickhead Bike Racer comes out. He's out of food. He has no water. And so naturally he asks me if I have anything I can give him. And I'm, like, 'Dude, don't get me wrong, but this is a *bike race.'*"

Marcin: "At this point, I felt really comfortable on the downhills so I think, well, okay, maybe I'll attack on the downhills."

Ira: "We were both going pretty good, but I could tell he just didn't have it on the ascents, so I tried to hammer it."

Marcin: "My idea was a good one, but he was just stronger. He pulled away from me on the hills, and then I would kind of catch up on the descents, and then I would get to the top of the next hill and see his light getting pretty far ahead of me. I was, like, man, I am not going to catch him, am I?"

Ira: "I kept trying to gap him off on the hills, and then I would look back to see his light—see how far back he was."

Marcin: "But I keep going after him. And then I get to the top of this one hill, and I look up, and there is nothing. He's gone."

Ira, once he'd left Marcin on the far side of that hill, had turned off all his lights. Out of sight, out of mind.

The last hundred meters of the Trans Iowa climbed a relentless uphill curve paved with rocks that averaged about half the length of my middle finger. At just about exactly five o'clock in the morning, twenty-five hours after the Trans Iowa began, Ira Ryan flickered into view at the bottom of the hill. He killed off the climb at an agonizing pace, his front wheel tracing a gentle zigzag. By the time he reached the little finish-line encampment, he already had one leg slung off his bike. The half dozen people gathered in the predawn cold—Guitar Ted, the race volunteer, Ira's dad, up from Iowa City, and a couple of buddies—gave him a round of applause. In a few minutes, he was sitting in the dirt next to his bike with his legs straight out in front of him, unstrapping his helmet, drinking his first beer in weeks.

"Guitar Ted," he announced, "you are a fucking asshole for designing this course." Then he looked over at me. "Zach," he said. "Dude, you made it. How're you holding up?"

Sometimes, you just feel stupid.

Macjei Nowak and Doug Pietz, the other two-thirds of Team Polska, drove up right about then. The boys now looked disgustingly well rested, fed, and bathed; just about human, I would say. Ten minutes after Ira's victory, Marcin Nowak climbed the hill. He later admitted only peer pressure and potential shame drove him to the finish.

"I almost stopped at the bottom of the hill," he said. "My knee was just exploding with pain and I was worried I wouldn't ride again all season. But I knew my brother and Doug would be up at the finish and figured they would swear at me or something if I quit then." He walked some of the way, rode some, walked some, and then saw the little tent and forced himself to straddle the bike one last time and dawdle up the hill.

"Oh, my God," Marcin said as he dismounted. "Okay, where is the Man?" He found Ira, and soon had a beer of his own in hand as he stood hugging himself and shivering, still wearing his helmet and staring into space.

Aaron Millberger finished an hour after Ira, with the ever steely Joe Kucharski just ten minutes behind to win the Trans Iowa single-speed championship. A few others, all riding alone, straggled in over the next few hours. In the end, nineteen of the sixty or so riders who started the 2007 Trans Iowa would finish. (Ken Yokanovich, he of the lovely orange Quickbeam with the attached lip balm rack, became the first ever to finish the race on a fixed-gear bike.) I kept myself awake, with bad coffee and worse breakfast at the only diner open in Decorah early on a Sunday morning, to see if Tim Ek made it. Thirty hours after the race began, Tim willed himself up the hill. I thought he might just keep going—he seemed almost unable to acknowledge the little knot of people sitting around the awning drinking beer and eating gross snack food like it was a nice day or something. He finally got off the bike, a vision of disarray, his black hair knocked into a crazy fright wig by his helmet. He slumped in the grass, leaning against a granite pillar in the cemetery fence.

"How'd I do?"

"Ninth," said Guitar Ted, who was bopping around the finish area like a cocktail host in a manic phase, cracking jokes and telling stories.

"Ninth," Tim said to himself. "Ninth. Ninth." I couldn't tell what he thought about this. Proudest accomplishment of his life? Stunningly dumb waste of a weekend? Perhaps he just felt numb.

By now, Team Polska had reappeared as a Euro-style cheering section. Doug and Macjei ran down the hill to greet incoming finishers, banging on a couple of cooking pots and yelling *"Allez! Allez! Allez!"* like they were full of lambic at a Belgian road race. Marcin limped around in jeans and sunglasses. (As it would turn out, Doug would be off his bike for six prime riding weeks, in physical therapy for Trans Iowa–inflicted injuries.) Marcin mostly wanted to talk about soccer. I would deduce from our later conversation that he was processing some Trans Iowan version of the stages of grief. "When I got done, I spent that whole day saying never again," he recalled. "But twenty-four hours later, I'm thinking about how we train for the next one."

Great idea, great idea. Why *not* do this every year? Why not do this every month? I found myself fantasizing about helping Guitar Ted launch a national, even global, circuit, with TV rights for sale to the highest bidder. The Trans Idaho! The Trans Delmarva! The Trans Manhattan! The Trans Bulgaria! I decided this was my cue to pack it in. At about eleven o'clock in the morning,

I drove down into Decorah, walked into Hotel Winnishiek, and begged for shelter.

No one died. No one even crashed, as far as we learned—a case of Guitar Ted's hopes overcoming his plans. The word *extreme* has devolved into a lame cliché, but the Trans Iowa was the real thing. Or maybe "extremist" would be more accurate. I came away wondering how many professional athletes, in any sport, could do exactly what Ira and Marcin and the other seventeen finishers did, pedaling a distance greater than the gap between New York City and Washington, D.C., without help. The average pro jock would wonder where his or her personal masseuse had gone. My search for renegade sportsmen had inadvertently turned up some real athletes.

More than anything, I came to think of the Trans Iowa as an odd and unself-conscious experiment in liberty. It emerged from nothing, owed nothing to any central authority, took shape first in Guitar Ted's mind, and then spawned an informal community. The race itself demanded an almost frightening level of independence. In a mediated world, the Trans Iowa came with almost no filter at all. Ira summed it up well the first time we met: "In a way that is pretty perverse, no doubt about it, what's appealing about this kind of event is that you can die. It's all about navigation, endurance, and self-sufficiency. It pushes you as animal."

FOUR

DERBY DAY NOTES

One week after the Trans Iowa came one of the high holidays of my personal sporting calendar, a prime chance to explore a more genteel approach to sports fandom, one that involves clever haberdashery rather than painting one's face in the old alma mater's colors: the Kentucky Derby.

I love the Kentucky Derby because it does not matter. Of course, very smart people could make a good argument that no sporting event matters. I mean that even within the context of sports—a context in which the 2004 Boston Red Sox are more historically significant than Metternich—the Kentucky Derby really does not matter. The derby just exists. Outside of career gamblers, plutocratic breeders, and scary Barbaro cultists, Americans just don't care much about horse racing anymore. We don't care that it was America's ur-sport, our first national organized competitive endeavor. We don't care about its history or tradition, tactics or nuances. Given a choice between wagering our cash on gorgeous, fearsome animals, piloted by tiny but courageous athletes in fantastic outfits, and buying one-dollar Scratch 'Em tickets from the teenage meth addict behind the counter at Kum'n'Go, we have collectively chosen the latter.

Yet the more the Turf declines, the more I like the Kentucky Derby. Its genius lies in the fact that you don't *have* to care. Most of our overblown Big Events depend on the fiction that the entire public mood rides on the outcome of months and months of excruciating buildup. (Yes, I'm thinking of the NBA Finals.) In contrast, one can enjoy the derby to the hilt while maintaining happy ignorance of all participants, human and equine, until about an hour before post time, when it's time to consume a mint julep and achieve the instant wisdom required to place a bet. This is the key to the derby's wonderful leveling effect.

Every other red-letter sports happening inflicts a surplus of knowledge upon us: not only do talking heads on TV know everything there is to know about the game at hand, but the squarehead on the next barstool, who spends all day combing the Internet for stats so he can improve his fantasy team, also knows everything. Consider the gauntlet of pseudo-expertise we confront at the start of every year. January begins with the big college football bowl games, the culmination of that sport's strange, Kremlinological competitive "structure." It would make more sense to ask the Hogwarts Sorting Hat to choose a national champion. The Super Bowl then unleashes two weeks of numbingly detailed prognostication, most of which turns out to be 100 percent bunk when the game itself finally occurs. Then, March Madness demands that every red-blooded citizen complete a tournament bracket, half of which consists of institutions of higher learning previously known only to their own alumni. And still there's always someone in your office pool who squanders enough company time trawling ESPN.com to know the Mount Saint Marys from the Coppin States. That guy takes your money.

And then—sweet mercy!—comes the derby, a certified Major Event too big to ignore, which no one, not even the craziest sports savant you know, can tell you a single intelligible thing about. Bliss. A whole hidden culture of superwealthy lunatics and their pint-sized, silk-dressed avatars comes into focus. For these people, Derby Day is a very pricey obsession. For the rest of us, it provides a rare chance to wear weird hats.

Portland warmed up beautifully for Derby Day '07, and my wife and I hit a race party thrown by a couple of friends. She was pregnant, so I found myself obliged to double my mint julep consumption. The all-important signature cocktail is a vital symbol of the derby's greatness. The julep's internal battle between sprightly mint, wintery bourbon, frigid ice, and syrupy sugar makes it a drinkable essay on spring. As I lounged in a lawn chair, frosty mason jar in hand and sun penetrating my psychic wintertime shell, I was tempted to think all sports events should have their own particular drink—except the Super Bowl would probably adopt the kamikaze.

The party's betting book operated in one corner of the yard, with a glossy white board with each horse's name and current odds graphed on it. Don't tell the federal or state governments, but the in-house system worked like so: Two dollars bought one share of a particular horse; punters could buy as many shares in as many horses as they wanted. Those who chose the winning horse would split the entire pot, with each share receiving an equal payout—in other words, if you bought more than one share of the winning horse, you collected multiple dollops of the purse. I liked the look of Cowtown Cat and plunked four dollars on him, which I knew guaranteed he would fail.

As post time approached, people milled around the backyard. Almost everyone wore a hat. The private derby party provides an excuse for midday socializing and low-impact merriment. This particular party was, to me, a vision of sports paradise, my private fantasy world in which no one ever again watches a game in the clutches of a corporate sports bar called Left Field or Champion's. I believe we need to reinvent sports fandom, which has become such a core part of American culture, just as urgently as we need to reinvent athleticism itself. If we're going to experience spectator sports primarily via video, because of ticket prices and simple logistics, we need to inject flesh-and-blood life into the experience. How much more fun would it be if every big event occasioned a theme party with a low-budget, fancy-dress component, plus traditional beverages as needed? A good Kentucky Derby party goes one better than the average sport-centric gathering, because the actual event is only two minutes long. That leaves at least an hour on either side to hang out.

This particular year, those two minutes proved quite incredible. Street Sense, next to last in the backstretch, took a slicing tack off the rail in the last curve, cannonballed through the front of the pack, and ran down Hard Spun on the curve. I'm pretty sure no one at the party had heard of either horse before that week, but we all lost our minds as these two exquisite animals, products of decades of carefully planned horse sex, dueled to the finish. Street Sense, Street Sense, Street Sense by two lengths! Then we took deep breaths and got back to our cocktails. It is, I tell you, televised sport at its finest. Mark your calendars for next May, and go buy a hat.

FIVE

STADIUM PUNK

O n a sunny June day in Our Nation's Capital, a blond guy with a scraggly goatee staggers up a weedy hill, toward the dilapidated '60s Modern bowl of Robert F. Kennedy Memorial Stadium. As I pass him, heading in the opposite direction, I speculate that the gentleman's pregame warm-up may have gone too far—whether or not he will still be conscious in an hour seems an open question. He drops an empty fifth bottle, which shatters on the gravel, releasing a potent cloud of booze vapor. His black T-shirt, an imitation jersey, reads, "BARRA BRAVA / 12 / D.C. UNITED." An RFK employee watches Blondie's unsteady uphill progress from the driver's seat of her stadium-issue golf cart. "Man," she says as we inhale the drunken man's aura, "I'd love to have some of what he's having." (Johnnie Walker Red Label.)

Blondie is ready for some football.

I've come to RFK to hang out with fans of D.C. United, which very attentive observers of the national sporting scene will recognize as a soccer team. From the earliest days of Major League Soccer, United's fans have distinguished themselves as some of the league's rowdiest and most committed. Two separate but allied supporters groups—La Barra Brava ("the Brave Fans"), largely but not exclusively Hispanic, and the Screaming Eagles, mostly but not exclusively Anglo—dominate one side of RFK, where their incessant mass jumping causes the entire bottom tier of stands to bounce in a most alarming fashion. The eight hundred or so members of the two groups account for about a twentieth of the usual United crowd, but generate about 80 percent of the noise.

On the day of my visit, United faces the Chicago Fire, a rivalry with some edge to it: United's faithful loathe Chicago, in part because of a series of recent playoff eliminations courtesy of the Fire, but mostly because they feel Chicago, a later addition to the league, is a bargain knock-off of D.C. United. "They've been a strong club from the beginning," one Screaming Eagle says, "but only because they copied us." The two teams do wear similar color schemes, and the Fire's heraldic badge, modeled on a fire department crest, might vaguely recall D.C.'s militaristic, eagle-emblazoned shield. What we're really talking about here, though, is an ineffable sense of identity. D.C.'s fans think of themselves as the most *authentic* in MLS, the closest to real Euro/Latin flavor. Chicago, in the form of its fanatical supporters in the group called Section 8, begs to differ.

This, of course, is the sort of feud no sports marketing department could invent, a sign of organic life hard to imagine when MLS hatched, fully formed and focus-grouped, over a decade ago. I've traveled to D.C. to see La Barra and the Screaming Eagles in action, to try to figure out what their existence, centered as it is on the most browbeaten pro team sport in America, might mean for fandom itself, now and in the future. And, of course, because a nerd loves nothing more than the company of other nerds.

I am a soccer fan, not an unusual thing here on Planet Earth. To many of my fellow Americans, however, this marks me as a possible subversive element, so maybe I should explain. A number of life experiences helped make me a soccer fan. Only the first involved a choir festival.

Every two years, my hometown of Missoula, Montana, hosts an event called the International Choral Festival. Understand that Missoula, though a college town urbane by Montana standards (and, in fact, viewed by much of the state as a bastion of latte-enfeebled Trotskyites), is not exactly cosmopolitan. There's not a decent taco truck within 150 miles. And so the Choral Festival, an invasion of pubescent vocal ensembles from all over the distant exotic world, marked both a high point on Missoula's cultural calendar and a rare opportunity for transnational lust. In the summer of 1990, I was an aimlessly hormonal and awkward fifteen-year-old, typical in every way except a little more pathetic, in that I had won a high school varsity letter in Thespianism. (Really.) The Choral Festival staged an open-air show in a park a block from my family's house. And there—squeezed into a program of warbling Estonian eunuchs, twee Japanese poppets, and the earnest local talent—I saw them: the lovely Uruguayan Girls. There couldn't have been more than a dozen of them. But the Uruguayan Girls looked, to desperate and clueless teenage boys who rarely set eyes on females born outside of the 406 area code, like a hallucinatory army of supermodels.

Talk to one? Please. But when the festival announcer mentioned that the Uruguayan delegation—they'd brought some male specimens along, too, for whatever reason—planned to challenge all comers in a soccer match the following afternoon, I knew where I would be. Never mind that my actual soccer résumé to that point ended in second grade. It was a World Cup summer (Italia '90: awesome mullets), and after many lonely hours spent watching the grainy global TV feed, I figured I knew more about the World's Most Popular Sport than the average Missoulian. In retrospect, of course, that claim seems a bit slight.

I have only sketchy memories of what went down on that sun-blasted field next to my mom's old high school. I recall the American team consisted largely of the hirsute developing-world groupies who infest crunchy college towns—the kind of guys who wear hand-knit ponchos for noncomedic reasons and bore friends, and everyone else, with tales from their semesters abroad in *Neeek-aaah-raah-guaaaah, Paaaay-ruh,* or *Chiiii-leeeeey.* Our self-styled creative midfielder yelled *"Centro! Centro! Centro!"* when he wanted the ball, even though all his teammates spoke English as their first language. I know I nearly puked due to exertion. I remember a Uruguayan forward's knuckleball shot, which produced an audible ballistic hiss in the air and almost decapitated me. And I know we Americans somehow defeated the Uruguayans, a triumph we celebrated as a signal achievement for the motherland until we remembered that our opponents were, after all, a bunch of choirboys.

None of this mattered. What mattered were the Uruguayan Girls, who lounged on the sideline and waved tiny versions of their country's cheerful sky blue and white flag. They sang football songs in professionally angelic voices; moreover, in sexy, sexy *español*. In the heat and glare of a Montana summer afternoon, the Uruguayan Girls offered a tantalizing glimpse of the world beyond. And have I mentioned they were devastatingly gorgeous and crushingly inaccessible, and yet deigned to watch twenty-two boys play bad soccer on a beautiful day? I found this very intriguing.

For a long time, we soccer fans were the Soviet dissidents of mainstream American sports culture: we did not exist, except when the authorities found it convenient to denounce our existence. That seems to be changing. The World Cup and other major tournaments now attract respectable stateside TV audiences. When Manchester United and Chelsea, both giants of English football and global brand extension, played in the 2008 Champions League final, my local pub was jam-packed with Yanks in newish red and blue replica shirts, shrieking and groaning with abandon. Just a few years ago, the same broadcast at the same bar would have drawn a couple dozen exchange students and trainspotteresque Americans eager to share their disturbing pre-Wikipedia mastery of trivia about both clubs ("Manchester United was founded by railway workers, you know . . ."). We would have spent two drowsy hours muttering "ooh, nice idea," into our beers, then departed in semifurtive ones and twos, without exchanging names.

Of course, I find this sea-change-in-progress gratifying. The dearest fantasy of all American soccer fans is that History Is Turning Our Way, as some obscure Marxian process plays out. It's also a little bittersweet. Like any cultural outcasts, we secretly reveled in exile. Soon, we won't be (un)cool anymore. For now, though, soccer still inspires situational rabies in some people, particularly in the sports media. Every four years, the World Cup rolls around, and the lead sports columnists of major daily newspapers unearth antisoccer diatribes from their hard drives, search and replace a few names and dates, and file them anew. Sportstalk icon Jim Rome, as just one aspect of his robust sense of self, views himself as America's soccer basher in chief. Representative Rome: "We all know soccer has an embarrassment of riches when it comes to problems. They have no goals, fake injuries, violent fans, the mullets, flares, blood and urine bombs, head butts, warm Capri Sun and zero fan interest, just to name about a dozen."

These are excellent enemies to have, of course, and there's something fishy and Freudian about the whole thing, like the guy who goes out of his way to tell you how so not gay he is. I would, however, admit that my kind, the homegrown American soccer geek, makes a tempting target. We may suffer from an unrecognized strain of post-traumatic stress disorder. We tend to be martyr-complex-beset paranoids who see conspiracies everywhere, yet remain convinced of our superiority. We write regrettable letters to the editor and hair-trigger blog posts. We wear seasonally inappropriate scarves. We are the uninvited fanatics who turn up on your doorstep, eager to share an exciting pamphlet on the True Way. We are also the insufferable pseudo-sophisticate who won't touch the Budweiser in the fridge because he only drinks microbrew. Without warning, we will divert a friendly conversation about the NFL playoffs into a rant about the grandeur of the English FA Cup. Above all, we disturb people. Our very existence implies that our fellow citizens' understanding of sports is built on a false or incomplete foundation, like pre-Galilean astronomy or Italian food before the tomato. So what if you know how the Tennessee Titans' 2005 draft choices affected the balance of power in the AFC South? What can you tell me about up-and-coming African midfielders playing in the French league?

I am sorry, though, because we are multiplying. Like cockroaches, another pesky survivor species adapted to the shadows of an abusive environment, America's soccer subculture is thriving. My self-assigned mission: figure out what that might mean.

At the bottom of the hill, RFK's parking lots stretch off into overgrown trees, dusty strips of dirt, and crabgrass. A little tent city clings to one side of the asphalt, spewing barbecue smoke, a couple hundred people in orbit from beer keg to grillside to cooler—almost all of them, like the Johnnie Walker drinker, dressed in black. Behind one parked SUV, a drum corps composed of two black guys and three white guys warms up. A pair of loudspeakers rattles out classic ska and New Wave songs.

I track down David Lifton, one of the Eagles' leaders, and a few other senior figures, all clutching plastic beer mugs. Forget team owners, forget managers—like all true fans of all sports teams of all kinds, these people view themselves as the guardians of D.C. United's soul. In this case, with better than average justification. "We go back to before this team even had a name," Lifton says. "As soon as word got out that there would be a team here, our founder got hold of the franchise president.

And to their credit, the front office here has always gotten it. They understand what we're about. I've heard horror stories from other cities, where the teams and the supporters end up at odds with each other, where there's just outright hostility. That's never been the case here at all."

Now both the Screaming Eagles and La Barra Brava are deeply enmeshed in United's operations. The front office delegates some ticket sales to the groups' elected boards and basically relies on them for street-level marketing. (Like other MLS supporters groups, the D.C. fans produce an extraordinary line of unofficial merchandise: scarves, shirts, stickers, hats, baby bibs, flags, beer steins, coffee mugs, bike messenger bags, shopping totes, barbecue aprons. . . .) Fan-operated websites and podcasts make up a significant segment of available United-related media. The two supporters groups organize large traveling contingents for away games—a couple hundred for a typical visit to the New York Red Bulls, D.C.'s archrival; a rollicking wall of over five hundred bodies for the 2004 MLS championship game in Los Angeles. Relations are as smooth as could be expected between a corporate entity and groups with an unstructured grassroots membership policy and a pronounced fondness for beer. "It's symbiotic," Lifton says. "We're unofficial. They don't fund us. But we're both after the same thing, which is basically an atmosphere that's hostile to play in for any visiting team."

When the night's match kicks off, I see what he means. RFK is a cavernous expanse, designed to host eight or nine Washington Redskins games per year, and dwarfs even a healthy-by-MLS-standards crowd of over twenty thousand. The humanoid clumps scattered around the lower decks would feel disconnected and straggly if it weren't for the solid center of gravity provided by hundreds of Eagles and La Barra members packed at the forward edge of the stands. Throughout the match, a man with a gleaming bald head and meaty tattooed biceps—exactly the guy you don't want to meet when you're in over your head with your bookie—stands with his back to the field. As "capo," he orchestrates the section's nonstop chants and songs, barking commands for choreographed banner displays and the joist-rattling bounce. From my seat three or four rows behind the Eagles and La Barra, I notice that other, more sedate fans spend about half their time watching the game and half watching the standing, heaving, singing mass in front of them. The supporters groups are part of the entertainment—maybe, given Chicago's weak display in a 3–0 loss to the home side, most of it. Even for the relatively small audience that devotes a lovely spring evening to a pro soccer match, the superfans are something of a freak show.

"In America, we have a tradition of being led as fans," David Lifton says. "People aren't used to seeing fans themselves initiate things. To be honest, we have more issues with people who think they want to join us, but don't really know what that means, than we do with stadium security or anything else. People need to realize that if they come to our section, they're going to be required to participate. You will stand up. You will sing.

"In most U.S. sports, the atmosphere is dictated by the franchise itself. That goes back to baseball and the organist, I think. Baseball, fundamentally, is a game where you go to sit back and enjoy it in a sort of leisurely way. And because all of our sports traditions come from baseball, that's the predominant style. It's what people are used to, and we are something completely different."

*   *   *

In 1996, I left North America for the first time. My longtime
partner-in-crime Dan E. and I jetted off to Moscow so we could
test our undergraduate Russian skills and lord it over the sissies
who went to places like France. The country was in the midst
of its post-Communist, pre-Putin experiment with terminal-
societal-death-spiral decline, and Moscow was full of tin-walled
kiosks selling counterfeit Stoli and parks returning to wilderness
and filled with drunk teenagers making out. Of course, the obvious destination on our first night in town was a fake Irish pub.

To look at, Rosie O'Grady's, with its wood veneer and retro
Guinness posters, could have been any pseudo-Hibernian bar
in the world. The clientele, however, more closely resembled
the patrons in the *Star Wars* Mos Eisley Cantina scene than a
jolly night out in Galway: rootless cosmopolitans, mysteriously
wealthy locals and their surgically enhanced Ukrainian "companions," and, on one occasion, an Englishman sporting the
T-shirt of the notorious Nazi skinhead band Skrewdriver. The
bar's main attraction that summer was the European Championship, a sixteen-team tournament held in England but beamed
to Rosie's giant satellite screens every bright midsummer night.
Football went very well with the prevailing Weimar-lite atmosphere and the giddy effect of drinking beer in a foreign land
for the first time.

I didn't realize it, but football, always a worldwide phenomenon, was hurtling into a period of lightning globalization. The
scene at Rosie's was a symptom, and not even the United States
proved immune. Earlier generations of American soccer fans

lived on a remote, chilly, off-world colony. They subsisted on local ethnic leagues and obscure tournaments, the occasional spasm of World Cup interest, and an eccentric PBS show called *Soccer Made in Germany*. Now that was going to change. Satellite TV and the Internet would transform a mere big-time sport to an omnipresent panglobal juggernaut. Just as the dregs of international society could enjoy Euro '96 from Moscow, fans all over the world could now follow every major competition, club, and player like never before. Today, U.S. cable TV supports not one but two full-time soccer networks, not to mention the extensive coverage available on Spanish-language stations. (In 2007, the *New York Times*'s excellent soccer blog reported that about eight hundred thousand people in New York City alone watched Univision's coverage of a match between Argentina and Mexico.) European superclubs like Manchester United, Barcelona, and Real Madrid enjoy sizeable stateside followings and can fill any stadium in the country. All major Mexican teams now conduct a lot of business north of the border, including competitive tournament matches. Throw in three successful World Cups in less than a decade (the 1994 men's Cup, '99 and '03 for women) and the well-attended 1996 Olympic tournaments, and it begins to look like our supposedly indifferent country harbors a major soccer nation within it.

Of course, none of this was on my mind in Moscow as I watched Jürgen Klinsmann's Germany roll to the title. Euro '96 catalyzed all my previous tendencies into full-blown addiction. I found the game itself, with its limitless elaborations and complexities, fascinating, and there was more. Somehow—thanks to the Uruguayan Girls, the wretched hive of scum and villainy in Moscow, and, probably, the game's air of exotic remove—my mind fused soccer with adventure, travel, intoxication, and intrigue. I didn't understand how it all fit together, and I still don't. It's a mystery, a fixation, and probably a folly. I guess that's a fair working definition of love.

In that same year, 1996, a small group of investors launched Major League Soccer, the latest in a long series of attempts at a national American professional circuit. Talk about post-traumatic stress syndrome: fear of joining many, many other American soccer start-ups in oblivion shadowed MLS's every move. The central league office controlled all ten original franchises, manipulating rosters for maximum ethnic-group effect, and tamping down any untoward *competition* that could lead to, you know, someone getting hurt. The new teams' names, soulless confections like "the San Jose Clash" and "the Kansas City Wiz," reeked of mid-'90s sports marketing. The league was antiseptic and artificial—by design. Remove the paprika, tone down the garlic, and maybe this "foreign" sport, with its reputation for threatening fan behavior and oddly low-scoring games, would become palatable to the mid-American consumer. Call it the Olive Garden model.

In reality, the mainstream sports fan has proved elusive at best. For years, the league's average attendance has hovered around fifteen thousand per match, sometimes a little higher, sometimes a little lower. The wider sports world pauses to notice MLS only when the arrival of a major star, like England's David Beckham or teenage American wunderkind Freddy Adu, basically forces the issue. The league's officials always say they want

to turn the traditional Big Four team sports into a Big Five. Suffice it to say that so far, hockey has more pressing concerns.

Meanwhile, something else happened. The league's advent
revealed that America did, in fact, breed soccer fans—a tiny
but resilient tribe, seldom before seen in the wild, that began
materializing at MLS games. These people were not necessarily
well-behaved. They wanted to stand up throughout games, sing,
drink, throw things. They wanted homemade banners, flags,
drums, smoke bombs, confetti—all the plebian uproar of European and Latin American football. They seemed determined to
inject some craziness into the business-plan-driven MLS, to love
the sterile little league in spite of itself.

In Chicago, they call themselves Section 8, in honor both of
their original seating arrangements at Soldier Field and the military code for mental instability. In Houston, the Texian Army and
El Battalion show up at the stadium in orange bandanas, looking
like outlaws from some acid-trip spaghetti western. Toronto's Red
Patch Boys achieved instant notoriety in 2007, their club's first season in the league, by burying opposing players under avalanches
of paper streamers. These supporters clubs, as they're known,
combine inspiration from the nutty "ultras" groups of continental Europe, the traditional working-class atmosphere of English
football, and the mob rule that prevails on the concrete terraces of
Latin American stadiums. Yes, sometimes you have to use your
imagination a little; even the biggest MLS supporters groups can
generally muster a few hundred emphatic souls at most. Still, this
subcultural mutt appears to enjoy hybrid vigor. Strong supporters groups can even be found outside MLS, in the obscure lower
divisions of American pro soccer. In Portland, for example, the
Timbers Army has become a thousand-strong embodiment of the

city's eccentricity, full of bagpipers and solo mariachi trumpets, dyed green hair and homemade T-shirts. You could say the Army is out of scale with our second-tier Timbers, a bunch of career journeymen whose schedule consists of unknown quantities like the Atlanta Silverbacks and Rochester Raging Rhinos. That would both miss the point and potentially invite physical harm.

The most depressing thing I've ever seen in a stadium happened several years ago, when I was covering the Portland Trail Blazers for the city's weekly newspaper. I forget every detail of the game in question (midseason NBA games actively beg to be forgotten), except this: in the last minute of the game, the Blazers neared the one-hundred-point mark, and for the first time, the entire crowd rose as one. The fans began to chant in unison, something they hadn't done all night.

"Cha-lu-pa! Cha-lu-pa! Cha-lu-pa!" What was this? Did the Blazers have a Mexican player I didn't know about?

"Cha-lu-pa! Cha-lu-pa! Cha-lu-pa!"

The reporter next to me explained that if the Blazers (or, for that matter, their opponents) hit the century mark, everyone in the arena would receive a coupon for a free Taco Bell chalupa. The coveted chalupa! Deep-fried wheat flatbread stuffed with meat, cheese, and Baja™ sauce! The crowd, so far a desultory presence at best—fans roused themselves when the PA announcer urged them to *"Make some noise!"* but otherwise seemed preoccupied with their refreshments—came alive to root for mass-produced indigestion. I found this pathetic, but not a surprise. Prepackaged entertainment larded the whole evening: gimmick prize races, shoot-from-the-center contests, cheerleaders tossing T-shirts, ten-second blasts of pop hits, whatever. Sometimes some basketball would break out, accompanied by an irritable buzz. People didn't quite know what to do without amplified instruction. If you've been to a stadium recently, you know what I'm talking about. The ball goes out of bounds, and some third-division radio "personality" pops up out of nowhere with a hand-held microphone for the Fan Trivia Challenge. It's as though Management doesn't really want the audience to watch the game—like it lacks confidence in its core product. Sometimes, you understand the concern. I found the barrage of Top Forty snippets annoying when I went to see Portland's pro indoor lacrosse team but—well, it was pro indoor lacrosse. Can't blame them for dressing it up a little. In most cases, though, the pre-programmed hoopla feels like an offense against common law. A citizen should be able to watch a minor-league baseball game in peace, unmolested by big-screen karaoke. (Indeed, Portland's Triple A team offers an annual "Nothing Night," turning a brief respite from marketing gimmicks into yet another marketing gimmick.) After 9/11, Major League Baseball turned the seventh-inning stretch, one of the loveliest traditions in sports, into a mandatory patriotic pep rally to the strains of "God Bless America." (I had no problem with this in the immediate aftermath, but years later, enough is enough. A friend and I have discussed launching a protest campaign, maybe a Savethestretch.com website, but don't want to end up on any Homeland Security watch lists.) An ostensibly important concern like the NBA should aspire to a certain gravitas, but yammering video screens and bossy PA announcers neuter that league's once raucous arenas. Fandom is supposed to be a sanctioned form of temporary insanity, but rabid mass hysteria just isn't what it used to be.

In part, I blame architecture. Old-school venues, like the crumbling Boston Garden or the overstuffed Pontiac Silverdome of the Detroit Pistons' "Bad Boys" era, were downscale, tumble-down rumpus rooms for the People. Slick, technologically plush, luxury-box-oriented modern stadiums are devices to separate customers from cash at as many points of sale as possible. In a 2008 article in the *New York Times*'s *Play Magazine*, writer Jona-than Mahler reported that the new Yankee Stadium—a $1.3 billion project undertaken with a sizable public subsidy—cut the number of seats available to ordinary fans by about seven thousand. (Handily enough, this reduction of supply provided a pretext for higher ticket prices—which turned out to be a less than brilliant idea when the economy collapsed, right on cue, almost as though some just deity wished to punish the Yan-kees' hubris. First time for everything!) In addition to more than fifty luxury suites, the ballpark includes a "New York Yankees martini bar, a steakhouse (NYY Steak), a grill room, a Yankees museum, a year-round banquet hall and a conference center . . . [and] many more opportunities to spend money inside the ball-park." Mahler's story quotes a gushing Yankees official on a tour of the construction site: "It's not going to feel like you're entering a ballpark." Joy.

The new superarenas complement a general move toward more sterile, directed fan environments. Bill Simmons, ESPN .com's popular "Sports Guy" columnist, calls this "the Jumbo-Tron Era." "By pricing out . . . common fans and overwhelm-ing the ones who remained, professional sports leagues in this country made a conscious decision," Simmons wrote in 2006.

"[They'd] rather hear artificially created noise than genuine noise." Stephen Wells, the late English journalist who worked in Philadelphia for years, put it like this in the *Guardian*: "This moronic circus has all but killed fan culture. . . . [T]he near-hypnotic state of focused concentration that defines the truly great fan experience is denied the American fan. . . . But the greatest horror is that, after decades of being treated like sugar-stoned two-year-olds, entire generations of fans have grown up thinking this brain-frying farce is normal."

In truth, big-league franchises now value ordinary fans more for the taxes they pay than their passion. Owners always want new stadiums, often to replace perfectly good old stadiums, so they can jack up revenues from "personal seat licenses" (an ingenious up-front fee for the right to buy actual tickets later), "club seats," and the all-important luxury boxes. Local governments are now expected—virtually required, in fact—to kick down nine-figure sweeteners if they want to keep their local teams. The usual talking points in favor involve jobs, economic development, and neighborhood renewal. However, independent studies consistently show that stadium construction delivers negligible economic benefit to communities. The lefty sports columnist Dave Zirin estimates that American taxpayers have shelled out $16 billion in stadium subsidies in the last decade. (Zirin writes: "The building of stadiums has become the substitute for anything resembling an urban policy in this country.") The demands keep coming even though leagues make scads of money on their own. In late 2007, Major League Baseball announced annual gross revenues of over $6 billion, a fivefold increase since the early 1990s. Meanwhile, Washington, D.C.'s city council "capped" public financing for the Nationals' new ballpark at $610 million. By way of comparison, D.C. budgeted $773 million for public schools in fiscal 2009.

Municipal bonds, zoning and land use, economic multiplier effects—debates over stadium projects tend to get complicated. This obscures the very simple system devised by team owners: they get their way, or they move. The Seattle SuperSonics, part of the Northwest sports landscape for forty years, relocated to Oklahoma City in 2008 and became something called "the Thunder." The Sonics demanded a new arena, with the number $500 million thrown around quite freely. Seattle governments declined. Oklahoma City, on the other hand, agreed to pay over $120 million to upgrade its arena. Sold!

When teams make no pretense of their willingness to pull up stakes for whatever city proves most accommodating, and when stadiums function as dull, orderly, money-oriented theme parks, it's no wonder local loyalties are disintegrating. Especially in an era of economic upheaval, many fans can't afford to see their hometown teams anymore. Fantasy sports encourage attachments to individual players rather than particular teams, and round-the-clock TV availability of all games everywhere works to break down sports' sense of place. "When I was growing up in New York," David Lifton of the Screaming Eagles said, "you were still fairly isolated as a sports fan. I watched the Yankees, the Islanders, and the Knicks. Even in the biggest media market in the country, your primary exposure to sports came through your local teams. Then *SportsCenter* came along and gave you access to every team in every sport. Inevitably you end up with a national sports culture rather than a local one, a sports culture more focused on individual stars rather than a team that

local people live and die by. The other day, I was walking down
the street and I saw a guy wearing a Cleveland Cavaliers hat
and an Atlanta Falcons jersey—and the guy was probably from
D.C. At one point in time, that would have made no sense at all.
Now it makes perfect sense: he's into LeBron James, and he's into
Michael Vick. He's a fan of players, rather than teams."

There isn't much the Screaming Eagles, or any band of a few
hundred soccer fans, can do to keep franchise owners' hands
out of the public till—Major League Soccer is as keen to pry dollars out of local governments as any other league. What soccer's
supporters groups do offer, though, is an alternative version of
American sports fandom: robust, engaged, creative, organized,
fanatically local, and zealous about the integrity of the sport.
(Pressure from supporters groups helped prompt MLS, which
experimented with a number of "innovations" in its early days,
to bring its rules into line with global standards.) With their DIY
merchandise and independent guerrilla marketing, supporters
groups point the way toward a sports nation that's more than an
inert mass of consumers and pliable taxpayers. The wider soccer world also offers a few inspiring models of a different kind
of fan/team relationship. FC Barcelona is collectively owned by
163,000 fans. Germany's league rules require that fans own at
least 51 percent of all pro teams. In England, the so-called "punk
football" movement is trying to build an alternative to the major
clubs, with grassroots-run teams like AFC Wimbledon and FC
United of Manchester springing up in the minor leagues.

Here and abroad, the steps so far may be small. But it is time
for fans to reclaim fandom. Maybe those Americans who rally to
one of the country's most maligned sports can help.

* * *

As soccer continued its stealthy rise in this country, the mainstream media increased coverage at a grudging pace. (In fairness, the sport's TV ratings, the only measure of popularity that matters in a commercial sense, never exactly posed an irrefutable argument for more ink and airtime.) Stepping into the vacuum, fans peppered the Internet with blogs and online forums. The Web being the Web, many are shambling amateur efforts (e.g., my own). The best, however, equal or exceed the pros. Adam Spangler's This Is American Soccer (www.thisisamericansoccer .com) offers both exhaustive interviews with MLS executives and media types and a fizzy underground-scene-report perspective on the game as lived and played in New York City. Run of Play, primarily written by Brian Phillips, offers a poetic and hyperintelligent meta-analysis of the sport's competition and culture. And then there is Du Nord.

Du Nord (www.dunord.blogspot.com) provides an object lesson in why many of us working hacks, reared on the Associated Press Stylebook and the inverted pyramid lead, both hate and fear the Internet. For one thing, its stream-of-consciousness blurt makes no pretense of consistency in matters of grammar or spelling. For another, Du Nord rules. The site consists of a daily roundup of news from around the English-speaking soccer world, with short summaries linking to stories in outlets ranging from London's *Guardian* to the *Daily Press & Argus* of Livingston, Michigan. That's it; dead simple—except no mainstream media outlet I know of provides the same level of service. That makes Du Nord, which a guy named Bruce McGuire compiles in his spare time, mandatory daily reading for several thousand soccer obsessives. The man is just bad for business.

Bruce and I hung out one night in Minneapolis, his hometown. We hit a sportsy pub, where Bruce, a big dude with a yard-long red beard, purposely sat with his back to the TV screens so he wouldn't accidentally see any of the New York Red Bulls game he planned to watch on his DVR later. A man who plans his evening around a digitally delayed match involving the Red Bulls—a team that has changed its name and entire brand identity more times (once) than it has won a championship (never)—has the disease for sure. Bruce told me he first played and watched soccer as a kid during the swingin'-'70s Pelé craze, kept the faith through the '80s dark ages (the *Soccer Made in Germany* era), and then, when the state of world media was ripe, struck.

"I always seek out things that just aren't there," Bruce said. "I've done it my whole life—it's just my pattern. I try to find something, I go to where I think it should be, and I end up being the only one standing there, wondering how I got there." The Internet put the once inaccessible British press and the once scattered American soccer underground at his disposal. "I was just reading so much stuff, just devouring everything I could get my hands on. I'm the kind of person that, if I like it, I want to know everything about it. If I get interested in a genre of music, I read everything I can find about it and listen to every band remotely connected to it. A couple of years ago, I was doing that with soccer."

Du Nord started in March 2005 with a daily readership of about twenty. Three years later, the blog attracted almost three thousand readers a day. McGuire pounds through scores of

straight news and feature stories and chases unending MLS roster and business rumors and vanishingly obscure minor-league
and college news. It seems impossible, given his real-world job
as a university tech administrator, but Bruce struck me as caffeine in human form. He didn't go to journalism school, and
thus never learned about cynical detachment: Du Nord's chief
joy, aside from its scary completism, is McGuire's enthusiasm.

"I'm constantly knocked out by the stories this game produces," Bruce told me. "I refuse to stop digging. The only thing
that's limiting Du Nord right now is that I only speak English.
Imagine what I could dig up if I spoke Spanish, German, French,
Italian, Portuguese . . . the site would be insane!" He would also
be jobless, homeless, and friendless, but this didn't seem to occur
to Bruce.

"I've developed this theory, which is that in America at least,
soccer is the sport of the Internet," he continued. "What I do
is just what every soccer fan in America has to do. The mainstream media is doing a better job covering the sport than ever
before, but the fact is, if you're not right on top of it, you don't
know what's going on. And what the Web allows for is all of
us who want to be involved to connect—I've met thousands of
people in soccer through the Web. We can organize, we can get
shit done. When fans think the league is out of line, they let the
league know, in force. And the league, even if it never admits it,
has changed policies several times because of fans. And that's
amazing—that a bunch of people who have no financial stake in
this multimillion-dollar business can effect change. And that's
one big reason things are changing so fast with this game, man.
So fast. Things that were true about soccer in America in the
year 2000 aren't even close to true in 2008. If you're going off

what you thought the sport was a few years ago, you're going to be wrong."

"I call soccer the Amway of pro sports in this country." So said a man named Bryan James, of greater Philadelphia and the Sons of Ben, that city's MLS fan club, when I first spoke to him in the summer of 2007. In the weeks before our conversation, Sons of Ben emerged as the fastest-growing and arguably most exciting local supporters club in all of American soccer. The fact that Philadelphia did not actually have a soccer team wasn't slowing them down.

James and a few other Philly soccer fans started Sons of Ben the previous winter in response to rumors that MLS might, maybe, possibly, if all went well, place an expansion team in Philadelphia. It would take a National Geography Bee champ to name a major (or mid-major, or minor-major, or major-minor) U.S. metropolis *not* identified as a potential soccer hotbed by league honchos over the years. Commissioner Don Garber will fly just about anywhere for the price of a Chamber of Commerce luncheon and hold forth on the glamour that could await Rochester/Tulsa/Sacramento/Cleveland pending the requisite stadium-construction assistance. Philly (in the form of Bryan James and friends) got tired of waiting around.

"A bunch of us were talking on the BigSoccer.com message board," Bryan James said. "There are always these rumors. We're going to be the next expansion team, or the Kansas City Wizards are going to move here. Whatever. We started kicking around names for a supporters group. No one was really taking the lead, so I finally said, you know, if I can get Sonsofben.com, I'm going to go for it. The domain name came available the next day. The next day! Fate. We thought, here's a name that accurately depicts who we will be. It recognizes a guy, Ben Franklin, who moved to this city as a teenager and became one of the foremost names in American history. And there's the added benefit of the acronym, which is what most people think of Philly sports fans already. It struck a chord, I guess. We went online in January and by March we had eighty-eight members. I thought it was going to plateau, but we kept building and building, and now we're well over four hundred. We've got branches in England, in Norway, in Japan."

This led James to his network-marketing metaphor. "It's multilevel fandom," he said. "You're not going to get into the game because of the media, because frankly the media has its head up its ass. And if you watch a game on TV, that's not really the way you absorb what the sport is all about anyway. You almost have to have someone drag you to a match. Once that happens, it's over. It is like a cult in many ways—you go from couldn't care less to total convert. If you get someone to the right match with the right atmosphere, you've got 'em."

With hundreds of members but no team, the Sons of Ben made the best of it that summer. They put together a caravan to the Meadowlands to jeer and mock the poor Red Bulls. They showed up to support Philly's tame pro indoor team until management essentially asked them to leave. Most of all, they agitated with league officials, cajoled local politicians, and generally kept the pressure on. In spring 2008, the universe capitulated to this irresistible force, and Philadelphia landed an MLS franchise for 2010. When it came time to announce the team, every suit in the room gave credit to Bryan James and the Sons of Ben—good call, since scores of SOBs turned up at the ceremony to chant, sing, and brandish homemade yellow and blue scarves, based on the city flag. When it came time to choose official club colors, the front office wisely didn't think it over too much.

All the spontaneous momentum got James dreaming about what Philly's as-yet-unformed club (later given the fairly boss name "Philadelphia Union," complete with a menacing crest featuring a Revolutionary War rattlesnake and a Latin motto meaning "Join or Die") could be. "When we do get into the league, the general-interest Philly sports fan is going to realize, wait a minute—here's a sport that actually encourages the kind of passion we invest in every other Philadelphia team," he said. "Here's a stadium where I can go stand with a bunch of other nutcases and chant and scream and sing for two hours. And they're going to find that in Sons of Ben, we have everyone. We have the typical travel-team soccer players, we have the suburban guys, we have union tradesmen who are as blue-collar Philly as it gets. We have blacks, Latinos, immigrants. Every symbol we've come up with, from the name to the logo to the colors, is totally representative of this city and this region. We are going to be the most Philly team in Philly."

A couple years ago, I spent a steamy night in Brisbane, Australia, drinking Dutch beer in a bar packed with Korean fans, watching Manchester United (owned by the same guy who owns the Tampa Bay Buccaneers) beat Birmingham's Aston Villa (subsequently purchased by the same guy who owns the Cleveland Browns). Rupert Murdoch's Fox/Sky empire carried the live feed from England, and I imagined the raisin-faced Aussie overlord rolling around on a giant pile of dollars, pounds, euros, and won.

This kind of scene endears soccer to some sectors of political thought, in that it seems to represent the triumph of the liberal free market, the end of history, et cetera. American author Franklin Foer devoted an entire book to this idea: *How Soccer Explains the World*. In Foer's "unlikely theory," the sport is a near-perfect metaphor and vehicle for globalization. It is certainly true that modern football is a churning sea of mobile talent and unfettered capital. Take my personal English Premier League favorite, Liverpool FC—a club positively briny with old-school cred and home to the Kop, a seething mob of fans who see themselves as the Praetorian Guard of football tradition. The club's obsession with its own history notwithstanding, a pair of Republican tycoons from Texas bought Liverpool in 2007. Surprise, surprise—they seem not to know what they're doing. (By the Premier League's standards, Liverpool's bumbling magnates don't even approach exotic. Other recent league owners include the exiled former prime minister of Thailand, Emerati sheiks, and a number of what one might politely describe as successful post-Soviet entrepreneurs.) A goateed Spaniard manages the squad, which is staffed with Scandinavian, Irish, Israeli, Ukrainian, Dutch, French, Argentinian, Spanish, and—oh, yeah—English players. One of the club's most promising youth-team players is half-Finnish, half-Italian. This internationalism is typical at the sport's elite level. If a European team doesn't employ a half dozen Brazilian teenagers, it's probably not serious. (Given recent economic developments, however, I must note that many of European football's biggest brand names now stand on precarious mountains of debt, which leaves the future of this go-go talent marketplace in some doubt.)

Meanwhile, every World Cup brings a barrage of TV ads that portray the sport and all remotely ancillary retail goods as a worldwide Kumbaya. The media package soccer as a refined but affordable international luxury, the Toblerone of sports, and I have no problem with that. Football serves as a very useful lingua franca, especially when you're in a foreign tavern and need to shift an increasingly drunken conversation away from U.S. foreign policy. But this vision of soccer as a benign amusement for interchangable consumers ignores the sport's essential dual nature. Even as it embodies the glossiest aspects of the twenty-first century, soccer also provides a habitat for strange archaic tendencies.

The British writer Tim Parks lives in Verona, Italy, where he has become devoted to the club Hellas Verona. His 2002 book *A Season with Verona* chronicled a year among the Hellas supporters known as the Brigate Gialloblù ("the Yellow-Blue Brigades"). Other Italians revile Verona fans as lumpen small-town bigots, and Verona fans do their best not to disappoint. Parks's team represents a backwater city, an afterthought in the minds of most Italians, let alone the world. And yet in the imaginations of Hellas fans, Verona is worthy of imperial prestige. The club wears the city's traditional blue and gold and is nicknamed in honor of the hardboiled dynasty that ruled Verona in its days as a pre-Renaissance military power. The Gialloblù boys make a point of speaking only the most pungent local dialect (including the incredible blasphemous oath "Executioner God!" which sadly loses something in translation). They pepper trash talk on their online forums with references to battles that took place in AD 1200. At one match, Parks sees a banner that declares "Verona: City and State!" The club's name, Hellas, literally means "homeland" in Greek.

As politics, of course, this verges on Dungeons & Dragons. On the other hand, on its best day Italy is a wobbly construct of feuding regions and mutually unintelligible dialects. As Parks writes, "[W]henever some inconvenient wild beast is slain . . . you can be sure it will turn up again elsewhere in some other guise." From the point of view of a nation-state trying to be an influential European citizen and a well-oiled cog in the global economy, Hellas fans evoke a ghostworld of warring cities, an ungovernable peninsula carved up by fratricidal tribes. A very inconvenient beast, indeed.

Somehow, this simple, global sport has become an ark for homegrown quirks, chauvinisms, and symbols that just don't fit into modern life. Fans live out the secret, intimate social histories of the places they live. They nurse ancient grudges and breathe on the coals of dying identities. In his book *Paris: The Secret History*, author Andrew Hussey notes that the chronically nasty fans of Paris St.-Germain call themselves "the Parisii," an intermillennial shout-out to the Celtic tribe in residence when the Romans first showed up. Speaking of Romans, AS Roma's club crest depicts the she-wolf suckling Romulus and Remus. In Germany, FC St. Pauli represents Hamburg's bohemian red-light district, its stadium terraces full of drag queens and crusty anarchist punks waving Che Guevara flags and the skull and crossbones. London clubs like Bournemouth and Fulham preserve villages long since swallowed up by the megalopolis. Soccer may look "global"—it may, in fact, somehow explain the world. But as far as life on the ground goes, football is all about Local. Specifically, it's about Our Hometown—City and State! The shape this medieval urban patriotism might take in the land of the Interstate off-ramp will be very interesting to see.

"There's one significant thing about United that I don't think anyone from outside D.C. would pick up on," David Lifton told me. "It is so important that the team is not called 'Washington.' In the District, we say there are actually two cities here. There's 'Washington,' which is the monuments and the tourists and the seat of power. And there's 'D.C.'—the neighborhoods and the people, where the soul is. I don't know if it was intentional at all, but for anyone who lives here, the name 'D.C. United' sends a very clear message: this is the people's team.

"I grew up in New York, and I have no idea what the city of New York's flag looks like. But I know that you'll see the District's flag at D.C. United games. It's an outlet for city pride. And for a lot of us, that pride has a lot to do with the fact that D.C. is basically a colony. It's a way to say, we may not get a vote in Congress, but we're here."

The world soccer explosion, well under way elsewhere, hadn't quite happened yet in late-1990s Missoula. Social trends tend to wash over Montana about a decade late. (About half the time, this is a good thing.) Isolation breeds creativity, so my friends and I were used to making our own fun. Sometimes that meant hauling a rented generator down to the riverside to power a show by an extreme-leftist punk band on tour from North Dakota. All too often it meant those weekends aptly described as "lost." In '97 and '98, it meant the Carnies Football Club. The Carnies wore black T-shirts. Our team crest consisted of a wobbly, hand-drawn shield bearing a skull, a switchblade, and a bottle marked "XXX." When I solicited a sponsorship at a sports bar, the owner gave me a blank look and said, "Soccer, huh? Well, I guess. We wanna see you guys in here after every game, ordering *puh-lenty* of beer. Think you can do that, buddy?" Yes.

I can't say for sure, but I feel confident that Missoula Co-Rec Division 1 never before saw and never again would see a team as awful as us. For our debut match, about thirty rookie Carnies, lured perhaps by the team captain's talk of puh-lenty of beer, showed up. Our sideline resembled a protest against the World Trade Organization, and every substitution opportunity devolved into total chaos. If memory serves, we trailed a well-kempt team from a law firm 5–0 at halftime. The referee—a tallow-skinned, fifty-something character who wore a vintage Santos FC warm-up suit and chain-smoked straight through the break—strolled over. "Captain," he said, "you've got to get your team organized." I didn't ask if he had any teargas I could borrow. We did bag a consolation goal in the second half. A Carnie striker, one of a handful of our players with real experience, nailed a scorcher from twenty-five yards out. A fantastic goal from any perspective, it must have looked especially beautiful to him. Before the game, he told me he had ingested halluncinogenic mushrooms.

As the season progressed, the Carnies improved—a little. A Belarusian named Pavel, a paternal gent with salt-and-pepper hair whom none of us had ever met, mysteriously started showing up promptly at game time to play for us. He proved good for a couple of goals a game. Our pugnacious goalkeeper, a National

Guardsman who both served in Afghanistan and played bass for Missoula's most venerable punk band, put a little muscle in our defense. So did the linebacker from the Montana Grizzlies football (the other kind) team, recruited by my brother, who spent much of his time in Carnies black trying to start fights with opposing players. Our female players, it turned out, were much better than our men—for some reason, the Carnie women tended to be more physically fit and less lifestyle-impaired than their male counterparts. I don't know why.

Other teams—genuine amateur athletes seeking bona fide recreational competition, I suppose—seemed unimpressed by our freewheeling approach. "This is ridiculous," one snotty hot-shot whined to a referee. "These guys don't belong out here." His team had scored three goals in fifteen minutes while dodging homicidal slide tackles, so maybe he had a point. That didn't stop me from screaming *"That was for you, motherfucker!"* when we (Pavel) leveled the score in a game that we (Pavel) almost stole.

The Carnies put together an immaculate winless streak. No other team, however, could match our party record. About half the core squad, including the hapless cap'n, lived in a nine-bedroom decommissioned nunnery behind Missoula's oldest Catholic church. By postmatch midnight, a choreographed wrestling match usually took place in the living room, with Heinz 57 used as fake blood. We chewed over tactics, technique, and lineups, but soon enough the day's result started to feel irrelevant compared to olive-oil belly-flop contests on the kitchen linoleum. Sadly, Pavel never joined us. I believe he was a religious man.

*   *   *

In the middle of my Carnies summer, a slim book by a Uruguayan writer I'd never heard of came my way. My reading
list at the time was heavier on novels featuring wisecracking
detectives with substance abuse problems than Latin American literary journalism. I didn't know Eduardo Galeano, but I
soon recognized that *Soccer in Sun and Shadow* would be the best
sports book I'd ever read.

The American title looks clunky and lead-footed next to the
book's true name—*El Fútbol a Sol y Sombra* captures its deceptively simple grace. Galeano writes mini-essays, some no more
than a few sentences long, delving into soccer's history and
lore. The scores of chapters include many biographies of Latin
American stars from the '40s, '50s, and '60s, many digressions
into the entanglement of *fútbol* and culture in all those Spanish-
and Portuguese-speaking countries stacked up below the Rio
Grande. I can see how this description would not necessarily
constitute a recommendation to an American reader, but *Soccer
in Sun and Shadow* is more than a reference source for pub-quiz
night in Buenos Aires. It articulates what sports should be about.

In the course of Galeano's career as a political journalist, the
right-wing dictatorship then running his home country kicked
him out. He went to Argentina, where, after one of that country's
serial coups, the death squads put him on their list. He lived in
exile in Spain; he returned to Uruguay; he survived to tell about
all of it in a series of fierce books on politics and culture. (In
2009, Hugo Chavez, *capo* of Venezuela, sparked a small Galeano
boom when he presented Barack Obama with a copy of the
writer's *Open Veins of Latin America*.) In *Soccer in Sun and Shadow*,

Galeano celebrates the game he fell for as a kid in Montevideo six decades ago, but that doesn't mean he goes easy on the hard stuff. In Galeano's view, global capitalism is destroying soccer along with everything else, crushing the game's inherent poetry and humanity in favor of brutal, results-oriented robo-football played by maltreated serfs. ("The history of soccer is a sad voyage from beauty to duty.") He lashes club owners, international sports bureaucrats, TV executives, corporate sponsors, racism, violence, the perfidious hand of the market, the society of the spectacle . . . to the barricades, Comrade Galeano! The book would fast descend to the entertainment level of a consciousness-raising at a cooperative vegan café if Galeano didn't write so well, and if he didn't filter his rage through love.

He calls soccer "the only religion without atheists" and writes with devotional clarity about players who inspire him. Of Lev Yashin, a legendary Soviet goalkeeper from the 1960s: "This giant with long spidery arms always dressed in black and played with a naked elegance that disdained unnecessary gestures. He liked to stop thundering blasts with a single claw-like hand that trapped and shredded any projectile, while his body remained motionless like a rock." (Yashin, Galeano reports, warmed up for every match with a shot of vodka.) Of Pelé: "When he stopped, his opponents got lost in the labyrinths his legs embroidered . . . those of us who were lucky enough to see him play received alms of an extraordinary beauty: moments so worthy of immortality that they make us believe immortality exists."

I think Galeano could convert anyone, but a reader could also hate soccer and all sports and still take joy in *Soccer in Sun and Shadow*. Over the last decade, I have picked up this little book hundreds of times, because Galeano finds the kernel of value

hidden in the muck of modern sport (and life). He loves players who play—those who create and invent, the improvisers,
the unlikely heroes from the ghetto, the working-class kids who
become poets on the field, rebels who defy the owners and the
pundits. In his eyes, soccer is an art struggling to escape the
clutches of commerce. The fact that it never will doesn't make
the battle less riveting. You could apply Galeano's vision to any
sport, and other human activities besides. Much of what we do is
irreparably flawed and compromised. Yet our endeavors remain
worthwhile, sometimes affording the chance, as Galeano puts it,
"for the carnal delight of embracing the forbidden adventure of
freedom."

Sports exist, in large part, both to generate and to settle arguments—Yankees or Sox? Venus or Serena? And, when they
weren't out musket-shooting Hessians, our colonial forebears
killed time with faintly similar questions. Who bred the nastiest
rat-killing dogs? Could that boy from Boston really eat one hundred oysters? Young Asa claims he could fight a brown bear—
true? The crucial barroom issue of who could pummel whom
into bloody submission fostered vigorous interest in wrestling,
boxing, and eye-gouging. Far back in pre-Revolution days, vil-
lagers played games in which a rough blueprint of baseball
could be discerned, though they inspired no blank-verse poems
or metaphorical literary novels. Folks also enjoyed watching
animals battle to the death.

I'm sure a good time was had by all, but the transformation
of these grog-sodden amusements into sports as we know them
required three time-honored catalysts: speed, violence, and New

York City. Horse racing and boxing took shape first. Thoroughbred owners—rich, literate, and connected, the proto-Stein-
brenners of their day—enjoyed ready access to the emerging
national media. Turf fans used newspapers as a forum for endless debates on, for instance, the relative merits of Southern and
Northern horses, making the sport a precursor to both the Civil
War and *Pardon the Interruption*. Boxing didn't quite have racing's
class advantages, and it remained illegal just about everywhere
through most of the nineteenth century. Outlawry only added to
the excitement and spectacle of big-time fights. The 1889 heavy-
weight title bout between Jake Kilrain and John L. Sullivan took
place in a secret location outside New Orleans, which five thousand fans reached via high-speed chartered trains that dodged
companies of armed soldiers. As for the crowd itself, one eye-
witness account reported: "Every man was afraid of the other,
for every one of them carried a gun." By comparison, a black-tie
night at Caesar's Palace sort of pales.

Those raw building blocks—rural "sports" and budding
national interest in track and ring—needed to stew together.
New York City provided the ideal cauldron, as Manhattan's
population quadrupled between 1830 and the Civil War. This
was not Edith Wharton's Old New York; more like Daniel Day-
Lewis in *Gangs of New York* New York, the pestilential Gomorrah
documented in Luc Sante's book *Low Life*. Early on, New Yorkers just transplanted outback bloodsports. Patsy Hearn's "Men's
Sporting Parlor" in Five Points staged rat-killing derbies for up
to two hundred paying customers at a time. McLaughlin's bear
pit operated on First Avenue and Tenth, and (according to Sante)
"dog vs. raccoon contests were popular." Kit Burns's Sportsman's
Hall spotlighted a chap name of Jack the Rat, who would bite the

head off a mouse for a dime. Meanwhile, a more genteel crowd codified baseball, with fraternal outfits like the Knickerbockers and the New York Club playing the first recognizably modern games in the 1840s. A saltier crew soon adopted the diamond, however; Sante notes that a Lower East Side criminal syndicate called the Midnight Terrors took great pride in its hardball squad.

This cross-pollination—middle-class outdoors fun meets the gutter—spawned the Fan. After the Civil War, a weekly propaganda organ came along to spread the gospel of fandom nationwide: a pink-paged newspaper, printed in "Little Old New York," called the *National Police Gazette*. The *Gazette* was possibly the most reprehensible paper ever to achieve mass appeal in the United States. Its pages seethed with psychopathic racism, enthusiastic coverage of lynchings, Indian killings, Chinese perfidy ("Slant-Eyed Oriental Entices Maiden into Sin") and Jewish conspiracies. The paper's proprietor, a bigoted Ulster brawler named Richard Kyle Fox, was a master of the publisher's dark arts. Ten bucks and a weekend's worth of booze was the going rate for *Gazette* stringers. In exchange, Fox's stable of anonymous, alcoholic hacks would sling ink on whatever atrocity came to hand: Moqui snake dances; "sheeny abortionists"; the evergreen Horrible Gallows Scene.

And yet this grapefruit-hued monster was also one of the most innovative forces in the history of American journalism. Fox created the gossip column and showbiz coverage. His genius woodcut artists set the template for *Life*, *Playboy*, and *National Geographic*. The "lad mags" of the 1990s would be the *Gazette*'s comparatively housebroken disciples. The blogger equal to the paper's quarrelsome swagger has yet to blog. And alongside pictures of "savages" roasting New Mexico ranchers on hot stoves and slobbery tidings from the ladies' backstage dressing room, Richard Kyle Fox and his intoxicated minions invented the sports page.

Fox sponsored gold medals and trophies for champions in a mind-boggling array of athletic and semiathletic endeavors. He goaded readers into bizarre proto–*Fear Factor* stunts. (A letter to the editor: "I will wager $100 to $500 . . . that I can smoke more opium in a 12-hour contest than any man in Colorado.") The *Gazette* labored to define and hype every sport Fox could think of.* Baseball columns like "Sparks from the Diamond" lavished Peter Gammons–ish attention on roster gossip and hot-stove action. ("Buffalo has released young Hodson and is dickering for a star.") As the National League established itself as the epicenter of sports, the *Gazette* was there to dish clubhouse trivia and pry apart every tactical decision.

At its prime, the *Gazette* distilled an entire dank cosmos into pink newsprint. Tom Wolfe—who, though unlike Richard Kyle Fox in nearly every respect, recognizes journalistic pathbreaking when he sees it—writes:

> The world of the Police Gazette was not merely a world of vulgarity and excitement but of illicit vulgarity and excitement . . . [A] style of living that was not so much the opposite of High Victorian Gentility as its underside, namely the world of the Sport, or the Sporting Man . . . who led the Sporting Life . . . an

---

*Kite flying. "The Belles of the Bowling Alley." A six-day walking contest at Madison Square Garden featuring Nitaw-Ey-Ebow, "the Chippewa Runner." "New Revised Rules for Wrestling on Horseback." Etc.

uncultivated macho dandy whose love of sports had nothing to
do with the High Victorian ideal of "athletics" and everything
to do with, simply . . . the eternal gamble against Fate . . . (most
ellipses original).

In its earliest incarnation, then, fandom wasn't so much a
default mode for normal suburban manhood as it was a quasi-
criminal underclass. Or maybe that was just perception and
self-mythology. Most of the *Gazette*'s readers probably had as
much to do with the sleazebaggery in its pages as the major-
ity of 1960s *Rolling Stone* readers had to do with Woodstock. But
one can imagine the weekly arrival of an out-of-date *Gazette* in
a small-town barbershop or saloon: a hot-pink contraband ship-
ment that gave staid shopkeepers, mechanics, and farmers a
taste of the fast life. (Maybe it wasn't too different from reading
punk-scene reports from Latvia or Argentina in *Maximumrock-
androll* on boring teenage afternoons in Montana.)

Times were ugly—after the Civil War, the nation spent most
of the 1870s, '80s, and '90s mired in the so-called Long Depression. Those who led the Sporting Life, though—they had an
escape route. The Fan knew the score, literally and otherwise.
Armed with cigar, whiskey, and (when crowd management
demanded it) sidearm, he was a world-wise independent opera-
tor. The Fan knew how to wring pleasure out of this otherwise
drab existence, even if only for the weekly half hour devoted to
the *Police Gazette* between swing shifts or fence-mending on the
back forty. His (given the gender dynamics of the time) opin-
ions re: ring, track, or diamond mattered. The Sporting Man was
disreputable, but free. It's a long way from there to chanting for
chalupas.

*   *   *

In a direct reflection of soccer's status in this country, the stadiums MLS does succeed in building tend to be in the middle of nowhere. In June 2006, I went to Chicago for the grand-opening game at Toyota Park, the Fire's custom-built new home. My mass-transit journey to Toyota Park from central Chicago involved riding the El's Orange Line all the way to the end at Midway Airport, on what most Chicagoans would consider the far South Side, and then a long wait, in a desolate parking lot, for the chartered bus to a place even further south, the Village of Bridgeview. After standing around for about an hour, I spotted four men in Fire replica jerseys at the other side of the lot. We agreed to split a cab. The cabdriver, a fellow who called himself Big Mike and showed us both his pistol and his straight razor as he held forth on some of the risks of his trade, seemed unaware of any major new sports complexes out this way. After we found the place, I understood how Toyota Park might slip below a local's radar. With a capacity of less than twenty thousand and faux stately brick façade, the pocket-sized stadium resembles an upmarket Target.

That did not matter to the Fire fans I rode with. "Holy shit," a guy named Dan said as we walked across the sprawling, and as yet unpaved, parking lot, "a real stadium." The Fire began its existence as a poor-relation tenant at Soldier Field downtown. "I was at the first game ever," Dan continued, "and it was great— forty thousand people going apeshit, Polish hooligans lighting off flares, security guards chasing 'em all over the place. But that was never our stadium. To see it come this far is pretty great."

At the Section 8 tailgate party, held next to a huge pile of dirt and an idle bulldozer, Liam Murtagh, one of the group's leaders, buzzed around with the overstimulated air of a man about to walk his daughter down the aisle. "Lots to keep track of, man—lots to organize," he said. "We've got tickets to distribute, all these special commemorative scarves people ordered. It's been crazy." Given a decade of die-hard support—games played in a 90 percent empty Soldier Field, games played at a high school football stadium in an even more remote suburb—Murtagh and his comrades obviously felt they weren't so much here because of Toyota Park as vice versa. "Section 8 started at the first Chicago Fire game ever played," Murtagh said. "We've had a presence at every game since. Every single game. The team has played in Central America, played in Portugal, and there are Fire fans there. No one knows how they get there or where they come from, but they're there."

As I researched this trip, something on the Section 8 website struck me: this was probably the first sports fan club in history to take inspiration from the words of an urban planner. At the time, the site quoted Daniel Burnham, the architect who devised the landmark Plan of Chicago in 1909 and captured the spirit of the Progressive Era in his vision of a graceful city of public parks, museums, and civilized boulevards. *Make no little plans. They have no magic to stir men's blood . . . Make big plans; aim high in hope and work . . . Let your watchword be order and your beacon beauty. Think big.* These people clearly had a sense of occasion.

Ten minutes before kickoff, crepe streamers piled six inches deep in the aisles at the end of the stadium reserved for Section 8. From my spot in the middle of the standing throng, I could see Liam Murtagh in a heroic battle with a colossal flag—a flag bigger than any I had ever seen up close, which threatened to either tear off his arms or carry him into the night. Polish guys draped in scarves emblazoned with Warsaw soccer clubs' logos poured beer down each others' throats and screamed "*Shee*-Kah-Go!" at random intervals. When the match began, a huge banner swept up the terrace, unfurled hand to hand until it covered the entire section; it felt oddly intimate under there, maybe because everyone was falling over everyone else.

Then Marcin* took over. Marcin, an imperious Pole with ice blue eyes, a jaw that could be used to plow up fields, and a definite air of command, hoisted himself up to tower above the section. "Alright, everybody," he barked. "Picnic is over! I want to see some moves over here! Everybody—jump! Jump!" The crowd levitated on command—Arab girls in head scarves pogoing next to skinheads in brimmed caps and flannel. A black kid with a huge Afro, multiple Fire scarves wrapped around his neck, stood alongside Latinos waving Mexican flags. The Polish fans, male and female, all wore stunner shades and tight jeans. A burly skinhead's forearm tattoo read "Working Class" above two crossed hammers. A jet-black Mohawk bristled in the air. In between outbursts of noise, the college kid next to me told me he was working on his poli-sci thesis, on the organizational culture of the wartime OSS.

I fell for soccer at a time when I thought sports belonged to other people. Soccer showed me a new and different way to be a sports fan, and by extension a new way to see the world. A poetic Russian professor once told me that learning a second language is like acquiring a second mind. In sports terms, soccer became

*This Polish guy named Marcin is not to be confused with the other Polish guy named Marcin who appears in Chapter Three. Popular Polish name, Marcin.

my second language—a vein of knowledge not superior to what I knew by near instinct about "American" sports, nor as intuitive and perfect as that of a native, but now essential to my mental architecture, to how I experience the texture of the world. That night in Chicago, I was with my people—all of us trying to figure out how to engage with this national and global obsession in a way that felt right and authentic to us, to create something our own and then see what happened.

Soon everyone started singing:

"Late last night / While we were all in bed / Mrs. O'Leary left a lantern in the shed / The cow tipped it over / She winked her eye and said / It'll be a hot time in the old town tonight."

A song about—what else—the Chicago Fire, about an old nineteenth-century urban legend. That night, though, it felt like a young, new city sang it—the soccer fans of Chicago, American soccer fans, thinking big.

SIX

EXOTIC DANCES

Soccer functions as a gateway drug. First you champion one sport most of your fellow citizens don't care about, and soon you fall into other dire habits. You develop a semi-self-loathing, jodhpur-licking Anglophilia, followed by a fascination with still *other* sports none of your friends and relations care about or have ever heard of. (Not only do I more or less understand cricket—at least the basics—I've also *watched* cricket for consecutive hours. And I think cricket is sort of cool, and I don't care who knows it.) You discover that the line between "lovable eccentric" and "town lunatic" is fine indeed.

For instance, not long ago I began hunting down YouTube clips of a man known (but not by many) as Phil "the Power" Taylor. I started searching for articles about Phil "the Power" Taylor, boring disinterested friends with breathless stories about how far beyond awesome Phil "the Power" Taylor is, and developing a real Phil "the Power" Taylor problem. Phil Taylor is an

Englishman, and not an Englishman of either the whippetlike Simon Pegg variety or the mirror-shade-and-Versace David Beckham variety. His body resembles a delicately balanced stack of pears. His complexion speaks of vitamin D deficiency. And— this is key—he has the word *Power* tattooed on his right forearm. With lightning bolts. He is almost fifty years old. He trained to manufacture ceramic toilet-paper holders, but fate decreed that Phil "the Power" Taylor, thanks to a combination of natural talent, dedication, and chronic unemployment, would become the greatest darts player in history.

In America, darts is a game for drunk people. In Britain, darts is a game for drunk people, but also a significant spectator sport. Even though major darts tournaments pay six-figure purses (and that's in pounds and/or euros, not the pretend currency we use over here), the typical male professional darts player looks exactly like the typical male recreational darts player: that is, he looks like he probably knows the people at his neighborhood pub extremely well. He carries fifty extra pounds on his lager-saturated frame and the general air of someone who may have committed grievous bodily harm in his younger, wilder days. I understand that elite darts players once smoked and drank *during* competition, until the game's governing bodies concluded those practices did not reflect a suitable image.

The case of Phil "the Power" Taylor—who found time to perfect his darts game thanks to the vagaries of the ceramic toilet-paper-holder market—convinced me that America needs darts. This is especially true in a time of financial meltdown and widespread layoffs, which among other ills threaten to accelerate our love affair with the Wii. We need darts because it is a game of cool nerves, finesse, and simple mathematics, three things our nation could use more of. Most of all, we need darts so we can get rid of poker. I enjoyed the Texas hold 'em boom when it began, but it took all of six minutes of media exposure to ruin the game forever. Pro card playing transformed from an interesting fringe novelty, populated by rakes and ne'er-do-wells, into another drab Internet diversion for Facebook addicts. And now, even though the poker boom is indisputably and completely over— finished! past it! done!—the stuff still infests TV, draining our strategic reserve of off-peak sports-cable airtime.

Like competitive poker, darts has its roots in licensed premises. Unlike poker, darts cannot be corrupted by the Internet; it still takes place in licensed premises. In England, major darts tournaments attract hundreds of sozzled fans who spend full days in darkened lounges, drinking and singing in unison. Every time one of their tungsten-throwing titans nails the game's maximum score, the improbable triple treble-twenty, an abrasive announcer screams, *"One hundred and eighty!"* and the place goes insane. Compare that to a few Rainmen in sunglasses sitting around a table, and you'll see that a better world awaits.

When Phil "the Power" Taylor walks onto the competitive stage, arenas often play that awful early '90s "I've Got the Power!" song, and fans chant that there is, after all, only one Phil Taylor. And this is true. Phil Taylor plays darts the way (uh, one imagines) Caravaggio painted: with saucy arrogance and a precision that renders impossible shades of delicacy, combined with a self-mocking wink. He annihilates opponents, frequently by reeling off the coveted nine-dart finish, the sport's perfect game, and then he gives them a matey hug. Once, when he needed a bull's-eye to win, his first two darts just missed, creating a near-impassable barrier around the bull. Taylor took a highly unconventional stance at the farthest legal edge of the throwing area. The announcer proclaimed that Annie Oakley, on her best day, couldn't hit that shot. Taylor hit that shot, winging his final arrow into the target's heart from an oblique angle. If it had happened before an engaged American audience, it would be remembered as a Jordan-esque moment, and Phil "the Power" Taylor would be an even bigger living legend than he is.

Best of all, despite the game's atmosphere of carefree hedonism, darts maintains a strong family-values ethic. "You'll always get people calling us fat bastard darts players, drinking beer all the time," a player named Colin "Jaws" Lloyd told the *Guardian*. "But I'll tell you what, you don't get darts players sticking needles in their arms or snorting coke." Right. Let's get this sport into ESPN2 rotation as fast as possible. For the kids.

Darts, cricket, Afghan goat-grabbing—none are destined for the limelight here, I'm afraid, but all serve as a reminder that the real world of sports contains more wonders than are dreamt of in our philosophy. The renegade sports fan needs to embrace the idea that Strange is Good—or, at least, more interesting than our usual repetitive TV-highlight diet of football, baseball, basketball, NASCAR, golf tedium, and hockey fights. Back in the day, we had ABC's *Wide World of Sports*. Along with the awe-inspiring sight of ski jumper Vinko Bogataj self-destructing mid-air in the opening montage, the show promised "the constant variety of sport." The show's rota of hurling, demolition derby, and the Penn Relays, all narrated with bemused authority by the late Jim McKay, had its ridiculous side, but at least *Wide World* treated its oddball subjects with respect. Today, even hockey, long tolerated, even cherished, as the strange, violence-prone Canadian uncle of the big-time sports family, is alternately neglected and attacked. (If you want a glimpse into conspiracy theory and persecution, ask a hockey fan about the media. They're getting as bad as soccer fans.)

This parochialism must be smashed. We should live in a more interesting, diverse sports world, and that means both looking beyond our borders and expanding the definition of sport itself. As my research continued, I decided a true sportsman doesn't let trivial matters like national boundaries, popular acceptance, or common sense stand in the way of his or her entertainment. I became an Internet-enabled armchair fan of all sorts of weird things, particularly things that prove that bold (even reckless), independent-minded sport is alive and well all over the world. Once you start spanning the globe for the constant variety of sport, it turns out there's some very interesting stuff out there.

Take sledding. I have always considered sledding one of the world's greatest sports. Snow and gravity are free, even if the former unfortunately grows harder and harder to come by, and the basic equipment is easy to improvise, if not always to steer. (During a recent New Year's Eve party in snowbound Montana, for example, my friend Leif requisitioned a living-room coffee table and took it to a nearby park.) The sport's most enthusiastic practitioners are children and drunkards. Actual competitive sledders tend to be hilarious. Every Winter Olympics, a vaudeville crew of beer-loving Austrian lard tubs, Jamaican novelty acts, and endearingly useless members of Monaco's House of Grimaldi skids through the world's Awareness Bubble for a few minutes, then politely vanishes for four years. Any sport governed by an entity called the Fédération Internationale de Bobsleigh et de Tobogganing deserves a lot of love. J'aime le tobogganing!

When I heard about the Cresta Run, the world's single most storied and dangerous sledding course, it fascinated me—and not just because the run is located in glamorous St. Moritz and attracts a louche gang of champagne-swilling aristocrats. The Cresta is an inspiring throwback to the original Renegade Era, when dotty amateurs free of health-insurance worries invented sports as we know them in an outburst of self-destructive Victorian exuberance. Each winter since 1884, the St. Moritz Tobogganing Club (SMTC) carves a suicidal trench in the snow above the resort, a 1.2-kilometer drop through a series of whipsaw turns that frequently launch riders into graceful pinwheels. Every single day during the winter season, amateur riders (there are no professionals) brave the Cresta on headfirst, skeleton-style sleds, and every single day a few end up doing the cannonball through the courseside hay bales at high speed. Thanks to the magic of YouTube, a global audience may now enjoy the Cresta's "Crash of the Day." Yes, the Cresta exacts a hefty toll: broken arms; smashed lumbar; cracked ribs; ruptured kidneys. . . . In the prehelmet epoch, riders frequently suffered the so-called Cresta's Kiss. This meant they lost chunks of their faces on the ice. Before the day's riding begins, the run's governing official enumerates all these bodily hazards in a mordant address called "the Death Talk." The Death Talk concludes with this charge: "Do enjoy your time on the Cresta, gentlemen. The Cresta is all about fun." It may be unnecessary to add that the Cresta is a British-run and -dominated institution.

Sadly, I lacked the financial wherewithal to experience Cresta culture firsthand. So I called Mike DiGiacomo, one of the relatively few American Cresta riders and author of *Apparently Unharmed,* a book based on his own experiences and Cresta lore. DiGiacomo discovered the Cresta in the 1970s, when it diverted him from the youthful ski-bum circuit. Now a New York business executive, he has not missed a season in twenty-five years. "The Cresta, and being a Cresta rider, was a big part of my identity and self-image for a long time," he said. "It's hard to explain, but it really gets in your blood—the run itself, of course, and the whole social scene that surrounds it. There are people from all over the world, and while it tends to be a fairly affluent group—it's an expensive sport to pursue, and there are no sponsorships or cash prizes—it's really a very diverse bunch. Anyone can show up and ride, and every year there are some guys who really come out of the woodwork. St. Moritz is a small town, and once you're there, you don't really go anywhere, so it's like being on an ocean liner. There are lots of parties. You're bound to run into everyone eventually. It's very social."

To judge by his own book, DiGiacomo understates the case. The Cresta is the focal point of one of the looniest sports subcultures anywhere, informed in equal measure by P. G. Wodehouse and Evel Knievel, populated by lords, barons, and other minor European nobility. The top American rider, a high-powered New York art dealer named Luca Marenzi, also happens to be a count of some sort. In the 2008 Grand National, the most prestigious Cresta trophy race, Count Marenzi finished

second to one Lord Wrottesley. That's Clifton Hugh Lance-
lot de Verdin Wrottesley, to be precise, whose membership in
the Peerage of the United Kingdom does not prevent him from
competing for the Republic of Ireland, both at the Cresta and
the Winter Olympics.* All about par for the social course at
the Cresta: rumor has it that a couple of Windsors have competed under fake names. In his book, DiGiacomo reports that
the grandsons of both Winston Churchill (named Winston)
and Nazi bigwig Baron von Ribbentrop (named Adolf, if you
can believe it) merrily rubbed elbows as members of the SMTC.
When not actively seeking injury (*Apparently Unharmed* is full
of impromptu bubbly parties in local trauma wards), the Cresta
crowd parties. Hard. All the Cresta season's many races lead to
wacky awards ceremonies, replete with kisses from "designated
females," bottles of claret, traditional cheers originated by exiled
White Cavalry officers in the 1930s, that sort of thing.

Appalling, I know. Elitist. Chauvinist—women may ride the
Cresta only by invitation. Granted. Still, in the age of dour, EU-
style bureaucrats and vulgar petro-oligarchs, the Cresta proves
that old-style aristos can still have the most fun. It may not make
sense to try to read deep meaning into the Cresta—DiGiacomo's
book tries to weave in Francis Fukuyama and the "post-histor-
ical" bourgeois' quest for thrills, but that seems a stretch. Still,
the sangfroid the Cresta fosters does have other applications. In
the 1920s and '30s, the top American Cresta rider was a young
gadabout named Billy Fiske, a sportsman of a now-extinct

*Wrottesley finished fourth in the skeleton in the 2002 Games in Salt Lake City.
Asked by the BBC how he planned to celebrate, he replied: "Some Guinness, along
with a couple of glasses of champagne, should do the trick nicely!"

breed. Fiske won Olympic bobsled gold at St. Moritz in 1928 at the age of sixteen, then did it again at Lake Placid in '32. (He got in trouble with American Olympic authorities for naming his sled "Satan.") He drove the 24 Hours of Le Mans, skied like a dervish, became an accomplished amateur pilot, and won a bagful of Cresta Run trophies. (Meanwhile, his brief stint as a Hollywood producer may have included an affair with Cary Grant's fiancée—quite the lad, Billy.)*

Fiske refused to defend his Olympic gold in 1936 at Garmisch-Partenkirchen, Bavaria—he had helped out the German team after it lost a sled and a couple of injured members in a crash at Lake Placid, but no way would he compete for the entertainment of Adolf Hitler. When war came, he connived to join the Royal Air Force—some accounts say he passed himself off as a Canadian, while DiGiacomo suggests that he leveraged Cresta Run connections. In any case, he soon joined a fighter unit known as the Millionaires' Squadron. On August 16, 1940, at the height of the Battle of Britain, Fiske was shot down while dogfighting with German Stukas over Sussex. He died of shock, the first American serviceman killed in World War II. At Fiske's funeral, Lord Brabazon of Tara, one of the leaders of the St. Moritz Tobogganing Club, said: "A very gallant gentleman, Billy Fiske, has given his life for us . . . We thank America for sending us the perfect sportsman. Many of us would have given our lives for Billy. Instead he has given his for us." Billy Fiske. Patriot. Playboy. Olympian. Martyr. Sledder.

---

*For these and other details on Fiske, see DiGiacomo's *Apparently Unharmed: The Riders of the Cresta Run*, and Alex Kershaw's *The Few: The American "Knights of the Air" Who Risked Everything to Fight in the Battle of Britain.*

You may have heard of the Paris-Dakar, the bombastic off-road endurance rally traditionally run from France to Senegal, in which well-funded daredevils plowed through the African desert via motorcycles, souped-up cars, and massive trucks. (The race recently announced a move to South America after some semicoherent threats from would-be terrorists. Sissies.) This is exactly the sort of brawny adventurism I would like to endorse, and I love to fantasize about outfitting a top-of-the-line Land Rover—at a generous sponsor's expense, of course—and barreling off toward the Heart of Darkness. But the Dakar leaves me a little queasy. Something about white dudes burning huge amounts of cash and petroleum to speed through dirt-poor Saharan villages just doesn't feel right, even before the odd six-year-old girl gets crushed by an SUV.

Fortunately, I discovered a much friendlier, goofier alternative on which to focus my impractical daydreams: the Plymouth-Banjul Challenge. The P-B, a sterling example of DIY sport, is like the Dakar with a sense of humor, founded, in the words of its official website, "to take the piss out of the real Dakar." Its rules require that cars cost no more than one hundred pounds and cap the "preparation" budget at fifteen pounds. (Some participants increase the degree of difficulty by driving Ladas, the Soviet Union's contribution to the Communist automotive tradition that brought the world the Yugo and the Trabant.) After the run from the English port of Plymouth to the Gambian capital of Banjul, cars are auctioned off to benefit local charities. Since the first P-B in 2002, the organizers (or as they prefer, "dis-organizers") have launched a couple of spin-offs, including a Silk Road Challenge to scenic Bishkek. (The website promises this route's Ukrainian section provides "a chance to see Chernobyl.")

While these rallies share a nominal every-man/woman-for-him/herself ethos with the Dakar, Plymouth-Banjul challengers travel in cooperative packs, with group departures staggered through the winter months. The rules allow plenty of time for en route sightseeing and partying—some groups time their finish to coincide with major African music festivals (pending mechanical complications). The concept is an adaptable success: copycats include a Budapest-Bamako rally and a Paris-Beijing route. Numerous loosely edited Web videos set to groovy world pop/techno suggest that a hazy, amiable spirit presides over Plymouth-Banjul. So does this report from the starting line of the very first run: "Those in attendance mingled, marveled at others' detailed vehicle preparation (and luggage) and . . . consumed a large quantity of alcohol late into the night . . ." *Allez!*

I became obsessed with the idea of meeting an athlete named Terris Tiller, a modern pentathlete. Likewise, I became obsessed with the notion that Terris Tiller's chosen discipline was secretly the greatest sport in the world. As a born dilettante, specialization bothers me, and American sports make specialization into a cult. Football's enormous rosters allow teams to carry both snappers and long snappers, while baseball bullpens divide labor as precisely as Taylorist assembly lines. The modern pentathlon, on the other hand . . . Shooting! Swimming! Sword fighting! Scary horseback riding! A long-distance run to the finish! Here was a sport for true renegades, an antispecialist festival of mustachio-twirling, old-world élan. Add the fact that the modern pentathlon is under constant threat of extinction, and I was sold.

You know a sport is in trouble when it was invented specifically

for the Olympics—by the very founder of the Olympics, in fact—
and arranges its entire existence around its quadrennial cameo
in the Olympics, yet must wage constant sports-bureaucracy
battle to stave off elimination from the Olympics. The modern
pentathlon, devised by the nutty Baron de Coubertin himself as
a test of nineteenth-century martial values, now barely escapes
the IOC budget cutters, eager to make room for the next BMX,
each Olympic cycle. Like a species of Chinese river dolphin, MP
could disappear at any time, with few tears shed on its behalf. I
find this a little puzzling, because in concept the sport sounds
like a terrific reality-TV show. Pentathletes begin their single-
day competition bright and early, firing touchy air pistols at tiny
little targets—which would appear to impose a zero-tolerance
policy for hangovers. They end by running three thousand
meters as night falls. In between, everyone faces off against
everyone in a round-robin fencing tournament, swims two hundred meters, and rides a completely unfamiliar horse. Sounds
fun to me. Modern pentathlon is like a batty private college
that insists every student learn to recite *The Iliad* in the original
Greek: admirable in its own fanatical way, but completely out of
step with the times. I had to learn more.

Terris Tiller was one of the top American pentathletes, and
notable for a few other reasons as well. One, he was an African
American civilian in a sport traditionally dominated by Eastern
European military officers. Two, he wrote hilarious online dia-
ries for the U.S. Olympic Committee, which focused on his love
of OutKast and the possibility that his pentathlon career could
impress women at his high school reunion. Three, his personal
website offered this description: *"Personality: Observant; Passionate; Vibrant . . . Resourceful, Smart, Driven."* The website also

offered half-nude shots of Tiller in his fencing gear. I gave him a call. Terris explained that the pentathlon's all-rounder demands helped him build his own solid-but-not-exceptional athletic abilities into an international career. After running cross-country in college, he stumbled into the sport—of which he had, of course, never heard—on a friend's recommendation.

"I came out of an agility and speed background," he said. "I needed to work on the skill sports, shooting and fencing. I was always a pretty good basketball player, and that helped me with the fencing. For some reason, I picked up riding really quickly, which is good, because that's what we practice the least. We ride a couple times a month to keep our skills up. Beyond that, if you draw a bad horse, that's just tough."

Terris described the elite pentathlete's life as a long slog between competitions held in parts of the world where you really, really need your *Lonely Planet*. He and his teammates usually lodged in the Collapsing Modernist dormitories so beloved by second-world architects. Sometimes they managed to take a day to see something cultural or historic, but mostly they saw each other. "It's a long day," Terris says. "On competition days, you're up at seven a.m. and competing until six p.m. When we have back-to-back events, we're basically on the road for a month. Right now, they're trying to grow the sport in Egypt and the Caribbean, so we're in those places all the time."

Egypt and the Caribbean—dream big, pentathlon! At last, a sport not yet preoccupied with how it should carve up the spoils from its global television empire. People like Terris form the real backbone of the sports world. They break themselves training and traveling, investing precious time in disciplines no one else cares about, idling away nights in sub–Motel 6 hovels in forgotten parts of the old Austro-Hungarian Empire if that's what their sport demands. For modern pentathletes, it *really* isn't about the money. It is about doing something for its own sake, and trying to do it well, for private glory and personal satisfaction—some version of that thing they used to call the Sporting Ideal. That the object of Terris's efforts happened to be a crazy, pre–Great War, total-warrior concept with sharply limited appeal only made his dedication more touching. He tried to make the Beijing Olympics, but injuries forced him to retire not long after we first spoke. He moved on to an office job with the U.S. Olympic Committee. "It's a new position that allows me to do some writing and creative work," he told me via e-mail. "Pretty fun gig, but nothing like being an athlete."

Why should anyone care if the modern pentathlon survives, or whether a bunch of rich head cases blast down some Swiss mountain, or about the boozy superstars of darts? To me, it's a question of biodiversity. Sport, like any cultural movement, relies on its own ecology. Football, baseball, and basketball are the all-devouring grizzlies; tennis and golf, the majestic, tawny elk grazing on the horizon. They're what you put on the postcard, but on their own they do not add up to a robust ecosystem. Athletes who play sports that don't make money for franchise owners or bestow reflected glamour on college boosters all too often find their pursuits pushed toward oblivion. In 2006, for example, Rutgers eliminated six varsity sports—introverted stuff like fencing and rowing that doesn't bring in much seat-license revenue—to achieve budget savings of less than $1 million. The school spent $13 million on its football program that same year, and handed its football coach a half-million-dollar pay raise. Amateur wrestling, one of the oldest sports in the world, finds itself on the perpetual defensive as high schools and colleges eliminate their programs, often blaming Title IX's gender-equity requirements even as they pump resources into all-male football and men's basketball. Too often, American sports mimic Midwestern agribusiness, eliminating diversity in favor of a few big cash crops. True health requires depth and complexity, mutation and adaptation, freaks and outliers, heritage crops and voles scurrying through the underbrush. To restore, invent, and nurture all this is a critical part of the Renegade Way.

SEVEN

HOW TO RULE THE WORLD OF SPORTS FOR FUN AND PROFIT (PROFIT NOT GUARANTEED)

Admit it. You've wondered what it would be like—how it would feel to ascend to the ranks of sports moguldom. You've envied the power, the prestige, the ability to roll into your luxury suite on game night and idly wonder if you'll fire the head coach just for the hell of it. Change team colors? Threaten to move the franchise to San Antonio? Why not? That power—what's it like?

I can tell you firsthand. It feels pretty good.

On the surface, I suffer from a distinct lack of Master of the Sports Universe credentials. I share little common ground with the likes of Mark Cuban, the Steinbrenner clan, Roman Abramovich, or those party-boy bros who own the Sacramento Kings. Even so, after checking out the inspiring examples of do-it-yourself empire provided by the likes of the alley cat racers, Guitar Ted, and the Hash House Harriers, I decided to give omnipotence a try. If they could create their own private sports worlds, so could I. It turns out that the real secret to athletic glory has nothing to do with how fast you run the forty. Sure, it would be nice to be a great athlete, but why limit your ambitions? Become an *owner*—it's easy. Just make common cause with a few other would-be plutocrats and start your very own league. Based on my personal experience as part of a circle of flamboyant, megalomaniacal tycoons, here's how you do it:

STEP ONE:
Pick a Sport (Preferably One in Which You Will Face No Competition from Real Athletes)

We chose croquet. And not the arcane, chesslike elite version involving laser-leveled courts and maneuvers with names like "the sextuple peel." No, that summer the Portland Croquet League would crown its champions and deify its legends in backyards and parks, using the nine wire wickets and crappy, supermarket-bought mallets and balls we all know from wasted afternoons of our youths. We had many reasons to embrace this great game. No one is actually any good at it. Men and women can play against each other, because the game relies more on deceit, cunning, and viciousness ("tactics") than physical strength. Alcohol consumption improves one's play. (Within reason, I would discover.) If there is such a thing as a famous croquet player, word has yet to spread beyond friends and relatives. I can't find any official figures, but I estimate the total value of the world's croquet industry at about $672. The biggest cultural splash for the game I can think of is the strip-croquet scene in the 1989 'burb-goth/teen-murder classic *Heathers*. Behold a sport ripe for appropriation by talentless jackanapeses.

STEP TWO:
Hold an Owners' Meeting, for Organizational and Egotistical Purposes

The six PCL franchise owners gathered one fine spring day at the café co-owned by the league commissioner, where we drank Miller High Life, hashed out a bunch of needlessly complicated scheduling and competition rules, argued about game format, and compared possible team names. Unfortunate local health codes, with no loopholes for robber-baron gatherings, kept us from smoking cigars. I still felt like a king.

STEP THREE:
Name Your Team

A mistake here can doom the enterprise. Your team's success, failure, and entire existence will depend on your ability to con friends into sacrificing afternoons they could otherwise spend doing something.

I was disappointed that the other five PCL franchisees all took the names of nominal "sponsors"—two cafés, a coffee roaster, a design firm, and a popular local blog. (This selection said a lot about the PCL's core demographic; no longshoremen.) On the upside, this gave the league a brassy Tour de France flavor. But given that league entry cost nothing, I considered it a craven bow to market forces. My team would have a real name—but what? Should we tap croquet's Anglophile connections with a faux-classy name like "the Athenians," "Wanderers," or "the Pickwick Croquet Club"? Or explore the surreal world of made-up animal species popular with American minor-league baseball clubs and Japanese teams

in all sports: NightFalcons; SuperPigeons; HyperCougars? In the
end, I chose an aggressive brand that suggested heavy mescaline
use and Latin American black-metal fandom. We would be known
as the Jaguar Realm. That this decision would be the high point of
our team's existence only underlines its brilliance.

STEP FOUR:
Launch a Media Onslaught

The National Football League thinks it's all high and mighty
with its own twenty-four-hour cable network. Thanks to the
wonders of technology, you can compete. With a league blog, a
YouTube channel, and an irritating Twitter account fed a stream
of delusional proclamations, it's easy to create an aura of hype
and excitement. Hone a few basic propaganda skills, and you
could soon crush the middling intelligences of professional
sports marketing—after all, they're the people who gave the
world a hockey team called the Mighty Ducks.

For example, when my brother and his roommate organized
a day of gaming at the park across the street from their house,
they barraged their wider circle of acquaintances with breathless dispatches and HUGE ANNOUNCEMENTS. Whatever
sport you decide to base your empire upon, I suggest the following as a model:

HEAR YE! HEAR YE!

We do hereby decree a grand festival of sport, fellowship, and
mirth!

To be known henceforth as the Northside Games . . . on the
grounds of the venerable Northside Park! Beginning at Midday

and progressing without respite until Sundown! With a reception to follow, to last until all have been sated or dispossessed!

Activities and competition to include but not be limited to:

Two-person double-elimination bocce tournament!

Sack race!

Egg 'n' Spoon run!

Basking!

Boozing!

Slow dancing!

Romance!

Intrigue!

Amity!

Particular style is less important than bombast and self-importance. If the so-called big leagues can go around pretending that everything they do represents a vital turning point in human history, why can't you? In the PCL's case, we documented our four-week season on a blog that did not let its approximate readership of ten discourage a portentous fake-British tone and dramatic close-up portraits of league players.

STEP FIVE:
Create Pomp and Circumstance

The first match in PCL history took place in sodden conditions, as late-spring downpours reduced the host team's playing field (the backyard of a ramshackle house inhabited by several PCL members) to a spongy mire. Even so, we all did our best to impress. One team swanned around the Players' Lounge (a back-porch table stocked with domestic twelve-packs) resplendent in thrift-store neckties. The captain of another sported a blinding white jumpsuit, matching headband, and a good-sized stogie. The host team made its entrance to the field through a haze of fog from a small smoke machine, intimidating the rest of us.

STEP SIX:
Revel in the Thrill of Victory

The PCL's season format required each team to host one day's action. When Jaguar Realm's turn rolled around, I scouted various neighborhood parks until I found a roomy, shady stretch of deep grass. On game day, my team and I arrived early to set up the course after I stopped at a convenience store for two bottles of cheap Spanish bubbly and some paper cups. One of my players turned out in full nineteenth-century regalia, complete with bowler hat. When our rivals arrived and proclaimed this the most impressive facility of the season, my inner Martha Stewart crowed.

The action commenced in a blissful neoarcadian stupor. I drank cava until I had a mild headache. The shaggy grass and sprawling course encouraged a lot of ill-advised long shots, a few instances of creative tree-trunk use, and a general atmosphere of shoeless camaraderie. Halfway through the match, a few fans showed up with a bag of Dairy Queen Dilly Bars. So what if Jaguar Realm lost miserably and finished next-to-last in the league? In the short annals of the Portland Croquet League, our performance would shine bright. Private jet be damned, I was now a full-fledged sports kingpin. And I felt confident that, of all the sporting events held in the world that day, ours was the best.

Over the course of a summer, as I steered my team to croquet iniquity and continued my pseudo scholarship on the sporting fringe, I developed a theory, which is the sort of thing that can happen to the best of us. I call it the Two Futures of Sports Theory, and it posits that the sports world will evolve on two parallel tracks. One of these Linnaean branches is easy to locate—just turn on the TV, and you'll see the unstoppable process of Big getting Bigger, Glitz getting Glitzier, and Alex Rodriguez already thinking about his next contract, which will stipulate that he gets George Steinbrenner's reanimated brain. Behold sports as we know them—the Show, which I was determined to ignore as much as possible as summer rolled on. I was interested in the *other* future of sports.

This alternative evolutionary line already exists; you can find it in just about every city in America. In the annual Idiotarod, teams of humans drag shopping carts through the streets of New York. The Scooter Cannonball Run, a biannual transcontinental rally organized by Vespa lovers, demands that these stylish but underpowered vehicles navigate some of the most remote highways in America. Such DIY efforts are essentially the sports equivalent of starting a band in your garage, brewing your own beer, or knitting your own scarves. According to my theory, these sporadic examples somehow add up to a potential movement, even if haphazard and decentralized to the extreme. I needed to test the hypothesis, so I spent much of the summer trying to see how an independent, grassroots local sports reality might look. This was, in part, a semiapocalyptic thought experiment that became slightly less far-fetched in retrospect, when global capitalism hit the minor rough patch known as 2008–2009–?: What would happen if mainstream sports disappeared? What might the world look like if people *really* had to make their own fun?

Lucky me, I live in a town full of idler misfits with surplus free time. As one of America's postmodern Left Coast cities, Portland's traditional jock culture is weak, while its willingness to sacrifice dignity in pursuit of a good time is strong. We have just one major-league sports franchise, but two competing adult kickball leagues. I figured that if an underground sports revolution could thrive anywhere, it would be here. I would make Portland my laboratory. Interesting complications ensued. For instance, I ended up sitting in a listing rowboat full of discarded shoes, with the fecal-bacteria-enriched waters of a Superfund-designated river lapping at the gunwales. This provided some insight on just how far DIY sports could take me. It also provided an excellent opportunity to contemplate the fact that I am a very poor swimmer.

I met Jay Boss Rubin for afternoon beers on a gray day in July. He sat across from me wearing a striped, sailorish shirt, his hair an uncombed chestnut explosion, with a frighteningly avid look in his eyes and a notebook full of scribbled ideas, which, to judge by the one we discussed in most depth, all involved strenuous effort and zero economic return.

Jay and I talked about the Portland Challenge, an event

(street theater? social activism? a quasi-spiritual exercise?) of his invention and relentless promotion. Jay wanted to make sure that I understood that the Challenge wasn't a competitive endeavor—that would be far too mundane, Western, and right-brained—and thus only counted as a "sport" under a very elastic definition of the term. I assured him that the Challenge met my criteria: it required all participants to cross the Willamette River, which bisects the city, without using money, motors, or bridges. In this, the Challenge's fifth consecutive year, Jay expected a couple hundred Challengers to take the plunge, with or without human-powered watercraft. Seemed pretty sporting to me.

Jay liked to think of himself as the pioneer of a new discipline, which he called "Challenging." He said he viewed the Portland event as a prototype and hoped the idea would spread. "You could do this anywhere," he said. "There are just three rules—it's simple. No money. No motors. No bridges. And you just apply those rules to any route from Point A to B, and you become a Challenger. True Challengers could make their trip to work a Challenge, as long as they applied the rules. Challenging turns any journey into a kind of empowering adventure. You develop a different relationship with your environment, especially a city environment. If you're trying to get all the way across town on foot, without using any money, you need to know, okay, this is the best route, this is where the public restrooms are, here's where my friend lives and I can bum a sandwich. You're cross-ing a piece of territory, but you need its help in return."

I didn't know if I found this as mind-blowing as Jay obvi-ously did, but I was willing to approach the Challenge in the spirit of inquiry. In fact, I was slightly disappointed to learn that the upcoming Portland Challenge would be a rather lite version of Jay's original concept. "It was winter," he recalled. "The time of year when you sit around and dream up adventures. And somehow I hit on the idea of crossing Portland, from one major geographical landmark to another, totally unassisted. And then I was like, what would that mean? Well, it means when you get to the river, you have to cross the river by your own strength and ingenuity. If you can't swim, you have to build a raft. That was the original idea, and I was excited about it, but it sat dormant for a while, you know how it is. . . ."

Sure, I knew how it was. I could tell a certain improvisational flow was inherent to the Jay Boss Rubin creative process. I was not surprised to hear that Sweet Mother Alcohol had helped midwife Challenging. "So it was, I think, May, and I was with a bunch of friends up on Council Crest, which is, like, the highest point in the city west of the river," Jay continued. "I'm sure we drank a keg of beer or whatever. And I was looking out across the city, and I could see Mount Tabor, the highest point on the east side. And I said, that's it. That's the Challenge: to go from here to there. I think I got about fifteen minutes of sleep, and at six a.m. we started out. There were five of us. Of course, the first part is all downhill, on park trails in the hills, and then through downtown. It was like we were just out on a walk. And then we got to the river, and we were, like, oh. Here we are. We're on the Challenge."

The Willamette is a sedate riband of sluggish-looking water, locally renowned for the unhappy fact that the city's sewage system overflows into it every time a heavy rain falls, which happens, of course, often. While various green-sensitive measures have improved the Willamette's health in recent years, one environmental group rates it as America's third-most-endangered river. The official stance on swimming in the Willamette runs something like, *Uh, sure . . . go right ahead.* Aside from the risk of topical infection or, say, cholera, Jay Boss Rubin and his fellow hungover-or-still-drunk, sleep-deprived Challengers faced more than a casual dip. At city center, the river is about a quarter mile wide, equivalent to eight laps in an Olympic-sized pool. As I would discover, at water level that distance becomes very daunting. "We didn't know anything about the river," Jay said. "We didn't know about currents. We didn't even really know how wide it was. You cross it every day on the bridge in your car, but how wide is it?"

Most of Jay's companions that morning decided that maybe the Challenge wasn't quite for them. Somewhere in that polluted quarter-mile plunge, though, Jay Boss Rubin discovered a calling. "The middle of the river is the crux of the adventure," he said. "It's psychologically hard more than anything—you're out in the middle of the thing, and you can't turn back, and you also can't see how you can make it to other side. It's great. I've probably done it twenty times now."

Jay went public later that year, inviting all comers to join him on a trip across town. In the next five years, the Portland Challenge became something of a local institution, drawing hundreds of participants—which, rather unfortunately to Jay's thinking, made it more street parade than rugged expedition. "Now that so many people do it, all that remains of the pure original concept—*orthodox* Challenging, I guess you could say—is the river crossing," he said, wistful. "I'm still attracted to the more extreme version. A friend of mine and I put together this trip we called the Oregon Challenge, from the headwaters of the Willamette all the way up to Portland. It took twelve days.

So that's what I conceive of as real Challenging. But the Portland Challenge, it's still true to the kernel of the idea. It's a pilgrimage. A real-life pilgrimage, wherever you live. You don't have to go to the woods to have an adventure—you just have to put yourself in that mental state. You just give yourself to the spirits of that place."

Heavy. But I was into it—here was a guy who carried an entire new sport (or something like that) around in his head, complete with a fully formed mythology. I was excited. Except, I told Jay, my lifelong tendency to sink like a stone concerned me. I didn't want to harsh the Portland Challenge's mellows by becoming its first drowning victim.

"Oh, man, no problem," Jay said. "I'll just put you on the Shoe Boat."

While Jay Boss Rubin's enthusiasm and loopy psychogeography appealed to me, I suspected that the Portland Challenge would be crawling with hippies, who would drive me crazy. On Challenge day, I arrived at the Slammer Tavern, a broken-down saloon that looks like a haunted barn transplanted into the city, and discovered I was not wrong. A couple hundred Portland Challengers coagulated in the roped-off street, checking out each other's costumes (yes, Jay encouraged costumes) and drinking Pabst. One guy had a red and black necktie around his head. A woman wore a Mexican wrestling mask backwards. Jay himself scampered around in cutoff jeans and a beat-up flannel shirt, distributing life jackets from a huge pile in the back of a graffiti-covered old wine truck. Meanwhile, a band composed of aged longhairs played on the Slammer's roof, whimpering out jam-rock critiques of national policy. One long, bedraggled anthem revolved around the singer's repeated declaration, "*I . . . con-shee-ent-ious-leee ob-ject! I . . . con-shee-entiously ob-ject!*"

I have a more robust tolerance for subcultural whimsy than some. In my tenure as an alternative-newspaper reporter, I interviewed many conspiracy theorists, third-party politicians, lifestyle activists, and self-styled "social change agents," and never let the fact that these sources often teetered on the brink of outright vagrancy prevent me from presenting their provocative ideas to the public. I filed many stories based on the views of people the *Wall Street Journal* would expel from its offices with armed guards. All the same, scenes like the Portland Challenge preparty tickle the more misanthropic chords of my being. When I see a grown man wearing a rainbow Afro wig in broad daylight, I am liable to start talking in a loud voice about general military conscription. I was very glad I had invited my friend Jeremy along as my Challenger wingman. Jeremy is one of the most good-hearted and good-humored people now living, and I hoped his unfailing cheer would see me through the Challenge. He's also one of those physically capable types—he builds things and so forth. I figured he could save me if I started to drown.

Jay Boss Rubin found us and handed us each an oar and gave Jeremy an orange hand-stenciled sign reading "SHOE BOAT." "It's tied to a rock on the riverbank, man," he said. "Little white boat. Can't miss it." The idea was that the Challengers could dump their shoes in our boat, and we would ferry the *chausseures* to the far side of the river. (Ordinarily, the hygienic implications might give me pause. The previous night's downpour meant a healthy combined-sewage overflow into the waves we would paddle, so I thought, what the hell.) While most of our fellow Challengers would swim, we would be part of a small fleet. Two canoes sat on the pavement next to a vessel fashioned from an old aluminum tub, lashed-together boards, and empty water-cooler jugs. This craft had its name, *Desolation Row* (ha!), spray-painted on its side and a tattered, homemade peace-symbol flag aloft.

At a megaphone signal from Jay Boss Rubin, a group called the Last Regiment of Syncopated Drummers, a corps of marching-band percussionists in matching black jackets, formed ranks and started pounding away. The ragtag mob took shape behind them, and we started off for the river about eight blocks away. Challengers at the front of the pack raised a huge banner with the enigmatic slogan "Gone to Bongo," and a couple hundred people in life jackets and quizzical headgear commenced to block traffic on some of Portland's busiest streets. The drum corps' cadences exploded off the asphalt and concrete overpasses along the Willamette's banks. Jeremy and I found ourselves next to the crew of *Desolation Row*, a grizzled bunch who pushed their tub at a deliberate pace, so as not to spill the cocktails balanced on its plywood deck. Three twenty-something kids, including the fellow with the necktie on his head, scampered past us with an inflatable raft. "I'm ready for glory!" he hollered. "I'm ready for glory!" Who wasn't? The spirit of Lewis and Clark was alive and well.

As we neared the river, unlikely people started to join in. A middle-aged couple, all in black, looked like they'd just stepped out of a suburban casino or a midnight public-access televangelism program: she had a big puff of frosted blond hair, strappy black high heels, and silver-spangled painted toes; he had a pattern-baldness pompadour, a black short-sleeve button-up, black slacks, and black tasseled loafers. Did they plan to swim the river? What about the gray-haired man in the kilt? Did the future of Challenging include unexpected popularity in the AARP demographic?

The Portland Challenge reached the riverbank, a tumble of grimy boulders underneath a freeway escarpment. Jeremy and I spotted a dubious little white skiff and made a dash for it—a few Challengers, confronted with the actual river, now struck me as potential Shoe Boat hijackers. I scrambled aboard, and Jeremy held up our sign. A rain of Teva sandals and mungy high-tops filled the shallow boat in about a minute. Challengers splashed past us into the water. The river now held a flotilla of bobbing, giggling heads, inner tubes, and rafts. Jeremy and I decided that the Shoe Boat was at capacity, and tried to shove off. A few last stowaways bum-rushed us, and we relented for two women with large sunglasses, digital cameras, and jarringly fashionable out-fits, and a grinning Tanzanian man named Elvis. We set sail.

With five people and uncounted shoes as cargo, the Shoe Boat rode pretty low in the water. I noticed this at about the same time I noticed that Jay's oars didn't fit the boat's oarlocks. Jeremy had handed his implement off to Elvis. Elvis and I sat next to each other and hacked at the water. In a photo Jeremy took from his station in the prow, our female companions look like they're enjoying a pleasure-craft outing on the Seine. Elvis looks like he is doing the most fun thing he has ever done in his life (though based on our brief acquaintance, I would say he probably always looks like that). I'm holding my paddle in a manner that suggests I am completely unfamiliar with boats, water, and elementary mechanics. Also, as though I'm about to cry like a small child.

At about this point, I glanced over my shoulder, to see a few gawkers scattered along the civilized shore, twenty yards behind us. I admit that I wondered what the hell I was doing—all very well for Jay Boss Rubin to dupe goofball Portlanders into the Willamette, but why me, hard-nosed cynic and confirmed hydrophobe? I looked to starboard and saw *Desolation Row*. Somehow, the empty water jugs strapped to the tub with duct tape provided enough ballast to support four people. Just. A man in tattered jeans stood on the narrow deck, waving the giant peace-symbol flag and whooping in the shadow of the hundred-year-old bridge above us.

Under ordinary circumstances, this sight would annoy me mightily, so I was caught off guard by a surge of benevolent goodwill. The *Row* and its crew, maybe because they could sink at any second, made their silly Boomer-nostalgia banner seem bold and forthright—the world would, I thought in this moment of either weakness or insight, be a better place if we were all out Challenging instead of killing each other. Certainly it would have been hard to find a group of two hundred people happier, on average, than the Challengers at that moment. Fifty yards off the Shoe Boat's port bow, I could see Jay Boss Rubin backstroking in his bright red life jacket, smiling like a holy fool straight out of Jack Kerouac at his most overwrought and excellent. The Challenge temporarily seized and reinvented part of the city, taking over streets and freeing ordinary places from their ordinariness. This is one thing the new world of DIY sport is good for: we Challengers changed the city's fabric, even if just for a few minutes, and made it more interesting. Maybe this wasn't strictly sport, but it was a very pure form of play, and I could see that it delighted those who chanced to see it. As the Shoe Boat crept along beneath the bridge, we passed a fancy sailboat, standing idle in the middle of the river. A man and a woman stood on deck smiling, applauding, and taking pictures. Maybe they would tell some friends about us over cocktails—about the mob of lunatics swimming the Willamette. Today, we were the Show.

No discussion of do-it-yourself sport is complete without skateboarding. I am, to be honest, slightly in awe of skateboarders, and not just because I can't even propel myself forward on their contraptions, let alone do a trick or get from A to B. Skateboarders are the masterless samurai of the sports world. Where others see disasters of modern architecture and city planning—wasteland lots, brutalist garages, concrete "park" benches strategically located where no human would ever choose to sit—skateboarders see the Elysian Fields. This attitude helps skateboarding maintain its semicriminal status, a notch above trespassing and loitering with intent, in many places. That guarantees a certain level of petty police harassment and parental suspicion—which, in turn, ensures a steady supply of new recruits for a movement that has survived successive waves of persecution and commercialization for almost half a century.

It so happens that one of the great world monuments of skate culture, and one of the most spectacular examples of hands-on sports ingenuity anywhere, hides deep in one of Portland's most unsavory pockets. The legendary Burnside Skatepark nestles under the bridge of the same name, surrounded by befouled concrete grottoes and weedy hillsides. The whole area looks like it recently got the Sarajevo treatment—and I'm not talking about the Olympics. Shiny-happy-progressive Portland sweeps many of its social ills under this particular rug, and for decades the bridge's grim underbelly attracted vagrants, prostitution, drug

use, vandalism, and all-purpose scumbaggery. The city government always has a plan in the works for this part of town, and I
suspect it always will. In the meantime, one genuine force for civic
order and improvement asserted itself here: skateboarders.

The legend goes that sometime in 1990, a few skateboarders
started hauling bags of cement down beneath the bridge and
building obstacles on a forsaken patch of ground. (How forsaken? The land sits at the dead center of an American metropolis, a ten-minute stroll from million-dollar condos and the city's
business district—and no one, to this day, claims legal owner-
ship.) They threw up a couple of little ramps and started skating.
Word spread. More wildcat construction followed, creating an
elaborate and ever-shifting complex of ramps and bowls. So, too,
did successful negotiations with surrounding businesses and
quite a few encounters with the local street wildlife, as skaters
faced down the disreputable element and made the place their
own.

One spring afternoon, I headed under the bridge to meet Chad
Balcom, a machinist from Nebraska who moved to Portland a
few years ago. He's obviously not one of Burnside's founding
fathers—in fact, he told me his status as a new arrival left him
with "total white man's guilt—like I gotta do whatever I can to
help out to make up for lost time." Since he showed up, however,
his natural get-'er-done leanings have established him as a part
of the loose community that, through a process that defies exact
definition, runs the park. (Or as he put it, "I've been pretty much
balls-deep in this project for a coupla years.") For example, he is
the master of the keys to the onsite porta-potty.

"This is definitely an organic thing," Balcom said, as about a
dozen skaters took turns lounging on a curb and cheating death

inside the park. "That wall over there is being built as we speak. It's a weird lack-of-hierarchy hierarchy. Like, that guy over there, he has influence because he's down here all the time. He's old-school and everyone knows it. And then that little guy over there is pretty young, but he's a total pain in the ass, so he tends to have influence because no one wants to deal with his shit. It goes like that. It'll be, well, we built this wall, but now we're all a little better, so it needs to be higher. We pass out a few keys to the porta-shitters, and of course everyone loses theirs but me, so now I'm the guy who distributes keys.

"On day one, the dudes who started this place just put up a little something against the wall. Then they added to it and added to it. The voice of reason at the time said, man, we'll get in trouble. And then opposite opinion said, fuck that, it'll be cool. And somehow that logic prevailed, and continues to this day."

Burnside not only survived, it achieved mythic stature. (Along the way, Portland's city council voted to give the park a kind of tenuous, don't-ask-don't-tell legitimacy. It could be revoked at any time—if the council wanted an unmitigated PR disaster.) Skating video games feature Burnside, and pro skaters from around the world make pilgrimages to the park. In *The Answer Is Never: A Skateboarder's History of the World*, skater/author Jocko Weyland describes Burnside as "a massive renegade wonderland" (be still, my heart!). "[T]he right fanatics built it for the right reasons," Weyland writes. "Their mission to make something out of nothing has been as influential as any trick or board-design breakthrough." According to Balcom, the park's only real revenue stream comes from Hollywood production companies that pay to film scenes there. A nonprofit board manages the funds, more or less. Balcom mentioned that he'd recently spent

thirty dollars for a new padlock for the caged enclosure holding the park's building and cleaning equipment; he would get
reimbursed, y'know, sometime. Volunteer labor and construction raw materials that appear, without explanation, in the dead
of night cover the rest of Burnside's needs.

Balcom took me on a walk around the park. For all its renown,
Burnside still resembles the kind of urban hellpit that inspires
people to move to gated communities and arm themselves. Spectator facilities, such as they are, amount to a couple of holes in a
retaining wall in the parking lot above the park and a scary concrete ledge where you could stand, if you really, really wanted
to. As we talked, skaters caromed around the park's complex of
bowls, walls, and ridges. Like the punk-rock world to which it
is forever wedded, skate culture isn't particularly interested in
sartorial evolution. The mostly male crowd (on an earlier visit,
I saw a predominantly female contingent) sported torn denim,
tats, and T-shirts referencing bands that would offend old people, except many of the band members themselves are now old
people. Slumped on the curb outside the park, they looked like
an old-fashioned after-school special waiting to happen. But on
the park's obstacles, the atmosphere bordered on studious—an
air of focused calm and deliberation. Despite the growth of various competitive promotions, skateboarding remains at heart a
matter of personal mastery, an art as much as a sport.* The park

---

*In a column for the May 2008 issue of *Arthur* magazine titled "Skateboarding as
a Mind-Body Practice," writer Greg Shewchuk offered this perspective: "Anyone
who claims to know what skateboarding is 'all about' is full of shit. . . . Skateboarding is inherently meaningless. Its lack of meaning is what allows it to be such a
progressive and influential experience." Shewchuk compares skating to tai chi and
yoga.

itself has an otherworldly sculptural beauty. In contrast to all the unconsidered and neglected ugliness around it, its undulating fantasy-forms show what concrete can do when applied with love.

"Skateboarding is like anything else," Balcom said, as we stood about two feet from a wall that skaters were rocketing over and along at thirty-second intervals. "It's precedent driven. As far as stuff to skate goes, there's way better, but people come here because this is the mecca. This is an experience. It set the precedent that showed this could be done—that a bunch of skaters left to their own devices could create something that lasts. Now there are places like this in cities all over, and some of 'em last and some of 'em don't, but this is the one they all look to."

At this point, we broke off our conversation to look up. Behind a half-built wall overlooking the park, we could see a man with a shaved head and squared-off shoulders—he was working on the wall until that minute—in a loud confrontation with another party. "Dude," Balcom said, "someone might be about to get his ass kicked." It seemed a resident of a nearby homeless encampment took exception to something the skaters were up to. Now the burly wall-builder found it necessary to enter into a spirited exchange of views. "Stuff like that is never-ending," Balcom said, peering up at the fracas. "Just the nature of the neighborhood. We've had people shooting heroin, all that shit. We run people outta here all the time."

When the city council considered Burnside's fate, it sought advice from law-and-order types. The police chief (he later became mayor) offered this: "Patrol officers report that since the park has existed, a previous pattern of theft from autos in the adjacent area has been significantly reduced." This represented, the city's top cop wrote, "an unexpected synergistic effect." In the great irony of the Burnside Skatepark, this child of anarchy became an experiment in bootstrapping good citizenship—in spite of the fact that, in Balcom's delicate phrase, "as skateboarders, we're somewhat desensitized to legality." Most hours of the day, the skatepark's disorganized guild of tattooed punks is effectively the only government that exists under the bridge. I hope the skaters don't take this the wrong way, but they appear to handle the responsibility quite well. Negotiations with business owners and the city turned Burnside's elders into adept students of municipal politics. Many of the founders now run one of the country's most-respected skatepark design firms and execute contracts with cities all over the world. Balcom sits on the board of Skaters for Public Skateparks, a 501(C)3 advocacy group that he describes as "sort of a think tank, I guess." In that role, he devised a formula to help cities determine how many skateparks they need to serve their populations. He also logs many hours at the kind of planning and public-comment meetings that form local governance's mind-numbing substance, trying to make sure cities do right by skaters.

"Our whole thing is just to make sure they don't fuck up," he said. "Because if left to their own devices, they will fuck up. For all the skateparks cities try to build these days, maybe 25 percent are any good. So our mission is to try to improve that, or at least not let it get any worse. Tacoma—great example. They put up antiskating barriers at the main street-skating spot in one of the parks. Then they were gonna build, like, fifteen skateparks. So we were, like, why don't you let us go back in, take off the skate barriers, and fix that place up? We can make it better *and* save you money. When we did it, I went up and set the granite at that spot, and I've never in my life seen people happier than the kids who came to see us do it. We just try to set the precedent that this shit can work."

At Burnside, human creativity took on a nasty environment and won. The park's existence proves a little anarchy can be a healthy thing. On any given day, some of the most dedicated athletes in Portland can be found in a setting that would otherwise be a minor lesion on the *forma urbis*—skating, hanging out, plotting. As one of several Burnside-oriented websites puts it: "The park is still not done. The beauty of Burnside is that it is never really complete. By being a nonsanctioned park, we are at liberty to destroy and rebuild as we see fit. It is how Burnside was started and it is how it continues to thrive."

On a cold but bright morning at the very beginning of fall, I stood in the middle of a deserted industrial street, beneath one of Portland's many bridges, and thwacked a tennis ball with a nine-iron golf club. The ball arced and hooked before plonking one of the bridge's concrete supports and dropping into a cordoned-off construction zone. I noted with satisfaction that the plastic bottle cap I'd used as a tee had not moved. It feels good to hit things. The visceral joy of abusing an insensate object with a weapon of choice, then seeing where it goes and what happens when it gets there, explains a meaty percentage of human behavior. To smack a ball true and clean is to experience a crisp lift to the entire organism—a sense that, ah, yes, now everything makes sense.

"Man," I said, as I handed the club back to Greg, its owner, "that felt pretty awesome."

"Wait until you get a few drinks in you," Greg replied. "Then you'll feel like Conan the Fucking Barbarian."

Greg wore a tweed vest, a green felt cap, and tight wool pants checked with a black and green plaid. He held a plastic cup one-third full of a martini, complete with floating olives, dispensed from a cylindrical cooler disguised as a golf club (the "Kooler Klub") tucked in his wheeled golf bag. It was about ten o'clock. The morning sun gave the giant brick storage building across the street a superreal glow. Greg's friend Robert looked almost as swell as he did, in a snappy brimmed cap, navy sweater vest, and pants refitted into knee-length knickers with some hidden twine. He also swirled the olive around his martini, took a satisfied pull of bracing air, and leaned on his driver—waiting for Gatsby to show up, maybe. Greg and Robert were ready for World Urban Golf Day, and now so was I.

In a few minutes, about seventy-five people would join our little party in Portland's old inner-city industrial quarter. Together, grouped not so much into foursomes as amoebalike pods, we would play eighteen "holes" plotted across a few twisting miles of city streets. In a concession to health, safety, and the windshields of parked and passing cars, we would use tennis balls; instead of little cups dug into sod, our targets would consist of found objects and hunks of municipal infrastructure marked with bright orange pennants. Maybe some people would actually keep track of their scores, but our main objectives were the five licensed premises en route, the beer and liquor for sale therein, and the amount of collective havoc and puzzlement we could stir up in between. Besides these obviously worthwhile goals, a hearty day of urban golf provided at least some players with a forum for statements of a kind. Greg and Robert, for instance, thought of themselves as walking fashion manifestos.

"Golf is a sport that is distinctly tied to the past," Greg said. He teed up a warm-up ball. "Players last a long time. Their careers span generations and tie together different eras. Unfortunately, the style doesn't always come with them. The '20s and '30s, those were stylish times, and the style found its way on to the golf course." He stopped to swing. His practice blast lanced down the center of a lane lined with old warehouses and hit a Ford Explorer about two blocks away.

"Nice," Robert said.

Greg shook his head. "I'm obviously going to lose a lot of balls today. Anyway, I guess we're trying to revive that spirit—you should play with a little bit of style. It seems like a shame to discard all that in favor of slapping on as many corporate logos as possible."

Style would not be a problem that day. As the eleven o'clock tee time approached, urban golfers streamed out of the brick-paved side streets. Soon, the first "tee" looked like a Scottish Highland clan gathering held in a fever dream. I have never seen such argyle, such plaid: chocolate brown, cocoa powder, robin's-egg blue; hot pink, salmon, maroon; latte foam, commencement-braid gold, sunburn. In this crowd, eye-bleeding neon stripes looked hidebound and conventional.

The first hole traversed a corridor of ragged asphalt laced with obsolete iron streetcar rails, ending in a ninety-degree dogleg down the actual working freight tracks along the Willamette. A woman in sky blue pants and pink socks teed up on a square-foot section of carpet laid over the asphalt and took a big slash at the ball. It dribbled about ten yards. She stepped up and went after it again, with a grinding thud of five-iron on concrete. A stocky lad carefully placed a crumpled Pabst can on the carpet section, put his ball atop it, and fired, ricocheting a fine hundred-yard drive off a wall.

"See," Robert said as we watched the next player clunk his driver against pavement to squib the ball fifteen yards to the right. "Urban golf has its own degree of difficulty. You gotta free up your swing and take it easy. If you try to murder the thing, you're just going to hit concrete. That's what makes alcohol so very important."

Fashion and chemical abuse aside, the interesting thing about World Urban Golf Day was that it was *World* Urban Golf Day. In addition to the Portland mob, urban golfers played in about thirty cities around the world that day. In Newcastle, Australia, festivities began with tea at nine thirty a.m., followed by nine holes, beer and barbecue, nine holes, beer and awards, and beer. In Portugal, players whacked through the medieval center of Caldas da Rainha, one of the country's premier cultural sites. The Parisian contingent golfed in the shadow of the Eiffel Tower. Depending on how you looked at it, this day of applied physics and wayward projectiles could be considered sport, a public menace, or a combination thereof. It was certainly an impressive example of Internet-enabled coordination. The whole thing came together in a matter of weeks—Scott Mazariegos, a Portland artist who started organizing regular urban golf excursions a couple years ago, got a MySpace message from Portugal. A few Xeroxed and stenciled flyers and many, many e-mails later, a true global event took shape.

In the days before the event, I learned that several impulses turned people into urban golfers. Ian Johnson, one of the organizers in Australia, cited exorbitant greens fees and a lack of accessible inner-city golf courses. ("I have no doubt some are in it for the lack of respect for authority," he added.) The Portuguese group seemed to consist of hyperenthusiastic artists and students with energy to burn. Mazariegos mixed high concept and low. "I started doing these things because I thought it would be cool to design a whole event around bars," he said. "I wanted to get people out into neighborhoods they didn't usually go to. We did the first one, and had twenty-five people hitting balls into traffic—beautiful. We invaded these bars that usually just have a couple people sitting in them. We've done a few of them since, and it just seems like it strikes a chord with people. We get people who've never played organized sports and people who are hard-core golfers. Men. Women. Lawyers. Mechanics. We had a guy who just saw us when he was driving to a wedding, stopped the car, got out, and played a couple holes in his tux. For the players, it's fun and it exposes them to different parts of the city. For everyone else, I like to think it shakes them up a little, but in a good way."

This was exactly what I was looking for: a bunch of people, armed only with the Internet, their imaginations, some cast-off golf gear, and an objectionable fashion sense, staging what could be seen, if one squinted just hard enough, as a large-scale global sporting event. Especially after the world's conventional economy smashed head-on into what E. F. Schumacher, in his great 1970s book *Small Is Beautiful*, delicately called "absurdities," World Urban Golf Day provided a bracing counterexample of international trade—a trade in wild ideas and cocktail recipes rather than complex financial derivatives or cheap shoes. Schumacher's book, with all its talk of "Buddhist economics," would seem like a relic of stoned hot-tub philosophy, except that he foresaw just about all of our current dilemmas, from global warming to the credit crunch. He believed small, decentralized institutions serve human aesthetic, social, and spiritual needs better than big, centralized ones. I don't believe he actually had drunken street golf in mind, but as I watched tennis balls carom down the street, I thought Schumacher would approve.

Now I had to play golf, which promised humiliation even under these circumstances. I borrowed a shot of Maker's Mark and a baby-blue-headed driver from a fellow player, and proceeded to shank a shot off a parked Jeep. In the next three strokes, I made it about a block and a half to a tough lie in a depression between a lip of asphalt and an old rail. I managed to dig out a daisy-cutter shot straight through a gaggle of pre-pubescent skateboarders. Greg, who stood next to me offering some advice and trying to force me to accept a martini, looked unimpressed.

"Failure to hit the kids," he said. "One stroke penalty."

EIGHT

THE PEOPLE'S REPUBLIC
OF ROLLER DERBY

E ven as I appreciated the charms of improvised events like the Portland Challenge and World Urban Golf Day, I was aware of a looming shadow on the horizon: a goliath of DIY sport; a living example of the heights a shambles like my little croquet league could achieve, given an infusion of organization, violence, and arguable sexploitation.

Roller derby. I knew I would have to come to grips with roller derby eventually.

Thus, on a Saturday morning at the end of September, I stood and faced the Stars and Stripes hanging above a cavernous hall in the Austin, Texas, Convention Center. Not far away, a woman with purple hair, cowboy boots, Daisy Duke cutoffs, and a shirt identifying her as "Hyper Lynx" joined me in placing hand to heart. A singer belted an emotional rendition of "The Star-Spangled Banner" through the crackling PA system, to hundreds of fans eager to see New York's Gotham Girls and the Kansas City Roller Warriors tear into each other on the white oval track at the center of the arena. The Gotham Girls featured a vortex of human flesh called Beyonslay, whose passage during pregame warm-ups all but caused a detectable geological tremor. The Kansas City Roller Warriors, a red-and-black-clad posse built around a lithe, pigtailed human torpedo, alias Snot Rocket, enjoyed a sizable and vocal fan contingent, already pummeling tribal war beats on mismatched tom-toms and snares in one corner of the track. In a few minutes, the first true national championship of the Women's Flat Track Derby Association—possibly the first national sports league constructed on anarcho-syndicalist lines—would begin.

Until just a few years before, my awareness of roller derby was limited to distant memories of '70s TV. I remembered guys with shag haircuts mock-fighting, blowsy chicks struggling to stay upright while pulling each other's hair and yanking at snugly tailored polyester uniforms. To the extent that derby penetrated my consciousness at all, it was as an oddment from America's Olde Curiosity Shoppe: the crossroads of carnie culture and very low-end sport, a realm where fly-by-night leagues coexisted with flea markets and players sold a little plasma on the side.

As it turns out, roller derby boasts a history that, if "rich" doesn't sound quite right, is at least interesting. Some say the game owes its origins to none other than Damon Runyon, the legendary sports journalist who created the fedoras 'n' highballs world of *Guys and Dolls*. Endurance roller-skating contests were a popular live diversion in the '30s (no television, remember). Runyon supposedly suggested that a little simple assault might spice things up. The resulting golem rampaged around sports' disreputable outskirts for several decades, the wheeled equivalent of pro wrestling, complete with manufactured feuds and suspect competitive outcomes. Despite the fixed matches and carnival antics, "classic" derby did possess its own charm. Fans still note with pride that the sport practiced racial and gender integration from the beginning. Even though vintage teams were usually co-ed, women were often the biggest stars. *Kansas City Bomber*, a 1972 Raquel Welch vehicle, reflected women's prominence in the sport with its bumptious track action and girl fights. And then, along about the Reagan era, derby more or less disappeared, sliding into the same cultural void that swallowed Yiddish theater and maypole dancing.

Yet here I was, decades later, surrounded by hundreds of roller derby fans, scores of roller derby players, in a trackside Press Row crowded with derby bloggers and derby photographers, in a city the announcers kept calling "the Republic of Derby." The Gotham Girls and Roller Warriors lined up for a game that wasn't fixed at all. In fact, they would fight it out with the savagery of Neapolitan alley brawlers. Six other teams from all around the country had gathered with them in Austin to cram a full three-round elimination bracket into two grueling days. Around the track, talk revolved around simmering rivalries—the hometown Texecutioners, the sport's reigning dynasty, didn't much care for Seattle's team, the Rat City Rollergirls, for instance—and which stars would stage breakout performances.

How did this happen? How did a forgotten bit of kitsch resurrect itself as a real sport, fishnet stockings notwithstanding? Early in the '00s, guided by the traditional process that transforms one decade's cultural embarrassment into another decade's retro cool, a few Austin women revived derby. They updated the sport, stylewise, into a punk-rock costume party. They chose team names like the Hell Marys (who dressed like Catholic schoolgirls gone wrong) and Honky Tonk Heartbreakers (bad-ass country chix). Nighttime matches, irrigated with cheap beer and featuring local bands at halftime, drew raucous crowds from Austin's sizable bohemian set. Most important, the revivalists wanted wheeled mayhem as real as they could make it. In other words, no more fake results or staged fights.

No professional trendspotter would have guessed, circa 2002, at the existence of a significant untapped roller derby market. And yet in city after city, women heard about Austin's new, alterna-inflected roller derby thing and, for whatever reason, decided it was exactly what they were looking for. A league formed in Tucson in 2003. The same year, the founders of New York's league rented an old disco-themed skating rink in the Bronx for their debut. "We thought we'd get maybe two hundred people—friends, boyfriends, friends of friends," remembered Natily "Ginger Snap" Blair, the Gotham Girls' captain for the Austin tournament. "We had five hundred or six hundred people lined up down the block, and by the end of the night, we probably had thirty-five new players wanting to sign up."

This happened all across the country. People—a certain crowd, really, what one might call the Semi-Ironic Mustache Nation—loved watching roller derby. Women, particularly the sort who spent more time in high school smoking cloves and listening to the Germs than taking full advantage of Title IX, loved playing roller derby. And the media positively adored roller derby. Derby's arrival in a given city usually inspired a rash of daily-newspaper features, alternative-weekly cover stories, and slobbery TV news spots. *Hot chicks on skates! Hitting each other! With tattoos!* Perhaps predictably, derby soon came to suffer from oversaturation. A friend of mine, a former editor at a major men's magazine, told me that by 2006, roller derby had displaced Burning Man as the subject of choice for hackneyed story pitches from freelance writers. In 2009, Hollywood got in the game a bit late and confirmed Austin's status as derby's mothership, setting Drew Barrymore's rambunctious derby movie, *Whip It*, in a fictionalized version of the city.

Still, derby thrived. City leagues multiplied, traveling all-star teams crisscrossed the country, and some players (and fans—derby now had fans) started to take roller derby seriously. Very. Teams learned how to skate, mastered tactics, and recruited players with real athletic backgrounds. The WFTDA ("woof-da") confederated the start-up leagues, standardized rules, sanctioned tournaments, and would now crown a national champion. To derby's longtime players and fans, this eight-team tournament, the Texas Shootout, represented a defining moment. "It's a big deal for us—a milestone," Jenny "Apocalipzz" Oleander, a veteran Austin player who worked the Shootout in the nonskating capacity of all-purpose problem-solver, told me. "It's the first time we've had a real chance to determine a champion, with regional qualifiers to cull it down to the absolute best teams. This will be a far more professional event than anything before." The tournament would thus provide an ideal opportunity to see what happens when a DIY sport tries to go national. Could WFTDA transcend its grassroots origins without losing its soul? And what was the crossover potential of a game played and followed mostly by women with a general preference for nonstandard body piercings?

Our national anthem ended. The crowd turned toward the track. New York and Kansas City took their final warm-up laps. His Honor the Mayor of Austin, wearing khakis and a kindly but nervous look, stepped to the center of the track to blow the ceremonial "first whistle." The male announcer perched on a raised podium set the stage: "Five years ago, here in Austin, Texas, the Texas Rollergirls began a revolution in roller derby! Today, five long years of blood, sweat, and tears culminate in the Women's Flat Track Derby Association National Championships—eight teams vying to go down as immortals in flat-track derby lore. Ladies and gentlemen, both bars are open!" A woman who sat in the next chair over and sported a huge pair of motorcycle boots began to scream obscenities. It was eleven o'clock in the morning, and the moment filled me with hope about the future of the American experiment.

I sat in the second row, separated from the chaotic first minutes of the Kansas City–New York quarterfinal by the length of a hurtling skater. If I understood correctly, this promised to be a mismatch: Gotham had won the WFTDA Eastern Region and was thus a top seed in the Shootout, while K.C. held the bottom seed out of the West. Yet Kansas City came out skating with far more aggression and speed, and built a quick 16–5 lead. Whatever that meant. I had no idea what was going on, besides a feast of impressive violence.

At first glance, roller derby looks a little like the Tour de France would if the *peloton* divided into two warring factions bent on mutual destruction. Each team tries to propel one of its skaters, the designated "jammer," through the pack formed by the other skaters, who all move at high speed and perpetrate brute force upon one another. Over the course of two days in Austin, I would learn a few of the nuances. At first I just enjoyed such golden moments as when a Kansas City player named Ami-Geddon hit the deck, slid across the floor, and smashed her helmeted head into the knee of a man sitting in the front row. As far as following the developments in the sixty-minute match, I relied on external clues.

The woman next to me, evidently a New York fan, soon descended into hoarse fury.

"Come *on*—stay in front of her! Jesus! No fucking defense in the back of the pack! What the *fuck* are they doing? *Move your ass! Move your ass!*"

Meanwhile, the Kansas City fans edged closer to the track's outside boundary line, hammering their drums. On the opposite side of the track, a visible pall fell over the little knot of Gotham fans. I took it things were not going according to plan for the black-clad New Yorkers, many of whom wore the name of their home borough stitched in ornate lettering across the backside of their shorts. Gotham couldn't contain Snot Rocket, Kansas City's star; she knifed through the pack again and again, despite Beyonslay's best efforts to disable her and one particular hit, delivered by a Gothamite named Surly Temple, that would have guaranteed me a weekend of Percocet and Alfred Hitchcock movies. The Gotham Girls, keyed by a tough, wiry little skater called Bonnie Thunders, mounted a desperate scramble in the final minutes. At the buzzer, though, Kansas City fans and players rushed the track as though the high school state hoops finals had just ended, their collective ticket punched for the semifinals.

Okay, then.

I barely understood what had just happened. I could see, though, that derby did have *something*—a visceral appeal based on the visual and skeletal magic that happens when two bodies mounted on wheels collide. Did the fact that those bodies came clad in skin-hugging uniforms help? I won't say it hurt. In any case, after game one, the Texas Shootout made a compelling— if not quite yet intelligible—case for a sport once consigned to history's Lost Objects closet. And I obviously had a lot to learn.

All sports invented in the modern era have some agenda. Basketball, for example, was created to give young Christian men a wholesome outlet for the wintertime doldrums. Roller derby came back to life for diametrically opposed reasons: a love of sex, drugs, rock and roll, and a latent desire to see young women in crypto-fetish wear hurt each other. When the first derby revivalists started skating in Austin, athleticism didn't really figure into the plan. "Early on, it was very campy," Apocalipzz told me. "There were pillow fights. There was 'Spank Alley' instead of a penalty box. That sort of deal."

The derby revival had everything to do with attitude and almost nothing to do with sports as we know them. The sexy uniforms and bawdy nicknames put down a generational marker. Not to delve into the complexities of third-wave feminism, but let's just say it is difficult to imagine Gloria Steinem's cohort embracing derby's self-promotional lustiness. The roller derby after-party soon attained legendary status among those in the know. (During the Shootout, a male photographer from

Kansas City asked me, awe in his voice, "Dude, have you ever *been* to a derby party?") Derby wasn't just different from mainstream sports. It was tailored for people who probably started to hate mainstream sports in eighth grade.

The scene in Austin proved that if nothing else, this unlikely concoction touched some nerve. Without garnering much in the way of mainstream media attention,* the tournament had become a sizable affair. The Austin Convention Center, plunked amid small historic buildings a few blocks off the main downtown artery like an invading alien mothership, resembles every other convention center in America: a shiny monolith from the Stalinist Rotary Club school of architecture. The weekend of the Texas Shootout, the center also hosted the National Association for College Admission Counseling's annual convention, a gathering of over five thousand very clean-cut people who scattered copies of *The Chronicle of Higher Education* all over the place. Around a corner and down a wide corridor, the roller derby nation milled outside Exhibition Hall 5 like a hostile tribe from the dodgy side of the Rhine—or maybe just the kind of high school kids who cause those guidance counselors nights of existential despair. Either way, the spectacle testified to Americans' capacity to draft banal places into the service of odd activities.

Merchandise tables flogged everything from Windy City Rollers onesies for ages six to nine months to copies of *Blood & Thunder* magazine, the derby world's glossy of record. (The

---

*By virtue of filing a one-hundred-word preview distributed only in an e-mail bulletin, I was accredited as a reporter for the *New York Times*. See, kids—work hard, take your vitamins, and you, too, can make it big.

cover shot for Issue #2 showed a Windy City player named Broken Cherry submerged in a bathtub full of actual cherries, displaying a generous stretch of leg, plus skates.) A company called Via hawked T-shirts with cartoon cupped hands on the chest and the slogan "Support Your Local Roller Girl." Skaters pawed over a bewildering variety of skates, wheels designed for different surfaces, pads, braces, and helmets, plus less utilitarian gear. On the tournament's first morning, I ran into Molly Wretzky, an attorney and Windy City Rollers skater (a.k.a. Ying o' Fire), whom I'd interviewed by phone a couple weeks earlier. She had just purchased a pair of black sequined bloomers, a new addition to the uniform she wears for hometown bouts in Chicago. (Too frivolous for Nationals, she said.) Fans could pick up giant foam axes emblazoned with the logo of Austin's own Texecutioners, or the Kansas City Roller Warriors' red and black scarves.

A quick T-shirt census among the crowd revealed a true continental congress: Big Easy, Houston, Minnesota, Boston Derby Dames, Green Country (Tulsa), No Coast (Nebraska), Sin City (Vegas, naturally), Alamo City (whose motto, "Puro Pinche Derby," I interpreted via my minuscule knowledge of Latino slang as "Totally Fucking Derby"). The derby demographic seemed to encompass a broad cross section of hipster America, appealing to women in both recognized alterna-cities like Austin and Seattle and more blue-collar places, where perhaps the game's rough-and-tumble nature outweighed camp as an attraction. I met two earnest and energetic women from the new league in northwestern Arkansas, who reminded me of what I already knew as a native Montanan: people in so-called flyover country bring a special zeal to organizing their own fun.

Both Seattle and Tucson traveled with full squadrons of "derby brats," tiny girls who never, ever removed their skates. The hyperenergized children swarmed through an adult herd rendered slow and bleary by the two bars selling Lone Star ("the National Beer of Texas: Drinking Anything Else Is Treason") and cocktails. The humid smokers' patio experienced a rush of black-clad, generously inked fans at every break in the action. The Shootout's security detail operated under the command of a woman whose T-shirt identified her as "Val Capone." Val looked like the wrong person with whom to bandy hostile words.

The only immediate indication that this was not, in fact, a family-friendly garage-rock festival came from the relentless clack of skate wheels on the track's plastic Sport Court surface. A tight schedule dictated that as soon as celebrating fans and weeping eliminated players cleared the floor after one match, two fresh teams began warm-ups. After Kansas City bumped off the Gotham Girls, Raleigh's Carolina Rollergirls stepped out against the Saddletramps, western-wear-decked pride of Tucson Roller Derby, WFTDA's second-oldest outpost.

The smattering of prematch gossip I picked up tipped Tucson as the favorite. Carolina, however, fielded a feisty, apple-cheeked projectile named Princess America, who paced her Rollergirls to a narrow win. After two matches won by lower-seeded teams, it seemed the form book was out the window—a sliver of hope for the Windy City Rollers. The Chicagoans, holding the modest #3 berth from the Eastern qualifiers, faced the most feared team of them all: the hometown Texecutioners, godmothers of the derby revival and the sport's would-be dynasty.

*   *   *

After a stirring performance by Satan's Cheerleaders—six women in black robes, faces obscured by giant druidic hoods, carrying plastic pitchforks—the Texecutioners rolled onto the track. At the front of the pack, a player carried a huge white flag bearing a black star, the profile of a cannon, and the words *Come and Take It*. Never say roller derby never taught you anything. In 1835, the citizens of Gonzales, Texas, unfurled this banner when a Mexican regiment demanded they surrender their single artillery piece, on loan from the Mexican government. The resulting one-sided skirmish failed to add a chapter to the annals of Mexican military glory, but did help kick off the Texan War of Independence and the state's affinity for prickly slogans.

The team ripped around the track en masse—a full roller derby roster, about twenty women strong, skating in formation, makes an intimidating spectacle. Texas fans along the boundary thrust their red foam axes aloft. As the music died, the crowd began to chant.

Texas! Texas! Kill! Kill! Kill! Texas! Texas! Kill! Kill! Kill! Texas! Texas! Kill! Kill! Kill!

Did the Texecutioners enjoy a home-track edge?

Texas! Texas! Kill! Kill! Kill!

Perhaps.

The Texecutioners' speed specialists, like team captain Bloody Mary and a deceptively petite Asian American skater who called herself Rice Rocket, looked like human bullets, optimized for speed and impact. As for sheer size and brawn, what rival would fancy an encounter with Sparkle Plenty, a mere five feet eleven? Or with Dinah Mite, a literally iconic veteran skater—her profile graces the WFTDA's pink and brown,

NBA-esque logo—outfitted with the shoulders and forearms of a dockyard union enforcer? Moreover, this was derby's flagship team. All forty-six city leagues in the WFTDA owed their existence, one way or another, to the Austinites. In some cases, the ties amounted to sporting kinship. Kansas City, I was told, was Austin's "little sister" league, its players trained through repeated maulings by the Texecutioners. The Texecutioners almost never lost. In the all-comers-welcome Tucson tournament that served as an ad hoc national championship in 2006, they pounded everyone without mercy, beating Carolina by a triple-digit spread and crushing the Saddletramps in the final. Any rare Texecutioners defeat—and in the '07 qualifiers, Seattle edged them for the top Western seed—sent a thrill through the roller derby world.

"Everyone's gunning for us," Apocalipzz said a week before the tournament. "Parity is coming along fast. The fact that people have learned we're not totally invincible, that's been a revelation. But of course, we're saying hell no—the trophy stays here. So this should be a very interesting weekend."

I walked down the sideline to the Chicago bench. The Windy City Rollers huddled up for a prematch pep talk, feigning unconcern. One of the bench coaches, Kentucky Dervish, wore a long wig in the same icy blue as the stripes on Chicago's city flag. The Rollers' mascot, a beanpole figure in a skull mask, gamboled around waving a plastic sword, and the Windy City fans gathered at the track's third turn tried to shout down the hometown mob. Still, it wasn't hard to spot the underdog here.

If Austin was derby's heartland, Chicago provided an apt snapshot of the sport's revival. The local league started in 2004, with a few thrown-together teams skating on a substandard-sized track and an emphasis on vaudeville shenanigans. (A WFTDA city league consists of a handful of theme-driven "home teams"; Chicago's league, for example, includes the Hell's Belles, the Double Crossers, the Fury, and the Manic Attackers. For intercity games and tournaments like the Texas Shootout, all-star squads pick the best players from all home teams, like World Cup soccer rosters.) They packed the house, had fun, sent a team to the Tucson tournament, and got blown off the track.

"We started in a beautiful old theater right in the city," Ying o' Fire said. "It was very campy. After we saw the level of national play, all of a sudden it got a lot more serious. Now we're in a sports venue out in the suburbs. Practice used to be like the bad girls in gym class—whenever the coach wasn't looking, you were screwing around. The first season we were all a lot more punk rock, but it's evolving to the point where we can attract different kinds of women—like, we have a Republican now. We're getting stronger athletically as a result."

Serious competitive derby entails serious injuries, including a pileup just a month before the Austin tournament that left a Chicago player called Tequila Mockingbird partially paralyzed. But the team's transformation meant that Windy City arrived in Texas with a recent streak of wins over top-ranked Eastern Region teams. If attitude meant anything, the Chicago girls, their faces done up in scary eye-black, might have a shot. A skater called Malice With Chains, a former goalkeeper for Santa Clara University's top-notch soccer team, wore cropped punkette hair and a glacial, thousand-yard game face. She looked like an assassin for hire.

* * *

As the match got under way, I again ran into roller derby's most significant entry barrier for the new fan. Until you've seen a few matches, it makes no sense at all.

The Shootout was not my first derby experience. About a year before the Austin event, I checked out a match between local Portland teams. The action resembled a disturbingly refined Japanese porn subgenre more than a comprehensible athletic contest. Skaters jostled around the track in short bursts of action, sometimes just thirty seconds long. A huge corps of zebra-shirted referees tracked their progress. (With about a half dozen officials skating at any one time, plus timekeepers and statisticians, roller derby may be the most intensely adjudicated sport in the world.) Whistles blew, followed by cryptic hand signals. Skaters left the track for the penalty box, bitching and protesting. Did *they* know what was going on? At breaks in the action, a scoreline somehow emerged from the fray. "Alright! Heartless Heathers twelve, Guns 'n' Rollers seven!" Sure. A few semiaudible explanations over the PA failed to sort things out. Still—the beer was cold, skaters sustained visible abrasions, and one player called herself "Vominatrix." I considered my sporting dollar well spent.

During the Texas–Chicago bout I made a concerted effort to decipher the action. Derby's basic idea is simple enough. Two teams—five skaters each on the track at any one time—contest a long series of mini races called "jams" over the course of the sixty-minute match. Most skaters on the track are part of the "pack," a phalanx of bodies to which each team contributes a "pivot" (charged with regulating the pack's speed, designated by a special cloth cover on her helmet) and three "blockers." Blockers are often, though not always, the game's most imposing physical specimens.

Each team fields a single "jammer," the attacking player who scores points. At the start of a jam, pack skaters line up at one starting line, while the two jammers square up at another line about ten yards behind the pack. At the starter's whistle, the pack takes off. Another whistle, two seconds later, turns the jammers loose. Both jammers try to navigate the pack and establish a lead. Blockers and pivots collude to impede the rival jammer and help their own. Usually this involves contact. The laws of the game do, however, distinguish good violence—clean full-body checks or stubborn rolling blocks leveraging the gluteal regions—from bad violence. Skaters who throw elbows, trip, hold, punch, push, or otherwise transgress go to the penalty box. In theory.

Once one jammer takes the lead (becoming, yes, "lead jammer"), she controls the action for the rest of the two-minute jam. Both jammers then start scoring points by lapping members of the other team. Each in-bounds pass earns one point; the ultimate achievement is a "grand slam," the five points a jammer earns by blowing past every opposing skater. At least a few points are scored on almost every jam, and final tallies usually fall somewhere in college basketball range. The lead jammer may terminate the action at any time by making a hand signal that looks like repeated karate chops to her own kidneys. When and under what circumstances one should "call off the jam" is one of derby's key tactical questions.

Teams rotate their five-skater lineups from jam to jam, like hockey teams switching lines. Any player can skate any position, but most teams rely on two or three primary jammers, the star quarterbacks of derby world. For jammers, timing and spatial sense are as crucial as speed—picking the wrong line through the pack can be as fatal as it would be on a bobsled run. The best leave a trail of flailing blockers in their wake. Meanwhile, the best blockers and pivots keep enemy jammers bottled up. Or writhing on the floor. Whatever works.

That much, I understood, sort of, after the day's first matches. It took seeing what the Texecutioners did to the Windy City Rollers, however, to appreciate derby's potential wrinkles. After just a few jams, it was obvious that the host team would now unleash several different flavors of practiced whup-ass on their rivals. The Texecutioners' experience showed in the psychic-link seamlessness of their pack. Depending on which players they deployed, they could emphasize speed to force Chicago into a mass sprinting duel, or slow the jam down to a grind. They could flatten Windy City's jammers, preventing them from scoring points. They muscled open huge holes in Chicago's pack for fleet scoring threats like Bloody Mary and Rice Rocket to exploit. I would learn that in general, bigger derby teams try to pummel opponents into submission, Shaquille O'Neal–style; smaller teams favor quick light-cavalry moves to overwhelm static opponents. The Texecutioners could play it both ways.

Windy City fought like starved cats—Malice With Chains, true to her fierce mien, took on the Texecutioners' pack again and again. It was for nought. The Austin juggernaut ground Chicago to dust as its adoring public bayed for gore: *Texas! Texas! Kill! Kill! Kill!* Final score: 108–56. It could have been worse.

* * *

The last quarterfinal match approached. By now, I'd wandered
the trackside scene for hours. Most of the Shootout's female fans
seemed like they were also derby players, retired or active. A
noticeable minority hobbled on crutches or wore full-leg casts
or walking braces. Off-duty referees, coaches, league volunteers,
and male "derby widowers" dominated the rest of the crowd. In
fact, even though I found my own enthusiasm for derby's possibilities as a spectator sport growing with every game, there didn't
seem to be too many *casual* fans at the Shootout. The atmosphere
reminded me of some living-room rock shows I'd attended, in
which a band would play, then just hand the instruments to the
five people watching, because they were the next band. While
I found this winning, it didn't make the sport feel like a hot
candidate for mainstream success. I was also now overfamiliar
with roller derby's pervasive smell: a rank sour-sweat, wet-fabric
stench, not unlike the infernal miasma of a hockey locker room.
I decided it was time to get off the floor.

I bought a Lone Star and retired to a spot high in the bleach-
ers to watch Seattle's Rat City Rollergirls, top seed out of the
West, take on Detroit. No one in Austin referred to Seattle as
"Seattle"; everyone called them "Rat City." I got the vibe that
the Northwesterners were not exactly the people's choice here-
abouts, maybe because they'd beaten the Texecutioners in the
qualifying tournament. Still, an impressive Rat City fan contingent crowded one straightaway, waving signs and cheering.
The team's mascot, Rat Man Houllahan, a greasy-haired spiv
dressed as a street pimp/rodent hybrid, paraded up and down
the sideline. The team itself emerged for warm-ups in a black
and forest green ensemble; players like Burnett Down, a towering, pale-skinned Valkyrie in pigtails, managed to make this

combination very intimidating. By comparison, Detroit looked like innocents in their white unis. It was as though the two cities had swapped civic personalities, Seattle exchanging its shiny twenty-first-century Pacific Rim soul for the Motor City's aggro. I sensed I was about to see something ugly.

The nosebleeds proved the perfect vantage for the clinical dissection Rat City performed on Detroit. Detroit tossed ragged scrums out on the track; Rat City blockers sheared them open with flexible, angular wedge formations. Rat City's clockwork attack broke the track wide open for its lethal jammers—notably Miss Fortune, whose liquid Olympic speed-skater stride made her the most elegant player I'd seen yet. Rat City rolled up an insurmountable lead within the first ten minutes, and the rest of the game assumed the indifferent air of an exhibition match. Beer lines swelled and the stands emptied. A distinct feeling of derby fatigue began to settle over the arena.

And then, just as I was about to wander toward the bar myself, Rat City pulled off the roller derby equivalent of the bicycle kick, the suicide squeeze, the one-eighty slam dunk.

Understand that a common derby maneuver, the Whip, involves a player reaching a hand back for a trailing teammate, as though expecting a relay baton. The players join hands, and the lead skater lashes the trailer forward, propelling her with centrifugal force. A further refinement adds a third player to the chain. (I overheard one player asking another, "Did you see the picture of our Triple Whip? We were all in bounds, too!") The Triple Whip rates a high degree of difficulty, but you see the basic Whip dozens of times in an average game.

A Rat City jammer wheeled out of a turn. A lone blocker in green strayed back out of the pack, lifted her right leg, and jabbed it out into midair, turning herself into a cockeyed capital *T*. The jammer grabbed the outstretched skate, then held on as the blocker executed a hip-high roundhouse kick, rocketing the jammer down the track. In my notebook, I scrawled, *"HOLY SHIT! LEG WHIP!!!"* The crowd reacted like recipients of a low-voltage electric shock, and Detroit's bench players looked like they had just studied one of GM's recent financial statements. Rat City's performance seemed, in part, a declaration of intent. Subverting the dominant sports paradigm? Furthering the derby sisterhood? All well and good. They, however, were in town to kick some ass.

The derby revival began with a schism. The first Austin bouts took place on a banked track, a piece of equipment that sells for fifty thousand dollars used. Nonplayers owned and ran the promotion, and they emphasized its gimmicky appeal. Austin may be in Texas, but it's a pinko town and proud of it. Not long after women started flocking to derby, this arrangement began to strike many as . . . disempowering. "Skaters just weren't happy not knowing where the money was going," Apocalipzz said. "We had no control over how bouts were organized or promoted, or how we as skaters were presented. It became an untenable situation pretty quickly."

A faction of Austin skaters split off to form their own league, Texas Rollergirls. They would skate on a flat track, meaning the game could now be played almost anywhere—in fact, the new teams started practicing on the roof of a parking garage. More importantly, the Rollergirls would be a nonprofit, owned collectively by players and governed through committees elected by the whole league. Existing members would vote in prospective new skaters. Besides skating, everyone would pull some kind of organizational volunteer duty. When the flat-track game began to spread, to Tucson and beyond, new leagues adopted the Austin model. By 2004, derby cities established full diplomatic relations in the form of a Yahoo! Group.

Not to speak ill of the dead, but most American sports leagues were founded by cartels of tightwad promoters. As much as providing a sensible competitive framework, leagues work to freeze out rivals, protect territorial monopolies, impose owner-friendly contractual rules, and make sure players don't get their meathooks into the cash flow any more than necessary. When the National Football League was founded at a car dealership in Canton, Ohio, owners cared more about preventing players from jumping from team to team in search of more lucrative contracts than whether every franchise played a complete schedule. When forty or so roller girls from across the country met in the basement of a Chicago hotel in 2004, they, like any would-be moguls, wanted to standardize rules, figure out national competition, and come up with a sweet name for their alliance. (The first attempt, "United Leagues Committee," obviously wouldn't cut it.) However, the gathering broke from sports history in one crucial respect. The formative association proclaimed that player control would be its highest priority. New leagues would have to prove that "the skaters' voice" guided their every move. Meanwhile, a national vote would elect WFTDA's board and thus determine the direction of the whole embryonic sport.

"It's pretty rare for a sport to maintain its independence," a Chicago player called Kami Sutra said, after Ying o' Fire introduced us. "Just about every sport ends up being owned by someone. But any hint of that in derby, people just freak out. I think we're especially sensitive, because back in the old days, roller derby was completely controlled by sleazy promoters. There's been a very conscious effort to avoid that."

Of course, at the time of the Chicago convention, WFTDA was a ramshackle assemblage of amateur outfits trading on sex appeal, vague neo-post-feminism, and the magnetic power of beer. That's still mostly true. It's worth noting, though, that roller derby aspires to be something radical, even unheard of: a national sport controlled by current and former players. And though men often act as referees and coaches, women hold just about every position of power within the WFTDA. "We work as one huge team to try to make our league solid, and WFTDA does the same nationally," Ginger Snap, captain of the Gotham Girls, told me. "Every skater serves on a committee, and we have thirteen members on our board. It's messy and hard to deal with sometimes, but it's a model no other sport can match. We're not a democracy, but we are a republic."

Not every player consciously regards roller derby as a political vehicle, but WFTDA's collectivist ideals influence the sport on issues not likely to cross the desk of, say, NBA commissioner David Stern. Derby leagues prefer to outfit themselves in the "sweatshop-free" products of hipster garment manufacturer American Apparel. The WFTDA is almost certainly the only sports organization in world history to persuade equipment suppliers to manufacture "vegan-friendly" gear, in the form of leather-free roller skates. Meanwhile, the ground-up, collaborative structure has implications on the track. Even though the WFTDA rulebook now runs to twenty-one byzantine pages, referees in different cities interpret crucial fine points differently.

Players and coaches argue nonstop, both face-to-face and in dozens of online forums, about how derby really works. The game itself remains under construction.

"People talk about how we're DIY," Sparkle Plenty said. "A big reason we're DIY is that roller derby was never 100 percent codified, even back in its heyday. I'm a total jock, so when I got involved, I immediately looked for the rulebooks. There weren't any. Old-schoolers would dig up the rules from the '50s or '60s, but they'd be so sketchy and vague they were basically worthless. So we have to figure this thing out collectively. We have nothing to step into."

For some reason, I don't sleep well in Austin—and while I have never been to Paris, Rome, Bangkok, Tokyo, Rio, Edinburgh, or many other great cities, for some reason I end up in Austin again and again, staring at the ceiling at four a.m. Maybe Texas makes me a little nervous, afraid I'll accidentally kill someone and end up railroaded to the death chamber without benefit of competent counsel.

In any case, the second morning of the Texas Shootout found me suckling at a tankard from some indie coffeehouse, blinking against the glare off the white-blue plastic Sport Court floor. A glance revealed much of the crowd in similar or worse condition, likely due to nocturnal misadventure—except for everyone with a rooting interest in the upcoming semifinal between Rat City and the Texecutioners. Those people looked jumpy, brittle with anticipation. The consensus seemed to be that only an unfortunate accident of the bracket prevented the tournament's two true heavyweights—teams already bound, as they say, by a "history"—from meeting in the final that night. Even with an exhausting day of skating ahead, the Austin–Seattle collision looked like it might settle the Shootout championship, de facto, by midafternoon.

Apocalipzz, whose official tournament job did not preclude rabid pro-Texecutioners partisanship, wandered the small press area, a no-frills corner in the arena's nether regions mostly occupied by team photographers and bloggers. Seemed like perhaps she'd consumed some caffeine herself. "That's the one, that's the *big* one," she said. "I got goose bumps, seriously."

Throughout the Shootout, many people told me that roller derby was in the middle of an evolutionary shift. As athletes migrated into the game from other sports—players like Windy City's Malice With Chains, the ex–Division I soccer goalie, and Gotham's Beyonslay, once a competitive figure skater despite not exactly conforming to Michelle Kwan–like physical specs—many first-generation skaters found themselves eased out. "We've lost quite a few girls over the last year or so," Bonnie Thunders of Gotham told me. "There are a lot of people who would rather just have a beer league. We're seeing a lot of the older players disappear."

Texecutioners v. Rat City, then, could be a watershed moment in this transformation: the sport's most athletic, sophisticated teams going at it with the national title essentially on the line. First, of course, there was the matter of the Kansas City Roller Warriors and Carolina, the latter representing the last gasp of the obliterated Eastern Region. I didn't hold out much hope for either against whichever behemoth survived the other semi. In their opening wins, both K.C. and Carolina looked feisty, scrappy, built on heart—a spit-and-baling-wire version of the game destined to disintegrate on contact with more advanced variants.

Still, this bout served as a bracing wake-up call. Carolina clawed out an early lead, dominating the opening ten minutes. Then Snot Rocket, Kansas City's star, racked up seven uncontested points on a jam in which Princess America, Carolina's spunky little talisman, went to the penalty box for a full minute. The Roller Warriors' other go-to jammers, Fearlys and Xcelerator, also began smashing the Carolina pack. Kansas City leveled the score at thirty-five by the middle of the first half. KC's drum-banging fans at the track's final turn started to overwhelm the little group huddled under the "Carolina Raise Up!" sign.

Then, in the thirteenth jam, Snot Rocket sliced up Carolina for three grand slams (five points apiece, remember) in less than two minutes, a one-woman tour de force that put the room of seasoned derby-watchers into hysterics. Xcelerator ended the half with a daring move past four Carolina skaters, sticking a four-point cherry atop Kansas City's 70–50 halftime lead. Carolina stumbled off the floor, dead team skating. They fought back, came within eight on the final jam, but couldn't dodge the inevitable. At the end of the match, Princess America slumped alone on the Carolina bench, a lost expression on her face.

After watching Rat City crush Detroit, I thought I had the Seattle team figured out. I pegged the girls in forest green as derby's cool rationalists—built on speed, precision, and advanced strategy: scientific roller derby, if you will. The Texecutioners, awesome in size and snarling attitude, might embody the game's inner Prussian dominatrix. Rat City played the game the stereotypical Pacific Northwest way, a bunch of cerebral nerdettes on wheels. Or so I thought. Maybe I was just too much of a derby naïf. In any case, I failed to detect an essential facet of the team's game: these girls were flat-out mean. They just needed a worthy opponent to bring out their dark side.

At the highest level, all games are played at the far edge of the law. Great players and teams probe any elasticity in the rules and search out opponents' weaknesses with as much ruthlessness as skill. Rat City and the Texecutioners did not disappoint. The first two jams set the tone: tight, violent, chaotic as a third-world election and about as friendly. The Texecutioners seemed determined to stamp the game with their physical style, and darted to a 21–7 lead. *Texas! Texas! Kill! Kill! Kill!* Rat City responded by incurring a series of penalties, which cost them early points as they skated at a numerical disadvantage, but also put the Texans on notice. Bodies ricocheted around the track. Burnett Down landed a pair of shattering body checks, dropping Texecutioners to the floor. The crowd sizzled—both sides already enraged at the referees, the Rat City mob by the penalties, the larger hometown contingent demanding more. Rat City's all-out assault brought them level at twenty-five on a scoring run by jammer Pia Mess. They executed their signature Leg Whip, touching off a frenzy in the crowd. Skaters careened off the track, creaming a cameraman. The Texecutioners rumbled back to an eleven-point lead. At one point, there were more skaters in the penalty box than on the track.

Even a derby novice like me recognized a gritty classic in the making.

I sat in a folding chair in the second row. I might have been on my feet, along with most of the crowd, except a Texas fan with chopped-off, bleach-blond hair had her hands on my shoulders, riveting me down as she leaned over me to scream at the refs, the players, everyone. After about twenty minutes, she twisted my shoulders to look me in the face. "Sorry, man," she bellowed, "but I'm just so fucking excited!" I told her not to worry about it. She wasn't about to stop anyway. By the end of the first half, with the Texecutioners up 48–37, this superfan had whittled her voice down to a rasp: "I love our sport," she wheezed to a friend standing next to her.

I turned to them to ask a bonehead, *Idiot's Guide to Roller Derby*–type question, i.e., wasn't Rat City absolutely killing itself with penalties?

"Dude, Rat City always skates on the edge of chaos," the fan said. "If they're gonna win, they're gonna win ugly. I love our fucking sport, dude."

The second half began, Rat City chiseling at the Texecutioners' narrow lead: 51–45 . . . 51–46 . . . 55–53. Burnett Down faced off with Dinah Mite—two of the most terrifying skaters in the tournament matched up as jammers. Every Rat City skater on the track took a shot at Dinah Mite in a series of flying tackles, hip checks, and body blows. The referees could barely keep track of the compounding penalties. . . . 60–53 . . . 60–55.

Rat City relied more and more on Miss Fortune, whose classical, measured stride and easy aerodynamic tuck served her well in the worsening bedlam—she could melt through the gnarls of fallen bodies. Midway through the second half, a beautiful Triple Whip launched her through the pack to ten unanswered points. Rat City, 66; Texecutioners, 60. About twenty feet away from my seat, Apocalipzz—wearing camo cargo pants, a black anarchy-symbol armband, and hoop earrings straight out of a Tupperware party—stood over the Texas bench, bug-eyed, shrieking at the refs. *Something* was going down over there. Confused referees buzzed around the sideline, while Texecutioners captain Bloody Mary stood with hands on hips, an eyebrow cocked in disbelief. Through the crowd noise, I heard the announcer say that Texas's bench coach, a slick-haired character called Punk Rock Phil, had been ejected.

One could say the tenor of the thing had taken a turn.

Rat City's slicker skating abilities and scary groupthink maneuvers suddenly had the Texecutioners against the wall. As Rat Man Houllahan stirred up their fans, the Seattleites burst to a sixteen-point lead before the hometown side managed to steady itself and start a comeback. The lead shrank to five, then swelled to nine—real spite in every hit now, every jam just about turning into a scene from *Road House*. And then came the Incident in turn four.

Lady X, the Texecutioners' jammer, came into the track's final turn behind the main pack, riding Miss Fortune's shoulder as the latter tried to make an escape. Ann R. Kissed, Rat City's pivot, slid back along the inside boundary, tracking Lady X, forcing her outside, zeroing in for the kill. One photo of the resulting collision bears suspicious resemblance to a soccer slide-tackle or the way Ty Cobb used to treat rival second basemen. Ann R. Kissed scythed Lady X down from the side, skate wheels up. Subsequent Internet debate revolved around whether this shot reflected (a) a near-capital offense or (b) just good derby:

"[A] perfect example of the complete disregard for the rules that Rat

City has a reputation for playing by . . . I've seen dirty, and this tops them all."

"If there's one thing this illustrates, it's that a single photo can't accurately judge an action in derby . . . it was simply a clean block that went bad when Lady X shrugged off the blow."

"Clean block? You must be out of your mind!"

What is certain is that Ann R. Kissed skated out of turn four. Lady X—a competetive speed skater—did not. A referee whistled the jam dead, EMTs crowded around Lady X, and the Austin fans blew out critical neurons. "Nice trip," they howled. "Nice trip, nice trip." I thought security (a.k.a. Val Capone) might be forced to remove Apocalipzz from the building. I feared construction engineers would end up prying the Texas fan behind me out of the arena's ceiling. "What! The! Fuck!" she demanded. "What! The! Fuck! Was! That?" Punk Rock Phil, the already-ejected coach, stood on the podium behind the statisticians' table, both arms raised in a double middle-fingered salute. Ann R. Kissed spent some time in the penalty box, but in some sense, her work was done. Only three minutes, nineteen seconds remained on the clock, Rat City led by twelve, and the injury to Lady X sent the Texecutioners into a terminal morale spiral.

A few jams later, Rat City's Femme Fatale laid out the Texecutioners' jammer. She cruised past the Texas bench, blowing kisses. Texecutioners fans hurled their red foam axes onto the track as Rat City advanced to the championship round.

After two days in Austin, it was obvious to me that derby's camaraderie was as powerful a draw to the game as any opportunity to do damage to others at speed. It was almost too easy to encapsulate derby's social side—per Apocalipzz, "When you become a skater, you instantly have hundreds of new best friends." (Ohmigawd!) But I saw its reality in Austin: a vast sorority in studded leather, screaming for each other's blood one second, communing over beers the next. Derby's intentional self-parody—the over-the-top aliases, bombastic team names, and concept costumes—works like a flashing "Weirdos Welcome" sign.

"When I went to my first derby meeting, I just felt this fire," Sparkle Plenty said when I called her a couple weeks after her Texecutioners went down against Rat City. "I closed my eyes and instantly envisioned a woman check-blocking another woman, and I was like, I'm in. That was my vision—not a man, not that I was going to be playing the female version of a male sport, but that this was going to be all about women."

To me, two subtexts seemed to be at play at the Texas Shootout: amazement at just how far this inclusive movement had come, tempered by concern about what might happen next. Sparkle Plenty gave me the most optimistic view.

"You saw the derby brats from Seattle and Tucson," she said. "If the junior leagues keep growing, we'll have an option for girls that is a pure women's sport—played by women, run by women. And the fact that I can take a piece of chalk down to an asphalt basketball court and lay out a track means there really isn't a limit to how far it can go."

"Move! Bitch! Get out the way! Get out the way, bitch! Get out the way!"

The Kansas City Roller Warriors always slapped a raucous

Ludacris song on the PA as they skated around the track for squad introductions. The announcer always hollered, "Ladies and gentlemen, here they are, *the Masters of the Universe,* your Kansas City Roller Warriors!" Score two to the Warriors in the chutzpah department, but I still figured the Rat City machine would destroy them. My hypothesis seemed confirmed when Miss Fortune took four effortless points on the championship match's very first jam.

Still, the psychic energy of the room ran all Kansas City's way. Rat City's cold-blooded takedown of the Texecutioners established them as the night's villainesses. Someone had a T-shirt hot press in the Shootout's vendor zone, and a quickie edition of "Rat City: We Be Trippin'" became a coveted item during the slow third-place match. (The Texecutioners disposed of Carolina despite skating in a disconsolate trance and using a bunch of reserve players.) The little-sister alliance between Austin and K.C. made the Roller Warriors the obvious choice for Texecutioners fans, effectively a proxy for the hometown team. Now hundreds of neutrals, the derby-world pilgrims from Minnesota and Fayetteville and Boston and everywhere else, also gravitated to the underdog. The Gotham Girls invaded the small trackside media area, packing the boundary line to support the Roller Warriors.

Kansas City enjoyed one other notable asset: Snot Rocket. She didn't quite have Miss Fortune's style, and she wasn't all that big. On closer inspection, though, she possessed a rangy athleticism that made her just about indestructible—a good thing when you're pinballing through a sentient meat blizzard like the Rat City blocker pack. On the second jam, Snot Rocket posted a stinging response to Miss Fortune, scoring nine points despite two migraine-caliber body checks. The Roller Warriors clamped down hard. After about ten minutes, they led 24–19. Though both teams had now skated for over an hour that day, bodies slammed around without mercy. The grappling packs rounded turns so fast they could barely hang together—always, a skater spun out wide, unable to contain her own momentum. When the jammer rotations brought Snot Rocket and Miss Fortune to the line at the same time, fans ratcheted the noise up to last-charge-of-the-berzerkers levels.

Penalties everywhere—Rat City whacked Snot Rocket again and again, but the refs tossed Miss Fortune into the sin bin, and Kansas City won the jam 7–3. The Roller Warriors then produced a secret weapon, a player called Dominant Jean, who hadn't skated as jammer at all during the tournament. She bagged two quick points and called off the jam, a crafty tactical move to stifle any counterattack from Rat City's Pia Mess. With Kansas City up 35–22, Rat City's fans looked grim as their team sent Blonde 'n' Bitchin' to the jammer line.

She swept to a five-point grand slam, the first of three Rat City racked up in quick succession. Roller Warriors jammers found themselves snared, pinned down by a succession of brutal sandwich moves. Even Snot Rocket ended up staring at the rafters every time she ventured off the bench. The same dynamic that carried Rat City over the Texecutioners looked like it might emerge here, as a permanent Rat City delegation took up residence in the penalty box and their opponents' rage mounted. Fans from every other city in the house might be on the verge of apoplexy—their teams would never, *ever* play like this, of course—but Rat Man Houllahan strutted down the sideline like he'd just collected on a long-standing street debt.

The Roller Warriors, however, didn't let Rat City escape. After trailing by as much as nine, they cut the margin to three by halftime. The teams headed for the locker rooms, leaving the crowd giddy, transfixed by this unexpectedly spicy finale, but also by the whole ever-drunker spectacle. "We got Chaser, we got Emergen-C, we got Tums, we got Pepto," a guy behind me said. "We got everything a hungover derby rat might need."

The second half turned on a pair of knockout hits. On the fifth jam of the half, Snot Rocket tossed her signature speed and finesse in favor of raw aggression. In the back of a tangled pack, she targeted Skate Trooper, Rat City's jammer, for a cutthroat check, springing herself into the lead and six points. Control of the chaos—broken skates flying, flurried jams ending in multiple penalties, arguments, an ejection—slipped into Kansas City's hands. Moments later, Patti Wackin, one of Kansas City's scariest enforcers, turned her head to pick out Burnett Down trying to gallop around the pack on the backstretch. Patti Wackin glided backwards and delivered a meaty hip that threatened to snap her lanky rival in half. Burnett Down clattered to the floor just in front of the ecstatic New York girls. This body blow had more to do with the game's gestalt—the ineffable but very real sense of who owned whom—than the scoreboard, but soon Kansas City pushed its lead to twelve points, an 89–77 margin with seven minutes left.

They would not score again. Rat City picked off points at an agonizing rate in the final minutes. Kansas City clogged the track, assassinated jammers, burned clock—anything. Miss Fortune brought Rat City to within four points with an exhausting white-knuckle run. One minute to play. I expected Miss Fortune to go straight back to the jammer line. Maybe she just had nothing left. Rat City instead sent out a skater named Voltron to face Snot Rocket—K.C.'s fans, drums banging, chanted *Snot! Snot! Snot! Snot!*—in the jam that would decide the title.

Voltron broke out of the pack. She needed to lap four of five K.C. skaters to force overtime. Snot Rocket elected not to pursue, but rather hang back with the Kansas City blockers as they set up a wary, slow-rolling rear guard. Voltron battered against the pack—and again—but could never snap the picket of bodies. Time expired. The Roller Warriors came off the bench squealing like preteens, jumping in the air—as much as people on skates, with legs rendered near useless by 180 minutes of rolling combat in less than thirty-six hours, can jump.

A photo I took in the ensuing celebration shows Snot Rocket, her sinewy arm wrapped around teammate Princess Slay-Ya, eyes closed, sweat, tears, hair, and mascara melding with the arena lights and the heated crush of bodies to gilded, beatific effect. She reminds me of Y. A. Tittle, the old Giants quarterback, in the famous picture showing him crumpled in the end zone as his last bloody season winds down. Her face says just about everything about what lies beneath roller derby's postmodern knowingness and madcap antics. A minute later, the Roller Warriors swarmed around, screaming in unison: "Move, bitch! Get out the way! Get out the way, bitch! Get out the way!"

Was the Texas Shootout the moment derby began its escape, however modest, from the alterna-ghetto? Or would it remain in comfortable obscurity? Either, of course, seemed possible.

However, I left Austin—clearing airport security just ahead of a late-middle-aged man with tired eyes and a Kansas City Roller Warriors cap—thinking it likely I had just seen a game come just a little closer to the moment when amateur hour ends.

For all its semiutopian politics, WFTDA was not immune to the charms of the snake. Before the regional qualifiers leading to the Shootout, the association signed a deal with a cable operation called MavTV, which bills itself as "TV Created by Men, for Men." Mav offered WFTDA the appetizing chance to join such programs as *Real Guys . . . Real Golf* and *Bikini Allstars* on its roster. After watching eight of the best bouts in the short history of the derby renaissance, I knew the sport's hectic speed and confusing rules could well look like mush on the screen. But I also knew it could be done. If the MavTV camera crew knew what it was doing, derby could make terrific television.

And then what? Two weeks after the tournament, I called Juliana "Bloody Mary" Gonzalez, the crash-'em-up captain of the Texecutioners. Bloody Mary, I heard, knew derby stem to stern, from intricate lineup rotation strategies to the dicey realities of running a sport like it's the Paris Commune. I also observed that she finished the Shootout with a Crab Nebula–shaped welt on the back of her thigh the color of Chinese eggplant. I wanted to get her tournament postmortem and see how she was healing. Plus I wanted to try to get her to talk some trash about Rat City. I asked Bloody Mary if the Texecutioners had "learned" anything from the loss—bait, I admit, deliberate bait.

"Rat City . . . ," she said with audible care. "We learned from Rat City . . . I guess you could say we learned about . . . the value of tactical penalties. Penalties above the waist, which we would be more likely to commit, are very easy for referees to catch, and seem to have a really adverse affect on a team without giving it much advantage. Whereas it seems that a foul below the waist, like"—again with the diplomatic pause—"a trip, say, seems to be harder to catch, and can give you a big advantage." The value of tactical penalties—I liked the euphemism, which spoke to a game shedding its youthful naïveté to acquire the murky undertones of secret tradecraft and devious human ingenuity that elevate sport from mere playtime to soap opera. I asked Bloody Mary just how much smarter—I meant, basically, how much nastier and more fearsome—the Shootout would make its eight teams.

"Oh, this will have a huge ripple effect across the country," she said. "The girls on the city all-star teams are already engaged in the sport on a much different level than the players who only skate in the local leagues. That will be more and more the case. Tournaments like this will make every all-star player an expert on rules and strategy, and the gap will grow.

"There's also going to be a huge alignment of standards in the way the game is played across the country. Right now, there's some flexibility in the way leagues stage their local matches— they can do three twenty-minute periods instead of thirty-minute halves, for example. Those things will fall into line. Our national rankings, which just started in the last year, will start to be based on tournament results more than one-off games between teams. The business model will become more standardized—how travel-team matchups are arranged, what constitutes a fair stipend for the visiting team, officiating, all those things."

In the 1920s and '30s, basketball's early pro barnstorming teams never knew what rules they would play under in Scranton, or which thugs they'd have to fight to prevent the theft of the box-office cash in Syracuse. In the Darwinian process of team spectator sport, games rationalize or die. The wild early days are fun while they last, but they don't last. Teams keep up with the state of the art or they dissolve. Players who just don't have it find themselves involuntarily retired or shunted to the rec league. The eight derby teams that played the Shootout would scatter back home knowing what they needed to do—Kansas City if it wanted to keep its crown, everyone else if they wanted to take it. Carolina would look for faster jammers. Gotham would hone its track tactics. The Texecutioners, Rat City—well, the mind reeled at the new angles those crews would devise.

The game would get faster, harder, more complicated and violent. It wasn't hard to imagine that an outfit much more august than MavTV might someday come calling. Some bright entrepreneur could try to lure the best teams—or maybe just the best players—into some kind of national professional league. A TV network could kick in cash purses for tournaments. If any version of this happens, it will be sold, as it always is, as an inevitable and necessary elevation of derby's status. And once the first check is cut to a player, the fundamental chemistry shifts forever.

The game's not there yet, and maybe it never will be. But according to Bloody Mary, WFTDA already faced choices about how, and whether, to grow, choices that cut right to the heart of the real question the derby revival raises. A national sport, owned and operated by players, a nonprofit, a democracy of sorts—is it even possible? "It's regularly very challenging," Bloody Mary said. "We're in deep discussions, all the time. Every time we talk about money, we are very aware that we could probably have a national sponsorship deal—if we had an owner. We could have all travel paid for—if we had an owner. But that's not what we want. It's hard. But if we can keep the two decision-making processes on track, the sport side and the business side, I think we have a chance."

And the leg? She sounded most concerned about how that mother of all contusions might look on TV. "I was wearing tiny shorts and I had blood running down my leg," she said. "Are they going to show that? Of course they are."

This took us straight from speculation about derby's future to the gloriously meaty reality of its present: mangled limbs and *joie de guerre* in an uncharted domain open to tough, smart, fearless women to define. Other sports should be so lucky.

NINE

FEAR THE KILLING CONE

G WACK-GWACK-*gwack*-GWACK.

A strange noise: a piercing, rapid-fire bark/squawk.

GWACK-gwack-GWACK. The two gyrfalcons sense something up there, an intruder, a wild hawk traipsing into their territory. They look at Bob Welle, their owner, and me with marble-eyed suspicion, like we're in league with the trespasser. Like if it weren't for us and this damned pen—a rough-beamed, man-made aerie out back of Welle's house, next to the corral occupied by his llamas and goats—they would damn well *do* something about it. Then again, these two birds look like they could be a bit touchy at the best of times.

"Easy, boys," Welle says. He pulls on a glove with an elbow-length leather gauntlet as he peers up around the pen's roof. Then he coaxes the younger of the gyrs, a bird named Seven, onto his fist. It's a pristine, frigid January day in the farm country just outside Portland. Beyond a frozen duck pond, Mount Hood's snowy volcanic jag pops against a blue sky. Seven's feathers are ivory white with sagey gray-brown speckles, his talons bluish bone. Given the backdrop and the airborne killing machine on his arm, Welle could strike a mythic pose. Instead he's all politeness and small-town understatement. Still, as one of only eighty-five licensed practitioners of the ten-thousand-year-old sport of falconry in the state of Oregon, he does qualify as a rarity, as does Seven. "Back in the Middle Ages," Welle says, "only the king could hunt with these guys. They're the largest, fastest falcons. They can do sixty miles per hour in level flight, and when they dive, it could be one hundred miles per hour, it could be two hundred. They're as high-octane as it gets."

At this point, I take renewed interest in the tether on Seven's leg. Worst-case scenario, it will prevent him from tearing my face off. I guess.

After my immersion into so many citified sports—roller derby, croquet, the Portland Challenge, urban golf, etc.—I felt the call of the wild, or at least the semirural, semisuburban cul-de-sacs of the northern Willamette Valley. I wanted to explore a sport that harked back to the most primeval definition of the word, something with nothing to do with organized teams or man-made competitions, a sport that brought its practitioners up against the rough skin of the earth. I wanted something completely different—something outré. So far, with a beaky promise of severe facial injury perched about two feet from my chin, falconry delivered.

Falconry seems more like the stuff of Saudi oil sheikhs and fictional oddballs à la *The Royal Tenenbaums* than low-key guys at the edge of farm country. Hunting with trained killer birds? For real? Before or after you transmogrify lead into gold? This is why I tracked down Bob Welle, who at first glance makes a somewhat unusual addition to my research. As one of relatively few native Montanan males never to have killed a beast in the field, hunting holds a vicarious fascination for me—but where does the oldest sport of all fit into my imagined pantheon of bike punks and roller derby belles?

Falconers are not easy to find, and I soon gathered that this is, to a degree, by design. The subculture does not exactly court the spotlight. Falconry websites tend to be low-tech and stand-offish, with password-protected, members-only forums and grudging "contacts" sections full of blind e-mail addresses and terse directives to call your state wildlife office for further info. The North American Falconers Association stages its big event, the annual Field Meet, over Thanksgiving weekend. The public is not invited. However, I decide Welle's duties as president of Oregon's state falconry association must entail some PR, like it or not, so I cajole him into inviting me out to his place. Bob does, in fact, say that part of him—the conscientious president-of-the-association part, rather than the devotee-of-ancient-arcana part—wishes falconers could be a little more outgoing, if only to push up their total numbers. (He estimates there are fewer than four thousand falconers in the United States.) Alas, sociability is just not really part of their deal.

"There is no stereotypical falconer," he says. "In our club, we have a fourteen-year-old girl. We have guys with gun racks in their trucks, and we have college professors. I would say the only trait that really unites us is that we all tend to be a certain type of independent person. This isn't something you dedicate yourself to if you're into group activities. With eighty-five of us in the whole state, what are the odds you're going to live next door to another falconer? If you're attracted to crowds, this is not really the activity for you."

Becoming a falconer is not like signing on as shortstop for your office softball team, either. The medieval sumptuary laws that restricted the mighty gyr to kings while the yeomanry made do with goshawks no longer apply, but falconry still functions like a guild, subject to a spiky array of state and federal regulations. Beginners must find another falconer to act as their sponsor, pass a written test, and show state wildlife inspectors where their birds will live. They can then trap a wild kestrel or a redtail, the "short-winged" bunny hunters that serve as falconry's starter kit. After two years' practice with those birds, a falconer may acquire, train, and fly a larger prairie falcon. At this point, the aspiring aviomancer could be forgiven for thinking he or she knew this stuff reasonably well—but it takes yet another five years to become a "master," allowed to fly anything from gyrs to golden eagles.

Falconry demands more time than money, more patience than anything. Welle's regime involves training sessions with giant red balloons, bouts with domesticated fowl ("They ultimately have to kill something to learn"), electronic telemetry, and long days out when ducks, his gyrs' primary targets, just refuse to fly. If dead mallards were his objective, he'd take his shotgun. "The worst gun hunter in the world can blast ducks out of the sky," he says. "With the gyrs, one duck constitutes a good day." Still, I think I see the point. Years invested in birds allow a falconer to mesh with the workings of the elemental. As Welle describes the sport, falconry sounds slow and quiet and lonely; it also sounds the opposite of boring.

"When you turn a falcon loose on a pond of ducks, the

dynamics are completely natural," Welle says. "The ducks aren't helpless. If they decide not to fly at all, the gyrs can't do a thing. If they do fly, the ducks can play the game. They don't have the falcon's speed, but they can try to outmaneuver them. They can scrape the hawk off on a fence or a building. They'll try to get up above the falcon and eliminate its gravitational advantage. A duck can hit the water, stop dead, turn, and take off in a different direction, which a falcon just can't do. If you're coming down at two hundred miles per hour, you need a hundred-yard run-out at least."

The ducks do lose, of course. Welle's gyrs look down on the world and see an ever-shifting matrix of slayable stuff; they're hunters, same as him. "Their vision is huge," Welle says. "So is their killing cone."

Welle recognizes that hunting of all kinds is in statistical decline. In Oregon alone, the number of licensed hunters has dropped, by some measures, about 40 percent over twenty years, a trend mirrored nationwide and one that undermines funding for all kinds of public conservation programs. Welle also understands that the urban-liberal world I'll return to in my forty-minute drive home from his place often considers people like him a throwback alien species. A lefty bookstore a few blocks from my house sells bumper stickers that say "I Love Hunting Accidents"—yes, a notional endorsement of Bob Welle's violent death. A sizable minority in urban America considers hunting morally wrong (while remaining generally silent on bulldozing wild habitat to grow commodity crops). Most of the rest of us are merely indifferent or bemused. We metro-moderns view hunting as a quaint anachronism or the vaguely threatening cultural practice of people who also hate gays and the French.

The antipathy becomes mutual, and hunters vote for right-wing politicians who wax eloquent about firearms rights on the campaign stump, then sell out habitat to developers, oil execs, and mountaintop-axing coal companies.

Maybe the renegade solution would involve the rediscovery of hunting's radical and reformist heritage. Why did Robin of Locksley cash in his nobility, adopt the far cooler name Robin Hood, and turn outlaw? Because evil feudal lords wouldn't let commoners shoot stag in Sherwood Forest. Speaking of France, when the revolution started to boil in the eighteenth century, restrictions on hunting enraged the half-starved populace more than any *liaison dangereuse* antics at Versailles. In less remote times, the modern, state-regulated American hunting system, with its licenses, defined seasons, and mandatory safety and ethics training, is one of the more durable achievements of the Progressive Era. Hunting provided the legal framework—and more importantly the money and constituency—to save many species from annihilation and preserve millions of acres of wild land.

In the 1950s and '60s, the pesticide DDT almost wiped out peregrine falcons. Now, after decades of collaboration between governments, the Audubon Society, and falconers (and let's just say the annals of politics have seen more natural allies), the species has recovered to the point that falconers can once again trap wild peregrines to train. Consider sociobiological justice done: falconers provided many of the birds reintroduced to the wild. This alone seems to me reason enough to hope falconry survives the twenty-first century, but there are others. Hunters—real hunters, not those who engage in the canned captive-pheasant massacres beloved by certain former vice presidents who lack basic firearm skills—depend on healthy game populations and robust habitat. If Bob Welle has ducks to chase, that means there are ducks, which means wetlands remain intact, which means total biospheric collapse can wait a day. In an age when free-range, low-emissions local food couldn't be trendier, hunters actually engage with the food chain. As writer Steven Rinella puts it, they are the original locavores.

Most of all, though, as I admire Seven and he evaluates me as potential prey, falconry reminds me that sport can serve as a portal to rare learning and genuine magnificence. If this small corner of the sports world vanishes, human culture as a whole will suffer a sad loss. I don't think it will happen—a few thousand passionate people like Bob Welle can keep almost anything alive—but it could. "We are a thin sliver of the hunting community itself, and we have no political leverage at all," Welle says. "If you look at hunting numbers in general, then apply those dynamics to a group of less than one hundred people, you see what can happen, and happen fast. We're a small group of people that's become the repository for a lot of knowledge. If we don't share it, we could disappear."

TEN

THE LONG STEEL THUMBNAIL

I n the corner of a block on Portland's far north side, a greasy spoon called Patti's Home Plate serves fountain shakes, broadcasts old-timey pop songs through sidewalk loud-speakers, and hosts weekly meetings of the Western Bigfoot Society. On the opposite end of the block, there's a Starbucks. In between stands a fencing club. Salle Trois Armes—"the room of three weapons"—occupies a narrow storefront, the kind of half-broken-down old main-street shop one might expect to sell disintegrating paperback thrillers or secondhand housedresses. Instead, the front window displays an arsenal of swords and masks. During business hours, steel clangs on steel and fencers, in tight white jackets and breeches (yes, breeches), battle on three long, narrow *pistes* that extend from just inside the door to the back of the room. Sword-fighting memorabilia—posters for *The Mark of Zorro*, starring Tyrone Power; for Errol Flynn and Gina Lollobrigida in *Crossed Swords;* souvenirs from 1970s fencing tournaments; rules for practice duels dating back to 1696—covers the east wall. One spring evening, I walked into Salle Trois Armes to meet the proprietor, a man named Rocky. I hoped Rocky would teach me to sword-fight.

After months mostly spent living through other people's sporting eccentricities, I decided it was time to develop one of my own. A core precept of the Renegade Way (as I imagined it) holds that it's better to do things badly yourself than pay to watch other people do them well. Given my long and dismal record of athletic incompetence, I was reasonably sure I could fulfill at least some part of this ideal. My brief exposure to the mysteries of falconry and the quasi-monastic questers of the Trans Iowa also left me convinced that we, as a culture, underrate one critical aspect of sports. Games don't have to be passive entertainment, or glorified exercise regimes. They can teach you something, preferably something odd. Anyway, that sounded good when I explained to my wife why I planned to leave her at home with our infant child a couple nights a week to learn how to duel with archaic weapons. Truth be told, just like every other American male born in the 1970s, I've always wanted to be Luke Skywalker.

When I entered the *salle* that first time, a lesson was in progress: two skinny little adolescents, a boy with his hair cut in a neo-mod shag and a bleached-blond girl with a junior-goth look to her, faced off under the direction of a tall, gangly man in his fifties, who wore a brush mustache and an air that combined quiet authority and amiable discombobulation in a manner that made me imagine him, instantly and inexplicably, as an officer of the Royal Canadian Mounted Police. Rocky, I assumed. I would soon dub the two kids, the boy A. and his female sparring partner E., the Punkettes. We would see a lot of each other over the next few months. I didn't know it yet, but the Punkettes had already achieved a level of fencing mastery I would envy and probably never attain.

I stood by the door. Two middle-aged adults—Punkette parents, I guessed—sat in folding chairs to my left. Both turned to me and stuck out their hands, reminding me that I startle easily. We all shook and mumbled pleasantries. This made me feel self-conscious, awkward, and conspicuous—the perfect introduction, I would later realize, to the sport of fencing.

Fencing intrigued me for a host of reasons, but I showed up at Salle Trois Armes that night in large part because I thought becoming a fencer would be supercool. I liked the thought of swanning around in those chic whites, theoretically capable of filleting all comers, making informed comments about parries and ripostes and whatnot *en français*. Great clothes! Swords! Foreign words! I could tell my friends, oh, man, I can't meet for drinks Tuesday . . . I've got *fencing*, you know. I chose Salle Trois Armes, over several other local fencing clubs, for two reasons: (1) it's close to my house; (2) it looked kooky as hell. I suppose I anticipated a lighthearted, fun lark in someone else's subculture, like joining an all-mandolin basement jam band or taking a few contra-dancing lessons. I would meet interesting people, they would stab me, I would stab them, and maybe we'd all go out for prosecco afterward. I am, of course, an idiot.

Rocky dismissed the Punkettes, then came over and shook my hand. The Punkettes gathered up their parental units and made to leave. Before exiting, they also both shook my hand, their small uncalloused mitts like a pair of hamsters in mine. As they left, an apple-cheeked young woman, maybe twenty, came in. She grinned and stuck out her hand. Now all my social-anxiety alarm bells officially reached full klaxon. "Oh," Rocky said. "We always shake hands with all our teammates when we arrive, and again when we leave." He turned to the wall and tapped a stapled-up list, a code of conduct. "That's the rule."

Teammates?

Rocky Beach started fencing in 1966. Now, in his own soft-spoken way, he waxed evangelical for a moment. "I'm fifty-eight years old, and this is all that's holding my body together," he said, gesturing at a *piste* where two adult men sparred. "It's one of the healthiest things you can do, and according to our insurance company, one of the safest." Salle Trois Armes, true to its name, offered instruction in all three of competitive fencing's weapons: foil, épée, and saber. Each blade has its own properties and its own rules, he explained, but we would begin with foil, the basic and classical weapon that provides a foundation applicable to the other two swords. I was fine with that— in fact, I was ready to don mask and hoist blade against the opponent of Rocky's choosing. Let the quirkily offbeat games begin!

I did not fence at all that night. I did not break a sweat, in fact, or touch a piece of equipment, or engage in anything resembling sport. Rocky wanted to talk. Better, he said, that I should understand the relevant philosophical underpinnings before I began my work here at Salle Trois Armes. "You already know a lot about fencing," he said. Interesting. I did not know that.

"You walked in here. Walking is a fencing move. You're standing there. That's a fencing move." I nodded and, I believe, looked
at Rocky with total incomprehension. He was already talking
about mechanics, physics, and the technical and social back-
story of the seventeenth-century dueling sword. He held up a
foil and explained how its streetwise forefather was the Glock
9mm of its day, a light and practical weapon for intimate urban
combat. "This sword was designed with one thing in mind," he
said, "and that was to pierce a vital organ as quickly as possible." He showed me how the sword's center of gravity resided
about two inches up the blade from the stainless steel bell guard,
creating an invisible pivot point and allowing a swordsman to
control it with a delicate precision grip. I guessed the meaty, satisfying, not-at-all-Freudian fist I envisioned was out, as was the
two-handed melee flail employed by Luke Skywalker just before
Darth Vader cuts off his lightsaber hand and (talk about Freudian) informs him of his paternity.

Rocky's disquisition then moved on to, oh, history, art, and
music. "A lot of what we do here is like when a musician goes
through classical training," Rocky said. "You start out knowing
nothing but how to hit notes at random. If you learn the classical principles, then you can eventually do everything—play any
kind of music you want, sit in with any band in any style. An
artist has to learn how to draw accurately from life before moving on to abstraction. The same idea applies here—we'll teach
you how to do things in the classical way, and then you can
adapt and see what works for you."

I wondered if Rocky was (or had at one time been) the kind
of guy to raise the subject of marriage when it's just about time
to order a second cocktail on a first date. Certainly, it did not

sound like he had my idea of a casual commitment in mind. He promised, for example, to rewire my nervous system.

"I see a lot of fencing instructors who just don't know how the central nervous system works," he said, shaking his head with the kind of oh-what-a-world look others might adopt to bemoan the fact that kids don't learn enough Latin these days. "A lot of the work we do is intended to shut down some muscular reflexes and hone others. Our lessons tend to be short, because there's only so much your neural pathways can absorb." I was pretty sure he was right about that. My neural pathways felt about up to the brim already.

As Rocky filled me in, another lesson—one that involved some actual swordplay—took place on the next *piste* over. The twenty-something girl jabbed at a wizened figure in a black tracksuit straight from the Gotti menswear collection. This stooped little man wore a fencing mask and a thick, rough-surfaced tan leather vest. "That's Maître Calvert," Rocky said— *Master* Calvert, in other words. He bossed the lass about in fierce Gallic fashion: "*Non.* Zeez is incorrect. *Non. Comme ça,* you see." Was Salle Trois Armes a sporting club, or something out of *The Story of O?* Maître Calvert, I learned, started fencing when he was in the French Foreign Legion and later trained the French Army team and coached the U.S. national squad. Now deep into his eighties, he still maintained an intimidating air of eminence. My introductory chat with Rocky ended just as Maître Calvert pulled off his mask. Rocky led me over to him, and we shook hands. Rocky leaned over to loud-talk to the master.

"This is Zach," Rocky said. "He's our newest victim."

Maître Calvert cracked a grin. "Very good, very good," he said. "So, *Zacque,* tell me. Are you a . . . sadist?"

* * *

My second lesson: I look like a fat twelve-year-old. I stand in front of a full-length mirror, holding a stick. Not a sword, but a yard-long cylindrical stick. Somehow, I can't hold the thing right, either. I'm supposed to pincer it between my thumb and the second bone of my index finger, with the shaft slotted into the groove between the big muscle at the base of my thumb and my palm, my other three fingers wrapping around the handle in an orderly row, knuckles flat, to provide control. My damn hand keeps balling into a baby's fist.*

Rocky, perched on a three-legged stool, tells me to adjust my grip as he instructs me on some basic poses and moves, starting with the en garde position. Right foot dead ahead, left foot at a ninety-degree angle—except that terminology is wrong. "You're a fencer now," Rocky says. "You don't have a right foot or a left foot anymore. You have front and back." He asks me to point the stick down and twist my body sideways by extending my left arm (would that now be my back arm?) behind me and crooking my elbow, allowing the hand to flop forward as though I'm trying to shadow-puppet a swan's head. I do this. It feels fey and ridiculous. Rocky explains that the floppy hand will provide counterbalance for forward lunges. Within thirty seconds, the muscles beneath my left (back?) shoulder blade start to lock up.

*After I advance to a real sword, I will use a foil outfitted with a "French grip," a phrase that does indeed sound like a euphemism for some kind of indecent act. This simple handle, gently curved to nestle into the inside of the wrist, is distinct from the Italian, Spanish, and pistol grips. There are at least ten different kinds of pistol grips, including Russian, Belgian, Chinese, and Hungarian varieties. In fencing, nothing can be simple.

Then Rocky directs me through a series of slo-mo moves to basic defensive positions—maneuvers that do seem vaguely sword-fighterish, but are difficult to imagine as the basis for a flowing act of aggression. I bend my knees, forming an elongated diamond between my thighs and calves. I keep pointing the stick at the wrong spot in the mirror: "No, that's offense. You want defense."

Behind me, the Punkettes canter like tearaway colts, merrily blasting each other with épée blades and giggling between points. I find several things annoying about all this. One, what I'm doing is so pathetically simplistic. Two, I cannot actually do it. Three, not only are these tweens having way more fun than me, I am not yet anywhere near the point where I could fence against them, kids twenty years younger than me, without constituting a danger to myself and others.

Rocky doesn't prolong my agony—in fact, the physical portion of the lesson ends after about ten minutes. "The length of our lessons is determined by what we need to accomplish on a given day," Rocky informs me, in his most gnomic mode. "I've given a four-minute lesson. Sometimes they last an hour. This is military training—important to remember. Our goal here is not to entertain the fencers. The fun part comes later." Certainly true, as far as I can tell.

I put down the stick. Rocky beckons me to the blackboard and says the words every student of every discipline so longs to hear: "Time to introduce you to some theory." He disappears into a cluttered back corner of the *salle* and emerges with a black three-ring binder. He opens it to reveal a dog-eared pile of Xeroxed pages set in an antique gothic font. "I gotta get more photocopies of this stuff," he mutters. The title page reads *Le Règlement d'Escrime*: The Regulation of Fencing, from a publisher no less imposing than Le Ministère de la Guerre, the French Third Republic's ministry of war. Year of publication: 1909. "This is the basis for what we do," Rocky says. "It's never been surpassed. It has been added to, but never surpassed." Part of me thinks this is cool—behold, a musty tome of antique wisdom. Another part isn't too sure about paying good money for lessons based on a French Army manual, published at the beginning of a century in which the French Army did not exactly establish itself as the last word in military know-how.

We study the technical names for different zones of a fencer's body: the upper-left-hand *sixte*, the upper-right-hand *quarte*. I remember enough high school French to notice that not only does this sport conduct business in a foreign tongue, it uses vocabulary that hasn't evolved since the sixteenth century. Soon, Rocky closes the binder and starts drawing little ovals on the blackboard. "These are muscle fibers," he says. Then he draws little tube-shaped thingies between the ovals. "These are the neural pathways . . ." Then ensues an explanation of how nerves fire, which quickly exceeds any anatomical knowledge I picked up about the time I was memorizing Gallic verb conjugations. The message seems to be that my neuromuscular connections need lubing up—and that repetition of various simple stances and moves will build up a nice juicy surplus of neurotransmitter fluid right where I need it, the better to flood the synaptic gaps on demand.

I nod. It occurs to me that this may not be quite what I was after.

*　　*　　*

The bookish sissy faces a tough choice when it comes to combat sciences. The Eastern disciplines—karate, tae kwan do, whatever trendy mess-with-your-opponent's-chi method happens to be in vogue—all seem way too useful and freighted, through no fault of their own, with an icky jarhead vibe. *No, sensei! Yes, sensei! Grasshopper can kill with one touch, sensei!* I'm sure they're excellent practices, but I'll pass. For one thing, any knowledge that fools me into thinking I could actually kick some ass could lead to dire consequences. Boxing and wrestling—to say nothing of the mad-dog scrapping of mixed martial arts—are way too butch for me. Fencing, on the other hand, offers aesthete anticachet in spades: it's historic, esoteric, French. Its most famous practitioners are all fictional characters who wear tights. The sport is a blank slate—good for me, since I am usually somewhere between mediocre and outright terrible at most athletic pursuits. I also take an immediate and instinctive liking to Rocky and Maître Calvert's operation, with its geeky clubhouse atmosphere and unself-conscious memorabilia. Salle Trois Armes feels more like a moody teenager's bedroom than a house of sport.

The night of my third lesson, chaos prevails at Salle Trois Armes. With a big tournament coming up over the weekend, kids and parents overrun the place, trying to extricate equipment from unkempt piles of gear, round up T-shirts, and sort out rules and schedules. Rocky, alone, struggles to manage, which gives him the air of the embattled maître d' at a slapstick French restaurant. Meanwhile, the Punkettes fight away on one *piste* and two experienced-seeming guys in their midtwenties spar with one another. I stop to watch. The veterans, both yardstick-skinny, dance at each other with pugilistic buoyancy, up on the balls of their feet, primed to strike. Swords clash and whip the air, evoking cymbal crashes and a seaborne snap of rope in the wind. That's fencing, I think—and I'll probably never, ever get there.

Rocky finds me and shakes my hand. "I forget," he says. "Did we go into delivering a touch last time?" No, last time I stood in front of the mirror, holding a stick, sir. "Okay. Why don't you find a mask that fits? I'll be with you momentarily."

A mask! Progress, indeed. I duck into the equipment rooms at the back of the *salle*, a mad-scientist-lab rumpus of old swords, ancient posters, overflowing toolboxes, one of those replica human skeletons that stand in the back of high school biology classes, fencing jackets, and helmets. I rummage awhile. Most of the helmets, sized *en français*, of course, squeeze my skull in an alarming way. An XG (*extra grande*) saber mask finally comes to hand. My head sort of rattles around in this one, but its stainless steel mesh and almond shape resemble the head from a manorial suit of armor, and I like that a lot.

Rocky hands me a foil, the sport's basic weapon. He leads me over to a wall and shows me how to hold the sword—and that takes about five minutes, as I try to place the thumb so, crook the index finger so, and curl the other three digits to form the proper delicate guidance system for the blade. Then he turns me to the wall and asks me to get into *en garde*. Ha, I think—we're getting somewhere. And then some fencing mom distracts Rocky with her need for a registration form, and Rocky wanders off. Halfway across the room, he turns back to me. "Remember," he half shouts over the din of swords and kids, "as a fencer, gravity is always available to you."

At this, A., the male Punkette, breaks off from his bout and looks at me. *"Gravity is always available to you!"* he parrots. "Not if you're in outer space, it's not!" Then he cackles like a fiend and returns to battle. I have no idea what they're talking about. I stand in the *salle*'s corner like the prime minister of Douchebaglandia, holding my mask, holding my sword, without the first clue what to do with either of them. Should I cut my own head off with the foil? Finally, Rocky ambles back over and explains: I must always remember that gravity is a fencer's first resort. If I can just let the blade fall into my opponent, without exerting myself at all, so much the better.

"Think lazy," Rocky says. "Always think lazy." Sure.

Then he orders me to stab the wall a bunch of times. After about a dozen attempts, I manage to do this half-correctly.

Hand level. Like I'm carrying, Rocky says, a dish of cookies.

Drive the blade forward like it's "a long steel thumbnail."

Use the arm, but not the shoulder, and don't use anything else.

No leaning. I don't know it yet, but avoiding the forbidden lean will become one of my most difficult fencing challenges.

The idea, Rocky explains, is to turn the arm into a smooth, independent piston that can operate without a herky-jerky, tensed-up body behind it. I'm listening. My goddamn nose itches. It requires every last shred of my presence of mind not to reach up and paw at my mask like an idiot. Rocky tells me that fencers try to "recruit forces in sequence," harvesting muscle potential latent in different parts of the body bit by bit, rather than all at once. If gravity alone doesn't get the blade in, use the arm first, then the lunging power of the legs. He goes into some detail about the automatic muscular reflexes your with-it fencer works either to suppress or to subvert to his/her own nefarious purposes. I must admit I am not retaining a particularly high percentage of this information. I take it, though, that the aim is to slide into movements rather than lurch, with a light yet tensile grace.

Then follows a bucketload of French terminology—more stuff about *sixte* and *quarte,* and yet my nose still itches. Maybe I should cut *it* off. Then—at last—Rocky asks me to face him *en garde,* to practice delivering a touch to an object both animate and mobile. He taps his thick leather safety vest to invite my attack. I am surprised to find that I have a real hardwired taboo against stabbing another human being. I am not surprised to find that I conquer it very quickly.

Salle Trois Armes is not my first exposure to the sport of the sword. In college, I briefly joined the University of Montana's fencing club, a nonsanctioned, student-run endeavor that met in whatever oversized liberal arts classroom it could cadge. I was a freshman, excited about any activity that did not require begging the twenty-one-year-old dude on the dorm floor above mine to buy beer for my roommate and me. *Fencing*—I liked the exotic sound of it, and insofar as I rapped on that twenty-one-year-old's door more than I now care to contemplate, I hoped the sport could help me maintain my svelte figure in defiance of the rest of my lifestyle. And I figured, to be honest, that it might involve some hot European girls. Unfortunately, the match just didn't take. Bless them for trying, but the UM fencers of the day lacked a coach, or anyone like a coach. I feared the shared, very used equipment would give me some kind of flesh-eating disease. The club seemed to me to consist, in large part, of Society for Creative Anachronism members—those jolly medieval recreationists apt to address innocent bystanders with questions such as, "Prithee, my good man—whither findeth one the restroom?" I soon found my interest in the campus swordplay scene on the wane. Fencing mostly vanished from my awareness at that point. Still, the sport would sometimes sneak up on me. I was in Croatia during the 2004 Olympics, where television coverage of the Games focused largely on team handball and table tennis (Croatian strengths—who knew?) but included a generous side order of fencing. I discovered that Portland was home to a disproportionate number of America's top *sabreurs* and wrote a newspaper story about their deluxe suburban training facility. Every once in a while, I would find myself checking a fencing book out of the library, without really knowing why.

Thus, I arrived at Salle Trois Armes with more-than-average passive knowledge of the game—knowledge which, in practice, turned out to be about as useful as having just enough of a foreign language to proposition an undercover vice cop. I knew fencing turned one of the most elemental human encounters into a hyperdefined and arguably fussy practice. (In foil, for example, a legitimate hit must exert no less than 4.9 newtons of force. Offhand, I don't know any other sport in which the newton is a relevant unit of measure.) Thanks to a book called *By the Sword*, by a British ex-Olympian named Richard Cohen, I also knew that at its highest level, the sport fostered a baroque culture of corruption, bribery, and gamesmanship befitting one of the more hard-boiled courts of Renaissance Italy. (Doctored weapons, bought-off refs, intricate match-fixing schemes involving scores of fencers and unfolding over years—these people know how to cheat.) I learned that the sport attracts extravagant personalities. Sir Richard Francis Burton, the Victorian libertine/scholar/ adventurer who traced the origins of the Nile and translated the Kama Sutra, was even more obsessed with fencing than with Indiana Jones–ish stunts and crafty Eastern sex tricks. Polish saber champ Jerzy Pawlowski, a florid 1950s and '60s bon vivant and scam artist who won five Olympic medals, also found time to spy for both Polish military intelligence and the CIA. And we consider Gilbert Arenas a racy character.

It did not surprise me to learn that fencing's past contains a few episodes that the Fédération Internationale d'Escrime fails to highlight in its promotional materials. For some reason, the sport fascinates totalitarian regimes and wannabe Great Leaders. British fascist Oswald Mosley competed for the national team. Reinhard Heydrich, the Nazi-*über-Alles* who held several high-ranking Third Reich jobs before Czech partisans assassinated him in occupied Prague, tried to bully his way onto the German Olympic team in 1936. Cohen's book includes a priceless photo of Il Duce himself, Benito Mussolini, engaged in a fencing practice. Most of the postwar Communist regimes went in for fencing in a big way, and in recent years the People's Republic of China targeted the sport in its government-mandated push to pump up its Olympic medal count. Fencing may be, as Rocky told me on my first visit to Salle Trois Armes, one of the healthiest things a person can do, but it has a definite unwholesome strain woven into its DNA. Even today, male students at certain German universities, dressed up like villains from steampunk scifi in mesh goggles and high-necked safety vests, fight illicit *mensur* duels with razor sharp sabers. The dueling fraternities go back centuries, and given well-known, unpleasant aspects of

German history, left-wingers tend to consider these clubs' sense of fun rather sinister. (The members, of course, say it's not like *that* at all.)

As I began my student days at Salle Trois Armes, I didn't know what to think of this high-strung affair, which seemed, from my reading, an ideal habitat for cranks. I turned to a classic treatise by the Italian master (and triple gold medalist) Aldo Nadi, *On Fencing*. Writing in the 1940s with an eye toward converting Americans to the sport, Nadi exhibits the imperious, paranoid, egomaniacal self-regard of an opera *divo*—he denounces all other living fencing instructors on approximately every other page—and thus seems a dubious choice for guidance. I found his attempts at practical instruction nigh on incomprehensible. On the other hand, on the psychological front, Nadi interested me. "Almost all of [the fencer's] ability," he writes, "depends upon the sudden release, from total relaxation, of highly concentrated nervous energy." Sounded good to me. Then this: "The fencing strip is the mirror of the soul." Then this: "The first rule of fencing is to remain relaxed at all times." Good to know.

"Now, imagine we're in seventeenth-century Paris," Rocky says. I stand with my foil clasped to my hip, in an imaginary scabbard. "You're walking out of a pub. I come out of the shadows. I want to kill you and take your money. What do I do?"

Now this is more like it. Death or glory in the scum-clogged back alleys of the ancien régime? I could get into that. Besides, over a period of a few weeks, my modest (veering toward imperceptible) advances have earned me the right to wear not only a mask, but a white jacket, too. Now I begin my lessons by step-ping through the crotch loop (which, I think we can agree, is an auspicious way to start anything) at the bottom of every fencing vest, zipping an odd zipper configured to prevent an opponent's blade from catching in its teeth, and fastening the high-necked Velcro collar. I may look like a line cook, but I feel dead cool. I've also learned how to respond to Rocky's ceremonial salute, a series of exaggerated moves that begins with swords thrust straight up and ends with a smooth sweep of blades to floor. Rocky insists on the full protocol, though I notice the experienced fencers at Salle Trois Armes satisfy etiquette with the most perfunctory of blade flicks in each other's general direction.

And now we're talking Parisian tavern muggings. I take this as progress.

Rocky: "I'm not trying to be fancy. I want you dead. My blade will seek the shortest route to a vital organ." He orders me to "draw" my sword, then parry his would-be lethal jab at my chest. That block prompts a second attack, and thus a second parry. As we move in instructional slo-mo, Rocky explains that we're progressing through eight basic defensive parries, from *prime* to *octave*, which unfold according to the logic of a mortal street duel. Besides saving my fictional life as a drunken *boulevardier*, Rocky says these protective measures also gather information: each contact with an opponent's blade betrays something about his tactics and intentions. All the nomenclature—labeling the left-hand side of the body *sixte*, and so forth—provides an ana-lytical framework, a system for processing that information.

"It's all about allowing the brain to make sense of a chaotic environment," Rocky says. "The blades are whipping around, like this." He breaks off our downshifted engagement and lashes his foil around. "You can't see it. But if you can contact it, you learn something about what's happening, and if you have a template in which to place that information, you can figure out what you need to do. It's like a road map to a city. If you don't have a map, you don't know where you are or how to get anywhere. But if you memorize the map and understand it, then not only do you know where the landmarks are, you can figure out the shortcuts." He adds something about fencing consisting of "a rapid sampling process." I think I know what he means. I think.

I often find that each little thing I learn about fencing only reveals another vista of incomprehension. (Make what real-life extrapolations you will.) For example, I've learned the three most basic forms of attack, starting with the *coup droit*, more or less a straight thrust. It doesn't get simpler than this: see opponent, stab opponent—just extend the sword arm straight at the target. In the *dégagement*, or "disengagement," the attacking fencer loops his or her sword around the opponent's in a clockwise spiral that ends, in theory, with the tip of the foil buried in the enemy's chest. My favorite, even though I find it just about impossible to perform, is the "cut-over," or *coupé*. With a split-second release of pressure from the middle, ring, and pinkie fingers, the fencer pivots the blade straight up at the sky; then the fingers close and the sword point descends like a guillotine blade on target.

Trouble is, those three little moves only begin to hint at the terrifying mathematics of fencing. Each of them—*coup droit, dégagement, coupé*—can also be deployed as a feint, a diversionary fake attack not intended to reach the target. Each such deception can then lead to the real version of any of the three attacks. So an actual *coup droit* might follow a feint of *coup droit*. Or a fake straight thrust can give way to a real *dégagement* (or vice versa). Three times three—that would be nine reasonably simple attacks, right? No. Because such creatures as the *counter-disengagement*—same thing, opposite direction—and *counter-cut-over* also exist, and can be combined with any of the feints, or executed as feints themselves. The exponential regress of possibilities grows dizzying as these moves and sequences of moves combine with all manner of footwork and defensive variations. I discover, at thirty-three years old, that both my control over my limbs and my ability to process directions are limited at best. Standing opposite me *en garde*, Rocky tells me to defend his disengagement with a parry in *sixte*, a lovely little counter-clockwise twirl—one of my favorites—that scoops away his blade, and to follow with a feint of disengagement, followed by a counter-disengagement. And even as I think, *okay, what would that look like?*, Rocky's blade is there, and my body grinds into action that may or may not resemble anything ever done on a fencing strip before. Compounding the simple challenge of mere execution, Rocky insists I should pull off all this choreography with smooth, minimalist precision, contracting only the muscles immediate to the task.

"This just needs to flow," Rocky says. "Bop-bop-bop-bop. It's nothing. Don't tense up."

Unfortunately, at this green stage of what may or may not be my fencing career, the mental gyrations behind *bop-bop-bop-bop* seem to be more than the old gourd can handle. If I control one thing, something else goes to hell. One day, I spend half an hour trying to brew together a feint of *coup droit*, a *dégagement*, and a forward-stepping lunge, while Rocky says "no" many, many times. Either the thumb of my sword hand strays out of the desired "supination," rotating from its appointed place between twelve o'clock and one thirty to something more like eleven o'clock, leaving open my *quarte* side, or my back foot drags Quasimodo-style behind the lunge, or something. At one point, Rocky mentions an old-time training technique: nailing a shoe to the floor to force the back foot to stay put. My laugh is about as convincing as my counter-cut-over. As is often the case on the *piste*, I sense my mental circuitry frying down to a viscous, carbonized pulp.

A few weeks after I started at Salle Trois Armes, Portland hosted the U.S. Fencing National Championships, a mammoth event for just about every competitive age classification. (This was the big tournament that had Rocky's *salle* in such a logistical uproar the evening of my third lesson.) Dozens of fencing strips carpeted a vast natural-light-free room at the city's convention center, around which whirled thousands of fencers, officials, coaches, and fencing parents, the latter distinguished by an expression of pins-and-needles concern and extreme mobile-phone usage. America's cellular network logged an exceptional volume of fencing-related calls that day, as breathless, biased oral histories of various junior competitions circulated the nation's living rooms and retirement homes.

I walked into this maelstrom, following a gaggle of kids with sword-sized rolling bags about as big as they were, past a couple of feline teenage girls locked in a foil bout. For an outsider, arriving at the Nationals was akin to an outing to a tent revival, swingers club, or Civil War reenactment festival:

I discovered a large and fully formed social world heretofore invisible to me. Miniature ten-year-olds slashed at each other just thirty yards from the *pistes* where crucial bouts determined the makeup of the 2008 men's Olympic team. Teenage fencers strutted around, each endeavoring to out-soigné the rest in his or her sleek white kit. The adolescent vibe was very twenty-first-century America, part Ellis Island, part Abercrombie & Fitch: young fencers with names like Etropolski and El-Saleh on the backs of their steel-gray target vests formed dense high-school-corridor gossip knots between bouts. The whole place, in fact, looked like a sociology master's thesis waiting to happen. In the long queue at the in-house Starbucks, I found myself between an Arab woman (who complained about the line) and a middle-aged Sikh man (who was chilling with his iPod). Enough world-weary, jowly Slavic gents milled around to staff up a James Bond villain's secret headquarters. The official judges, one of whom stood glowering beside every strip, all wore extremely bad black suits two sizes too large, which the women spruced up with spike heels. This created a jarring effect. The fencers themselves evoked an avant-garde fashion designer's Astronaut Collection, while the referees looked like a Romanian agricultural trade delegation circa 1985.

With at least twenty bouts—different weapons, different genders, different age categories, some individual, some team—unfolding at all times, it was hard to know what to watch. Then, when I forced myself to stop and concentrate on a single sword fight, it was outright impossible to know what to watch. Competitive fencing makes few concessions to the casual spectator—on the solid assumption, I suppose, that casual fencing fans do not exist. Two people with swords dance back and forth, surge into each other, then both turn to the referee, screaming in triumph. Fencers are very demonstrative: just about every point ends with guttural hollers and fist pumps from both involved parties. Salesmanship, it seems, is key, because it's not just about who hits whom first. Complicated (or, let's be honest, incomprehensible) rules about "right-of-way" and "intention" determine the validity of each hit* or who scores if the combatants strike each other at more or less the same time. This renders just about every point a judgment call, which guarantees drama-club-caliber pouting in the face of impassive and unfeeling referees—all of which, I guess, could be part of the fun.

So why did hundreds of people from around the country/world bother to dedicate a sunny weekend to this very tough-to-crack nut, let alone their whole sporting lives? (I'm sure that nightmarish "fencing parents" must have something to do with it, at least in some cases.) Even though it baffled me, the know-nothing, I could see fencing enthralled everyone who knew what was going on. And I could see why. Blades sizzled through the air and clanked against each other with satisfying metallic ker-rangs. Spectators crowded around the day's glamour events—especially the high-level bouts in saber, a Zorro-ish weapon that lends itself to explosive action and all manner of swashbuckling theatrics—and shrieked at every split-second exchange of steel. It was boxing conducted at fluttering ping-pong speed; chess with pointy things; the lonely psychological tension of singles tennis translated to direct physical combat. Fencing wasn't much

---

*Most of the time . . . in foil and saber, at least. Épée's different. Something like that. As one measure of fencing rules' opacity, in three months of lessons, Rocky explained none of them.

of a popcorn sport. As a defining obsession, however, I began to see the potential.

At Nationals, I met a fencer named Lindsay Campbell, in the quiet corner of the room reserved for her event, women's épée. (One thing I learned at Nationals: fencing's internal hierarchy of cool derives from the dynamics of the sport's three weapons. Saber—which I would later hear an NBC Olympics commentator describe, in all seriousness, as "the punk rock of fencing"—ranks very cool indeed. Artsy, classical foil is cool in a Rilke-reading way. Épéeists, who fight under rules that encourage slower, more deliberative tactics, are like engineering grad students—respected for their cerebral skills, but not exactly the bleeding edge of hip.) Lindsay, a thirty-year-old native Clevelander, fences for the venerable New York Athletic Club and for the United States. I got to know her a bit in the course of a conversation between bouts—the most relaxed chat I've ever had with an athlete in the midst of a national championship—and e-mails and phone calls after the fact. Through Lindsay, I learned a little more about fencing's inner workings and what it's like to compete at a high level in a sport that, for Americans at least, remains an amateur pursuit in the most important sense of the word. She, like most top American fencers, mostly pays her own way.

Lindsay first picked up a sword as a highly competitive kid who hated anything involving a team or a ball. "I was always picked second- or third-last for kickball," she remembers, "and I was always told to 'keep it on the ground.' It made sports really annoying." In fencing, she found her niche and some superb revenge. She can now see her playground kickball rivals' callousness and raise them an All-American collegiate career at

Princeton and a passport worn to a frayed husk by jet-setting international competition. During college study-abroad stints, she tracked down fencing opportunities in Cape Town, South Africa, and a little town in Alsace. "Fencing's such a tiny sport," she says, "that if you go somewhere and find a club, there's pretty much an unwritten rule that they'll let you fence with them." While many American fencers retire after college, Lindsay managed to launch herself on the sport's World Cup circuit while simultaneously completing a master's degree at MIT.

International competition is by no means straightforward for an American fencer. Unlike the major European federations, U.S. Fencing doesn't have money to fund most travel or much of a coaching structure. That means Lindsay and her U.S. teammates run on their own steam much of the time, sometimes competing in Europe with no coach at all. Some fencers from New World sword-fighting nations move to Europe; Lindsay says she's considering it for the run-up to the 2012 Olympics, which she hopes to qualify for after missing out in '08.* So far, she manages a highly selective, time-zone-strategic approach to the World Cup schedule—tournaments in Montreal and Havana, good; China, not so much—with help from her parents and a flexible, understanding employer, the United States Forest Service.

Just hearing Lindsay describe her daily schedule left me in need of a cooling beverage. She lives in Red Hook, Brooklyn, and fences in midtown Manhattan. "Commuting cuts out tons

---

*Fencers face an Olympic squeeze: as the International Olympic Committee expands the number of sports in the Games, it slices away at the number of medal events in fencing. Beijing 2008, for example, omitted a team event in women's épée, reducing the total number of available roster slots and making qualification more difficult.

of time in my day," she says. She fences three or four times a week, three hours a go, and does other training two to four times a week. She runs with her boyfriend, a regime that includes a sprints-and-agility sequence he dubbed "boyfriend boot camp." She and a friend bike through urban patchworks like the Brooklyn-Queens Greenway. She swims in Red Hook's city-run pool. Then there are those little things, like full-time work and a viable social life. "I often get home after ten at night and eat dinner at eleven—this is routine," Lindsay says. "All my friends know that I'm always carrying either a bag full of snacks, a bag of clean or dirty workout clothes, or both. I always find myself trying to convince people to put off their dinner plans until nine thirty so I can join them, and basically running from practice, still unshowered, to make it. It's ludicrous. Of course, I always wish I was doing more—if I could get by on, like, four or five hours of sleep, then I could get everything done I need to get done."

A few weeks after the Portland tournament, I caught up with Lindsay on the phone. She was sitting in the departure lounge at LaGuardia, waiting to buzz up to Montreal for the only World Cup held on the continent that season. It sounded like a prototypical Lindsay Campbell weekend: fly to another country; stay in some random B & B; a little top-flight international competition; back home; back to work. In Montreal, Lindsay won enough of the round-robin qualifying bouts to move on to the sixty-four-fencer knockout grid, but her low seed meant she faced the world's ninth-ranked female épéeist, China's Zhong Weiping, to whom she'd lost before. Lindsay kept it close, tying Zhong at seven hits apiece with twenty-six seconds left in the nine-minute bout, but Zhong stabbed Lindsay in the ankle with

eleven seconds remaining to decide the matter. (Lindsay finished fifty-seventh.) The U.S. épée team—four fencers fighting
in succession against rivals from another nation—beat Sweden
and Hong Kong, but "got served" by Romania and Ukraine, finishing eleventh out of fourteen.

The whole regime—the training, travel, and pummelings
from world-class Chinese and East Euros—seems daunting.
Lindsay's international rankings rarely climb out of the triple-
digit range. (Her national rankings are much higher, and in
Portland she helped the New York Athletic Club win the épée
team championship.) Lindsay recognizes different forms of pay-
off, though, beyond outright victories and the incremental battle
to boost her World Cup standings. She's competed in Havana
three times, checked through Customs with a special Treasury
Department dispensation. Barcelona, Izmir, Budapest, Leipzig,
Prague, Paris, South Bend—for Lindsay, fencing provides a
means (or, perhaps, an excuse) to see the world. At tournaments,
she tends to hang out with a ragtag anglophone posse of Brits,
Aussies, Canadians, and Kiwis, who face more or less the same
funding and logistical challenges as the Americans. This gang
warms up together, rooms together, and eats together, stimulat-
ing the tight team structure enjoyed by their rivals from richer
fencing powerhouses like France, Italy, and South Korea. "The
major teams, they're essentially pro athletes," Lindsay says.
"We're up against that, and sometimes that's a pretty intimidating prospect when you're basically there on your own. But we
can't build a European system here overnight, so we all do the
best we can."

And then, besides travel, adventure, and awesome white
suits, she finds fencing has other benefits. "It's become a lifestyle

thing," she says. "As I've become an adult, fencing has helped me realize how much I care about fitness and being active, and I think it's helped me set a baseline that won't go away, even when I stop competing. There's the discipline of having to work very hard to realize goals, in most cases goals that you set for yourself. People talk about how fencing makes you a creative problem-solver—I can't say that it has that effect for me. What I do know is that fencing has forced me to reckon with a lot of psychological challenges. I've done a lot of visualization, relaxation, and meditation to cope with the anxiety of competition. It's all to quiet a really crazy mind that I felt was hindering me. Ideally, you want to attain that feeling of losing yourself in a kind of flow state. The mental side—that's what I've worked on, really, as much as anything."

"Okay, we're going to do that again. Except this time, close your eyes, please."

Rocky and I are crowded up against a wall—strident, fast-flowing bouts between real fencers take place on the *pistes*, squeezing the novice's lesson to the margins. He's trying to guide me through a choreographed parry/attack drill, but my attention just isn't there. (You try concentrating with two guys saber dueling three feet away.) I keep hunching my shoulders and leaning forward into my thrusts, rather than sliding into nice clean lunges. Rocky promises that these habits will lead to me falling straight on my face. And now he wants me to fly blind?

"Yes, close your eyes." I'm all for using the Force and all that, but this seems unwise. I am, however, in no position to debate.

I close my eyes and blunder forward into the blackness. I whip Rocky's blade aside with the little parry *sixte* and attack with a *coup droit*. Rocky parries, then I block his attack and riposte from my *quarte* side. Our blades sound like huge but delicate shears: *snick-snick-snick*. My riposte drives the foil's tip into Rocky's chest, and I open my eyes and smile with the delight of a kid who just made it around the block without training wheels. "See?" Rocky says. Sure, I knew what he was going to do, and what I was supposed to do, and I suspect he exercised some professorial discretion to make sure our swords met at the appointed places. At this point, though, I'll take my breakthroughs where I can get them.

Of all the bad habits writers indulge in—trashed hotel rooms, nonstop groupie sex on piles of hard currency, leather elbow patches—one of the worst is our tendency to impose epiphanies on ordinary experience. My nights at Salle Trois Armes served as weekly reminders that not every activity yields a moment of limpid emotional clarity, insight into How the World Works, or even anything worth so much as a blog post. I often left the *salle* frustrated, confused, and nursing a wicked ache between my shoulder blades caused by that stupid floppy left hand.

In the meantime, a miserable rainy spring went by. My son progressed from gooey near-silence to prolix baby babbling. I harvested two crops of arugula, but the other residents of my haphazard little vegetable garden hid out from the cold for weeks and weeks before, at last, they appeared. If I envisioned fencing as a dashing, escapist fantasy of some kind, I was wrong. It turned out to have a lot in common with that other stuff, the incremental processes of life in general. I now recognize that I expected both too much and too little when I showed up at Salle Trois Armes. I thought fencing would be both an entertaining romp and a shortcut to some kind of mind/body-nexus enlightenment. I thought I could both become Errol Flynn and skip straight to the end of *Zen in the Art of Archery*, when the German writer Eugen Herrigel advances so far in his lessons with a spiritual Japanese bowman that "the soul, sunk within itself, stands in the plentitude of its nameless origin."

But no—no plentitude of nameless anything for me. I ended up where Herrigel found himself early in his studies: "I went on practicing diligently and conscientiously according to the Master's instructions, and yet all my efforts were in vain." (Maybe I just needed to get superhigh before a lesson.) Of course, Herrigel kept at it for years before the Zen Fairy alighted on his shoulder. If it takes that long to become "egoless," maybe I'll just stick with my ego and have a martini once in a while.

It's not that I thought fencing would be easy—no Olympic discipline is to be taken lightly, not even ice dancing. I just did not approach it with the proper respect. I went in looking for some low-demand fun and easy answers, as a sporting tourist. Fencing doesn't do easy answers, and it doesn't reward tourism. Instead, the *piste* poses a host of problems simultaneously concrete—in the sense that you literally, physically cannot fence until you figure them out—and intangible. How do you persuade your sword arm to extend in perfect timing with your legs' explosive lunge and a subtle, articulated little flick of your fingers? And then reassemble *en garde* as though nothing happened, while analyzing everything that did, in fact, happen, so you can plan your next move and respond to your opponent's forthcoming attack? Drawing on one quarter-year's knowledge—which is to say, almost nothing—I would guess that a fencer can't solve these problems until he or she can first think them through consciously, and then discard all that conscious thought in favor of pure intuitive action. That said, I have no idea if I'm even conceptualizing these difficulties in a way that makes sense. Ask me again some other time.

Life intervened, in the form of the realization that I couldn't really fence, father, work, and live a semblance of a normal life at the same time. After several months (but zero competitive bouts) at Salle Trois Armes, I put my fencing career on prolonged hiatus. So, I failed. The strange thing is, I liked the process. I liked that fencing refused to offer up tasty little nuggets of achievement and validation at Pavlovian intervals. I found myself looking forward to my brief immersions into an atmosphere that combined the intent, studious sleepiness of a college library with the nasty charge of combat. And I did surprise myself sometimes. When I succeeded in marshaling all my limbs into some semblance of the desired moves, the sensation of my blade bending against Rocky's safety vest filled me with childish glee. As we repeated the same sequence of predetermined parries and thrusts again and again, in silence, I began to perceive some dim outline of what Rocky was up to. He was trying to install some new software in my head—to imprint the memory of what an opponent's thrust looks like under controlled conditions, so I would respond instantly when (if) I ever saw it live.

Maybe a tiny bit of new circuitry did take shape in my brain. In any case, my internal chemistry always seemed to balance when I stepped into the *salle*. I experienced the satisfaction of taking on a formidable beast. Maybe I failed in the end, but so what? My brief fling with fencing provided me with both a grand adventure (on a small scale) and a bruising encounter with humility. The sense of adventure is one of those mysterious capacities that distinguish humans from our fellow animals. The more I see of current affairs, the more I understand the value of humility. I may not be much of a fencer, but my fencing experience helped me become a slightly more circumspect thinker. All in all, not a bad trade for a weekly session in a knight's war mask.

A renegade sportsman should always crave new challenges and unprofitable hobbies with cool fashion components. I didn't conquer fencing this time—and maybe I should leave the sport to the spry likes of the Punkettes or ascended masters like Rocky. Still, I'm glad I tried. And, as of right now, my membership in the United States Fencing Association is still valid, so you never know.

ELEVEN

THE SPORT OF KINGS

The man called Wheelie Mark sat next to me on the porch, cradling a Hamm's tallboy and smoking a roll-your-own cigarette as the stereo blasted an old Fugazi song. He talked of athletic excellence.

"The best players in the world are right here, man," he said. "Right here." He gestured out into the street. The cul-de-sac curb formed a natural barrier at one end of a little court. A curving, low wall of cobbled-together plywood blocked off the rest of the street to enclose a rectangular asphalt playing field. At either end, a pair of traffic cones served as goalposts. As I talked to Wheelie Mark, six riders carrying homemade mallets clashed for control of a bright orange street hockey ball, part of the regular Wednesday-night bike polo action at the Polo Haus, stronghold of Portland's bike polo elite. The action bore some resemblance to hockey, soccer, and a freeway pileup. Astride specially geared bikes, two teams of three swirled and sparred, trying to prod the ball between the cones amid shoulder-to-shoulder, axle-to-axle collisions. Up on the Polo Haus's porch and scrubby yard, a small crowd of fans and players grew as the first warm evening of spring turned into a humid night. Empty cans and expended cigarettes scattered on the ground.

The Wednesday Polo Haus crowd is a young and rather aggressively bohemian crowd—it makes a formerly marginally cool person now suffering incipient middle age, like myself, feel about as hip as an undercover narcotics agent. *Hey, right on, brothers, anyone know where a jonesin' cat can "score" him a crazy reefer cigarette?* But they come every Wednesday night, rain or shine, to watch bike polo, and if you want to talk bike polo, the Polo Haus will embrace you. A giant replica bike-polo mallet—equipment researched and developed, in part, at the Polo Haus—hangs over the porch. Giant lights bolted to the porch roof, donated by Wheelie Mark, flood the street and allow polo play late into the night. (Everyone claims the neighbors love it. They would have to.) Games go to five goals, teams fluctuate depending on who chucks a mallet into the cul-de-sac to claim a spot in the next match, and anyone can show up and play. The Polo Haus rolls democratic like that—except any rookie can expect a royal hiding, because like Wheelie Mark said, these are at least some of the best bike polo players in the world, right here.

Street bike polo has rattled around urban cycling scenes across the country for a few years. The night I visited, the most dedicated Polo Haus players were deep in preparation for a big tourney in Portland, two weeks later, against teams from several other cities. Bike polo's lively and growing international network revolves around tournaments, often held over long weekends and in conjunction with other bike-centric events. Despite that increasing cross-pollination between cities, the game had yet to develop a standard rulebook, organizing body, or social taboo against playing under the influence. If anything, the lack of a canonical version of bike polo seemed to sharpen the Portland players' appetite for competition against other cities, because it wasn't just their ability on the line, it was their entire conception of the game.

It so happened that my primary Polo Haus contact was my old alley cat race pal, Drew Kinney. It turned out that alley cats were a mere diversion for Drew, who by this time had quit bike couriering entirely. Polo, however, was his life. "This is focus week, man," Drew said between games. "We already took an upset this season—Vancouver beat us at a tournament up in Seattle. Can't let that happen again." Pride is at stake. Teams composed of Polo Haus players ran roughshod through the previous year's tournaments, confirming Portland bike polo's* state-of-the-art reputation. To the (very great) extent that the Polo Haus *is* Portland bike polo, city bragging rights matter a lot to Drew, Wheelie Mark, and the other top players.

"Everyone's getting better," Drew said. "Some cities, we've gone and played 'em and it's been like playing children. But every year you see 'em coming along. The whole West Coast is pretty much in the same place now—we all play by pretty much the same rules, with minor variations. The East Coast, I've only seen on video." Drew and Wheelie Mark mentioned that Seattle,

*See http://axlesofevil.org.

an up-and-coming force, featured a player called Dead Baby Peter, maybe the best sports nickname since the retirement of Oil Can Boyd. There was no room for complacency. There was, however, room for beer.

Despite roughly similar lifestyle and music preferences, Drew didn't sound like he harbored quite the same antiestablishment views as, say, the roller derby nation. And forget the purist, amateur zeal of the Trans Iowa. Drew handed me a Hamm's as he told me about his ambitions to take bike polo to the commercial promised land. "My dream in life is to be a professional polo player," he said. "That's it, that's my passion. I want to be sponsored—I'm more than willing to wear a Red Bull T-shirt if that's what it takes. I want to see this sport become a real national sport. The problem is, we need the investors. We're a poor breed. We're blue-collar. Like, I'd love to go to the tournaments in Chicago, in Toronto, but I can't do it. I want to see us get to where skateboarding and snowboarding are. I know what needs to happen—I have the whole list of things we would need to implement to take this game to the pro level, but someone's gotta step up to make it happen. Shit, dude, it would be cheap—we could start a pro circuit for dirt cheap, relatively. I'm just glad I'm young. I'm not even in my prime yet. And if it doesn't happen until I'm beat up and torn down, maybe I can be a coach."

Wheelie Mark jerked his head up. "Dude, don't say that. Coach? C'mon." I don't know why, but Drew's speculative suggestion seemed to offend Wheelie Mark's very sense of decorum, like he'd just mused on a possible future career as a street hustler.

"I'm serious, dude," Drew said. "I can't think of anything else I'd rather do with my life." Then he wheeled off to join the next game. In action, Drew combined finesse—bike polo players are penalized if their feet touch the ground, putting a heavy premium on balance—and Gretzky-esque court sense with raw, charging aggression. The game itself consists of a series of elaborate one-on-one duels, which require a rider to manage bike, ball, mallet, and opponent, and orchestrated plays involving a team's whole trio. The evening's action proved highly entertaining. What bike polo could be like if the players weren't all half in the bag, I can't say.

I couldn't tell if I was seeing the next great street sport in its infancy, or a passing sub-subcultural fad bound for Friendster status in the not-distant future. Given the unprepossessing surroundings—at one point, a neighbor's pit bull ran into the fray, interrupting a nice give-and-go—it was hard to imagine Drew's dream of a pro grand prix polo circuit coming to pass. Then again, I could tell Drew was a damn good bike polo player. So were his Polo Haus mates, and the evening's female players looked just about as tough as the boys. So why not? Some crazed millionaire or opportunistic corporation could swoop in, cut some checks, mandate sobriety, pay for snazzy uniforms, and catapult bike polo into the realm of well-behaved normalcy. (Or, at least, the wild 'n' crazy poseur paradise of "extreme" sports.) Alternatively, all the bike polo scenesters around the country could take inspiration from roller derby and form some kind of national federation to determine, in part, if these Polo Haus hotshots really were as good as they claimed. (At the time I visited the Haus, very loose talk of a national organization was circulating on the bigger polo websites. At the time of this writing, www.leagueofbikepolo.com is the place to check in on these efforts.)

By now, I recognized this state of fertile chaos. In a way, delving into America's sports underground is like traveling back in time to the 1840s, before sports standardized and rationalized. With players in different cities playing under different rules on whatever courts they could borrow or improvise and no formal competitive structure, bike polo looked a little like baseball before the Civil War. Back then, before professionalism brought about the Fall of Man and the three-strikes-you're-out rule, wherever you lived you played, and the game changed at the county line.

Here, tonight, a couple dozen kids were sprawled out on the stoop, drinking beer, socializing, watching a game unrecognized by the world. All sports begin in places like the Polo Haus. For now, bike polo belongs to the hands-on tinkerers, who make it up as they go, and the streets and neighborhoods where it's played. In the future, who knows? Like all the DIY sports I investigated, bike polo is writing its own history, and like the whole grassroots, independent sports scene, its ultimate potential cannot be known. After a couple of Hamm's, it became just possible to believe that someday, the people in the yard that night would look back in wonderment on the days when they could watch Drew Kinney—*Drew Kinney, dude!*—every Wednesday night, for free. My journey into the sports netherworld deposited me here, on a mangy street just a couple miles from my house, where some charming kids play bike polo once a week. Both the hidden promise of a stranger, freer, more creative future for American sports and the stale scent of cheap beer infused the scene with its own epic quality.

"We're pushing each other relentlessly," Drew said, after the pit bull cleared out and one game ended and another began.

"The people who always turn out, we could all be pro polo play-ers, right now. Nights like tonight, we play a friendly game. No one gets hurt. But in a tournament—fuck it. To the death. To the death."

Onward, then, to the revolution.

WHAT THE UNICORNS KNOW

Most Thursday nights find me drenched in sweat, screaming nonsense at friends, flailing at an elusive spheroid without accomplishing much. I do this while wearing a sky blue shirt with a picture of a unicorn on the chest, and I consider it a very important part of my life. My indoor soccer team, the Albina Going Football Club (long story, but no, *not* "albino"), affectionately known as the Unicorns (even longer story), plays its matches on Thursday evenings, against the sharks that dwell in the Portland Futsal Men's Fourth Division. This league sits a mere 9,874 levels below the professional game, and thus we often find ourselves matched against players much, much better than us. Okay, *I* often find myself up against players much, much better than *me*. At the moment, I haven't scored a goal in about six months, in a variant of soccer that sometimes generates twenty or more goals in a forty-six-minute match. The Unicorns could improve immediately by cutting me loose and replacing me

with just about any available human being. They can't do that,
though, because I'm the manager. Ha!

Futsal, a kind of indoor soccer (the name compresses *fútbol
de salon*, literally something like "room football") invented by
bored Uruguayans during some 1930s wintertime, features five
players a side, tight boundary lines, and superspeedy play. Its
compact spaces and scherzo tempo are supposed to work wonders for one's ball-handling, passing, and tactical skills. South
Americans love futsal—in Buenos Aires, you see five-a-side
courts stuffed into every available nook of urban space, including underneath freeways—and the game allegedly helps foster
the continent's trademark soccer finesse and artistry. That's the
sales pitch, anyway, which I'm not sure I buy. I've now played
for about two years without any detectable improvement whatsoever. Caveat emptor, I guess—though other Unicorns' results
vary. One of our former mainstays, a Croatian American tower
we call Big Nick, found it necessary to excuse himself halfway
through our very first game to run into the alley behind the arena
and vomit. Big Nick matured into a very capable performer,
with something of an iron constitution. I once found him sitting
on the curb before a game, power-drinking from a large brown
bottle, and he played just fine that night, with no digestive ill
effects. Such are the character-building wonders of sport.

Besides our liberal policy regarding pregame lubrication,
the Unicorns operate a vigorous diversity program: we have
Americans *and* Englishmen on the squad; the Flying Dutchman,
a Michigander who might conceivably qualify for a Netherlands
passport; and one guy, Liverpool Mike, whose national origin
is an indeterminate blend of England, Ireland, and New Hamp-
shire. Our Italophile Nebraskan, Nicolhino ("Little Nick"), left

the team some time ago, and an early Chinese-Jewish-Vermonter recruit didn't stick around long. But the intermittent presence of the Stag,* an Arizonan, and your bumbling correspondent ensures that our pan-U.S. contingent remains strong. The Ginger Prince, some kind of rocket scientist from England, tends to score the most goals; Iron Jan, an Anglo-German who spawned an American family, scores from midfield regularly; the Berkshire Bomber, from the wilds south of London, sends the most surreally brilliant mass e-mails. We even have an Oregon native in the ranks: Dangerous Dave is perhaps our fiercest competitor. The problem with Dangerous Dave is that he's often out with injuries suffered playing with his gay softball team or some damn thing. He plays about four sports a week and hurts himself all the time. We once considered signing up his one-man hairstyling business as our shirt sponsor—we thought "A Flair for Hair" would look good in an italic script—but now would be content if he could heal up long enough to play a whole season. We need all the help we can get. A twenty-two-year-old with sharp reflexes and zero regard for his own physical safety comes in handy, even if he does have a fauxhawk.

I would venture to guess that a Unicorns game makes an unedifying spectacle. A bunch of slow, sorta-kinda in-shape men, most in their thirties, some beyond, struggling to string three passes together, employing a when-all-else-fails-foul-them defense, screaming "Who are you marking?" and "I've got no movement, Blue!"—not exactly a treat for the neutral spectator. We yell a lot—shouting is my main contribution—and sometimes

---

*On the subject of nicknames: an automated online "Brazilian soccer name generator" bequeathed me the highly unfortunate "Zildo." It seems to have stuck.

collapse into mutual recrimination after surrendering a goal. We consider a season in which we win as much as we lose a success, provided we also defeat our archrivals to claim the informal trophy we cleverly dub "the Rivals Cup." Still, from time to time the so-called Beautiful Game ambushes us out of nowhere. The Berkshire Bomber executes a pretty step-over. I kick a ball through a snarl of defenders and the Stag one-times it into the net. A backheel pass connects. Big Nick, drafted into semipermanent goalkeeping duty because his wingspan is roughly as wide as the goal, delivered many improbable acrobatic saves.

In any case, the game itself is not really the important thing—that would be going to the pub afterward. Our bar of choice stands just down the street from the futsal arena. It's not one of those shiny imitation British or mail-order Irish joints where the bartenders carve little shamrocks in the foam of your six-dollar Guinness, but rather a friendly, scuffed-up neighborhood tavern. They serve beer in mason jars when they run short of pint glasses, and the food menu comes straight out of the deep fryer. (The owner once told us that he's had two requests for salad in two years.) It's an all-American place in every way, no less so for the fact that it keeps at least one TV tuned to an all-soccer channel. We show up, battered and sweaty, grab mason jars, commandeer a table, and talk for an hour or two. I'm not a sports-medicine expert, so I don't know what this regime—run around for less than an hour (with frequent breaks on the bench); drink two or three pints of grainy microbrew; eat French fries—yields in terms of a physical-fitness dividend.

Cardiac health and body-fat considerations notwithstanding, we do reap some remarkable benefits from our postmatch routine. One night, we heard the tale of how one Unicorn accidentally discovered, via an office-computer indiscretion, that his boss was an avid female impersonator. The Stag once told a story about a college lacrosse injury that lasted about half an hour (the story, that is) and left us all amazed that he went on to father two children. We all get to make fun of Dangerous Dave for not recognizing the Doors when they come on the juke-box. He really is disgustingly young. To me, this beery leisure makes the mundane chaos of life—jobs, businesses, families, taxes, houses, aging bodies, et cetera—look amusing rather than overwhelming. While we know each other, in various configurations, from civilian life, the Unicorns do not exist as a group outside the context of soccer. I've known Liverpool Mike for years, for example, but he pulled Big Nick into the team, and Big Nick, in turn, recruited the Berkshire Bomber. I know the Stag; the Stag knows the Ginger Prince; ergo the Stag is indirectly responsible for a hat trick in our average game. We win or lose as a social organism rather than a squad assembled with anything like athletic ability in mind. Without the team, I never would have met most of these guys. My life would be poorer, and I wouldn't even realize it. Facebook has nothing on the Unicorns.

After a year spent in Iowa cornfields, on Texas roller derby side-lines, hanging out with D.C. soccer fans, braving the Portland Challenge, and failing to sword-fight, I realized that the only thing wrong with sports was how I approached them: as a product I enjoyed as a passive spectator. Now my understanding of the sports world begins with what happens to the Unicorns on Thursday nights. Even when our economy goes insane, Americans in general have plenty of chances to kick back. What we need are more chances to act. That deficit obviously reaches far beyond sport, but I learned that sports do afford a rare opportunity for intimate, visceral, free experience. In an increasingly mediated, prepackaged, artificial world, the real renegade move is simple: do something.

I may always be a terrible player, but I consider my soccer career a success. The same could be said for my overlapping stints as a Hash House Harrier, fencer, roller derby correspondent, croquet team owner, bike polo pundit, field hockey has-been—all the illogical, impractical, and absurd roles sports play in my life. These adventures, among other things, provided a fresh lesson on how great life can be away from the electronic haze that has become our shared ambient environment. Life is short and uncertain. Sports offer many different opportunities to taste more of its flavors.

I'm not against mainstream sports—in fact, I love them. Sometimes you need to absorb the majesty of the best in the world. Usain Bolt losing his mind twenty meters from the Olympic finish line (and crushing his rivals anyway); Lionel Messi lacing through a defense like the world's most mild-mannered jewel thief; the homeschooled human circus that is Tim Tebow— all provide illuminating glimpses of human potential, physical grace, and raw emotion. But other times there's no substitute for firsthand experience. You need to stick your own head between two rugby players' legs and let them compact your skull. You need to gamble dignity and sobriety against the possibility of a good time with a profane drinking/running club. The back roads of Iowa hold just as much potential for grand accomplishment as major stadiums, and a championship roller derby bout easily matches a Yankees–Red Sox series for ferocity and drama.

The major leagues provide finely honed entertainment and riveting stories. But a journey to the outer fringe of American sports supplies something more: a reminder of just how diverse, kinetic, funny, and creative our country can be. Alley cat racing and fencing with your eyes closed may not be for everyone, but we all need to engage the world, both for our own health and sanity and in the name of the general welfare.

Sports exercise our higher social functions, fuel our dreams, and trigger the sensory animal pleasures that give our evolved consciousness its earthy roots. They remind us both of the body's capacity for excellence and its frequent and often hilarious fallibility. In the last story in his *Sportsman's Notebook*, nineteenth-century Russian writer Ivan Turgenev takes a ramble through reality as experienced by the old-world outdoorsman: "You walk along the forest edge, you watch your dog, but all the time . . . the imagination hovers and darts hither and thither like a bird. . . ." The world has changed since Turgenev's day—unfortunately, vast snow-white beards no longer figure in the literary man's uniform—but it's still out there, as rough textured, brawny, and delicate as ever. Too many forces in our lives push us inside, away from that world and each other. Take a walk. Go horseback riding. Throw a rock at a river. Join a team. Start a team. Start a league. Chart your own path to athletic glory. It's time to live the Sporting Life.

NOTES, RESOURCES, AND CONTACTS

My analogy between modern mainstream sports and stadium rock owes a debt of inspiration to a column by *Guardian* journalist Richard Williams. Read his piece here: guardian.co.uk/sport/blog/2008/may/12/stadiumrockoftopflightloo.

1. ON THE HASH HOUSE HARRIERS

Every major city in the United States boasts at least one Hash House Harriers kennel, as do many minor ones. Most kennels welcome new members. An exhaustive global directory of HHH kennels can be found at the World Hash House Harriers Home Page: www.gthhh.com. A comprehensive collection of other contacts and background information can be found at http://harrier.net.

Advisory:

Local authorities may take an unwelcome interest in hash-related activities. After the September 11, 2001, terror attacks, for example, police investigated a number of hash trails, suspecting that the white chalk or flour trail markings might, in fact, be anthrax.

A Few Hash House Harriers Songs

(Adapted from the Boston Hash House Harriers Hymnal, available in its
rude entirety at http://bostonhash.com)

"Why Are We Waiting"
(Melody: "O Come, All Ye Faithful")
(Traditionally sung when a hasher is taking too long to guzzle a beer)

Why are we waiting?
We could be fornicating
Oh, why are we waiting
So fucking long?
(Repeat ad nauseum)

"Meet the Hashers"
(Melody: "The Flintstones Theme")

Hashers
Meet the Hashers
They're the biggest drunks in history
From the town of _____
They're the leaders in debauchery
Half-minds
Trailing shiggy through the years
Watch them as they drink a lot of beers!

"The Visitors Song"
(Melody: "Ach Du Lieber")

Here's to brother (sister) hashers
Here's to brother (sister) hashers
Here's to brother (sister) hashers

> May they chug-a-lug
> They're happy, they're jolly
> THEY'RE FUCKED UP, BY GOLLY!
> Here's to brother (sister) hashers
> May they chug-a-lug!

A Few of the Many Drinks Mary Lou and Pabst Smear Have Consumed During Hash Runs

Margarita and daiquiri buckets

Jell-O shots (various liquors)

Boilermakers (one shotglass of whiskey—bourbon, rye, Scotch, Irish, whatever—dropped into a ten-ounce glass of beer)

Red Bull and vodka

Jägermeister

Mike's Hard Lemonade

Irish car bombs (equal parts Jameson whiskey and Bailey's Irish Cream mixed in a shotglass, dropped into a pint of Guinness Stout; to be consumed as quickly as possible)

Bloody Marys (ingredients will vary)

"Delicious fruity drinks"

"All kinds of crappy pints and fifths of booze"

"That doesn't even begin to include the beer. We're pretty snobby about beer here in the Pacific Northwest. I've heard that other hashes don't really drink high-end beer like we do."

2. ON BIKE MESSENGER RACING AND RELATED SPORTS

The International Federation of Bike Messenger Associations' schedule of upcoming national and international alley cat racing events can be found at www.messengers.org. The Portland United Messenger Association's website is http://portlandmessenger.org.

Joel Metz's history of cycle-messenger racing in Paris between 1895 and the 1960s can be found at www.blackbirdsf.org/courier racing.

3. ON THE TRANS IOWA

At the moment of this writing, the Trans Iowa's electronic headquarters can be found at http://transiowa.blogspot.com; the site includes ample information on logistics and complete results of all past versions. After expressing some doubt about whether he'd ever do the damn-fool thing again, Guitar Ted staged Trans Iowa Version 4 in the spring of 2008. Ira Ryan did not return to defend his title. The race, truncated by severe weather conditions, was won by someone called John Gorilla. In Trans Iowa Version 5, in spring 2009, a rider named Joe Meiser took first place. Tim Ek finished in a tie for second.

The Trans Iowa, the Dirty Kanza, the Red ASSiniboine, and other similar races owe at least some debt to the "Curiak rules," a philosophy of self-supported racing developed by legendary mountain biker Mike Curiak. Curiak, a mountain-bike wheel builder based in Colorado, explained via e-mail: "The underlying idea is simply for each racer to be 100 percent responsible for themselves from start to finish. . . . It's a higher standard than racing has had in a long time (ever?) but it's extremely rewarding to finish an already difficult race even under these sorts of rules. And that's attractive to a lot of people."

Ira Ryan's workshop website is http://iraryancycles.com. Ira's blog, wherein he recounts rides and offers thoughts about the state of cycling, resides at http://iraryanbicycles.wordpress.com. Find the Rapha Continental ride documentation project at http://rapha.cc/rapha-continental.

The Paris-Roubaix road race, otherwise known as "the Hell of the North," is the subject an excellent 1976 documentary, *A Sunday in Hell*. The film achieves a near-hypnotic pace and tone, and features an incredible shot of Eddy Merckx chilling in a powder blue denim jacket and awesome sunglasses, looking like a thug from a Tarantino movie. Check it out.

Geoffrey Wheatcroft's *Le Tour: A History of the Tour de France* is published in paperback by Pocket Books.

4. ON THE KENTUCKY DERBY

Here's how to make a mint julep:

> Make simple syrup by boiling equal measures of sugar and water for about five minutes. Cool. If possible, steep fresh mint in the syrup in the refrigerator overnight.

> Fill glasses with crushed ice. Pour in one part syrup to two parts bourbon. Stir.

> Garnish with mint and let stand to chill.

> Consume. The author suggests a two-julep maximum, but consenting adults can make their own decisions.

5. ON SOCCER FANDOM

Among many, many Internet sites created by and for Major League Soccer supporters and other soccer fans in North America, I commend the following to your attention: http://section8chicago .com; http://screaming-eagles.com; http://talktimbers.com; and www .ultrasmontreal.com. A true free-for-all of debate, rumor, ad hominem attacks, and other Internet mainstays can always be found at www .bigsoccer.com.

Along with books cited in the chapter (Tim Parks's *A Season with Verona*, Eduardo Galeano's *Soccer in Sun and Shadow*, Franklin Foer's *How Soccer Explains the World*), the author found the following works helpful:

> *Rammer Jammer Yellow Hammer* by Warren St. John (New York: Three Rivers, 2004): a firsthand account of a year with fans of University of Alabama football (the other kind) and a meditation on what fandom means.
> *Better to Reign in Hell: Inside the Raiders Fan Empire* by Jim Miller and Kelly Mayhew (New York: New Press, 2005): a harrowing look at the untamed culture of Oakland Raiders football (the other kind) fans.

Welcome to the Terrordome: The Pain, Politics, and Promise of Sports by Dave Zirin (Chicago: Haymarket, 2007): Zirin, who writes a regular column accessible at http://edgeofsports.com, analyzes the culture, business, and history of sports from a left/liberal perspective. He is particularly incisive on the subject of public stadium subsidies.

The Ball Is Round: A Global History of Soccer by David Goldblatt (New York: Riverhead, 2008): a stunning history of soccer worldwide, with in-depth consideration given to fan culture and globalization.

6. ON THE FOREIGN AND ARCANE
Please see:

http://philthepower.com
http://cresta-run.com
http://plymouth-banjul.com
http://terristiller.com

7. ON DIY SPORTS IN PORTLAND AND BEYOND
The official rules of nine-wicket croquet can be found at www
.croquet.com/croquet/ninewicketarticle.cfm. For croquet hospitality provisions, I recommend the Pimm's Cup: three parts Pimm's No. 1 to two parts soda, garnished with fruit, herbs, and (most importantly) cucumber slices, to taste. Be careful with croquet, however: the sport is more subversive than one might expect. According to an 1878 edition of the *American Christian Review* (cited in Dave Zirin's *A People's History of Sports in the United States* [New York: New Press, 2008]), croquet poses a critical danger to female virtue in particular. The *ACR's* twelve steps to moral downfall include:"#3. Croquet party. #4. Picnic and croquet party. #5. Picnic, croquet and dance. . . . #12. Ruin."

For another game with DIY league potential, check out cornhole. It's not what you think. See www.playcornhole.org for more information. A friend of mine constructed his own cornhole set, spending less than fifty dollars on materials. His membership in the American Cornhole Association allows him to host sanctioned tournaments in his driveway.

The extensive chronicles of the Portland Challenge reside at www.portlandchallenge.blogspot.com. Jay Boss Rubin billed the 2007 Portland Challenge, in which I piloted the Shoe Boat, as the "fifth and final" installment of the series. He also promises, however, to revive the Challenge in a new form. A Swahili-language enthusiast, Jay used the Challenge as an opportunity to collect donations for an orphanage in Tanzania. (Hence, I learned, the presence of my shipmate Elvis.) After the Challenge, he explained that the phrase "Gone to Bongo" refers to a Swahili slang word for "brains." I still do not understand it at all.

The Burnside Skatepark traditionally celebrates its anniversary with a huge street party on Halloween. Make it if you can. Among the many fictional and nonfictional representations of and references to Burnside, see Gus Van Sant's film *Paranoid Park* (which offers some excellent action footage, if not any particular insight into skate culture) and the documentary *Full Tilt Boogie,* which can be viewed at http://burnsideproject.blogspot.com.

The world of urban golf relies heavily on MySpace. Check out www.myspace.com/nwurbansports for extensive links and listings. A brand-new Kooler Klub or similar product costs somewhere in the neighborhood of fifty dollars. Assuming forty-eight ounces of liquid carrying capacity, a Kooler Klub should hold about sixteen standard martinis. Please plan accordingly.

8. ON ROLLER DERBY

The Women's Flat Track Derby Association can be found at www .wftda.org, a site that links to all the association's member cities. A number of significant sites offer derby news and comment, including www.derbynewsnetwork.com. *Blood & Thunder* magazine can be found online at http://bloodandthundermag.com.

I count two book-length examinations of the roller derby revival: *Roller Derby: The History and All-Girl Revival of the Greatest Sport on Wheels* by Catherine Mabe (Golden, CO: Speck, 2007) and *Rollergirl: Totally True Tales from the Track* by Melissa Joulwan (New York: Touchstone, 2007).

As intercity competition grows within the United States, international competition may be next. In 2008, an all-Canada team traveled to Great Britain for matches with Glasgow's Irn Bruisers, London Brawling, and Birmingham Blitz Dames.

The 2008 WFTDA National Championship was held in Portland. The Gotham Girls defeated Windy City in the final round. Olympia, Washington's unheralded Cosa Nostra Donnas came out of nowhere to win the 2009 title.

9. ON FALCONRY

More information on falconry can be found at the website of the North American Falconers Association: http://n-a-f-a.org. The site notes: "Few people thrilling at the brief, intense magic of a trained hawk in flight realize the intense demands placed upon one who aspires to be a falconer. Even fewer are willing to make the necessary sacrifices."

10. ON FENCING

The United States Fencing Association can be found at http://usfencing.org. You can watch fencing to your heart's content—albeit with a characteristic lack of commentary, explanation, or other helpful hints for the outsider, at http://fencingchannel.tv.

Richard Cohen's *By the Sword* is published by Random House. Aldo Nadi's *On Fencing* is published by the Laureate Press.

11. ON BIKE POLO

For more on the street bike polo movement, see http://nycbikepolo.com (info on the New York devotees who gather at a park on Hester Street in Chinatown), www.madbikepolo.org (the Madison, Wisconsin, scene), http://seattlebikepolo.com, hardcourtbikepolo.com, etc., etc., etc. . . .

ACKNOWLEDGMENTS

Many people helped make this book what it is—whereas the Author assumes sole responsibility for anything it is *not*, if you get the drift. I preemptively regret any omissions from the following Renegade Roster of Honor.

This tale would not exist without its protagonists: the bold, creative, and welcoming men and women of the American sporting underground. I thank the Cross Crusade and Oregon Jesters Rugby Football Club for shedding invaluable light on just how fun it can be to get dirty. Tyler Lynch and the Portland Humpin' Hash House Harriers then taught me what "dirty" really means. Joel Metz and Drew Kinney helped me understand alley cat racing. The men of the Trans Iowa—Ira Ryan, Mark "Guitar Ted" Stevenson, Tim Ek, Marcin Nowak and Team Polska and the rest—deserve to become sporting folk heroes; they were certainly generous with their time, insight, and passion. David Lifton, Kim Klyberg and the rest of the Screaming Eagles and the staff of DC United made my visit to RFK possible and enlightening; the staffs of the Chicago Fire and Portland Timbers also helped out along the way. The likes of Bruce McGuire,

Bryan James, and Liam Murtagh are turning America into a soccer nation whether anyone likes it or not. Respect is due to the Timbers Army. Mike DiGiacomo, Luca Marenzi and Lady Brabazon of Tara graciously provided insight on the phenomenon of the Cresta Run. Terris Tiller took time out from Olympic training to talk to me when this project was in its most embryonic and vague phase. Jeff Heisler, Mike Merrill, and the rest of the Portland Croquet League allowed me to join their coven of tycoons. Jay Boss Rubin should be an inspiration to all of us. Chad Balcom served as guide and bodyguard at the Burnside Skatepark. Scott Mazariegos introduced me to a worldwide conspiracy of urban golfers, who helped with wit and enthusiasm. I am deeply indebted to the women of roller derby—Apocalipzz, Ginger Snap, Ying o' Fire, Sparkle Plenty, Kami Sutra, Bloody Mary and many others—for explaining their sporting revolution. Bob Welle kindly welcomed me into his home, shared his love for falconry and kept Seven from attacking me. My failures as a swordsman are not the fault of Rocky Beach, Maitre Calvert, or anyone else at the Salle Trois Armes Fencing Center. Lindsay Campbell interrupted her national championship and World Cup quests to talk about the adventurous and hardworking life of a competitive amateur sportswoman. Thanks to the Polo Haus and the Axles of Evil for their hospitality. Thanks to the gentlemen (and lady) of the Albina Going Football Club for continued tolerance.

Behind the scenes, Melissa Flashman has worked tirelessly on *Renegade*'s behalf for nearly four years, with the able assistance of Adam Friedstein and many others at Trident Media Group. A writer could not wish for a better consigliere. Megan Lynch and Riverhead Books took a chance on a rookie from the provinces; Megan turned out to understand this book better than I did. To paraphrase Wooster, the woman must practically live on fish—she has an enormous brain. The indefatigable Sarah Bowlin and Riverhead's sharp design, editing, and marketing staffs saw this enterprise through. The pleasure is all mine. The fantastic collections and helpful staffs of the Multnomah County Public Library and the New York Public Library served up the archival goods. Steve Rinella, William Finnegan, and Bill McKibben kindly read the manuscript and left me blushing. Corey Arnold took an overly flattering photo.

As a freelance hack in what might euphemistically be described as "challenging times," I am indebted to the steadfast journalists, editors, and publishers who fostered me, trained me, and now keep my small artisan's shop in business. Wayne Seitz at Hellgate High School and all the fine profs at the University of Montana School of Journalism got me started. The old-school crew at the *Missoula Independent* gave me a tumultuous cub reporter's entrée to the trade. At *Willamette Week*, I worked with superb writers and sharp, patient editors—Brooks, Zusman, Schrag, and Stern, among others. During this excursion, *Good Magazine* and the late, lamented *New York Times Play Magazine* provided invaluable support in the form of assignments. As for the rest, you know who you are. Keep the ink-stained flag flying.

In matters personal, I am, naturally, tempted to thank everyone I've ever known, because I am the luckiest guy on earth—top percentile, anyway. As for proximate factors, Taylor Clark did yeoman work to help me launch this book; between them, he and Chris Lydgate had the dubious pleasure of sharing my workshop through years of laborious construction. Dan Oko and Christina Willis provided the finest of Austin crash pads; Matt Marden and Bobby Graham did the same in New York City.

I am rich in friends and family, and happen to come from a line of writers and readers who have encouraged and mentored me for decades. Undying thanks go to my mom, Laurie, and stepdad, Tim; my dad, Jay, and the lovely and talented Mary-Anne; my ever-nurturing grandmother Peggy; Uncle Harry and Aunt Patty; and aunts Vickie and Suzanne. My brother Chad's talent, brains, and lifelong comradeship are a permanent inspiration. Cousin Grady deserves special mention because his sporting outlook on life helped spark this book; Cousin Ali because she has been a model of madcap creativity for three decades now. Aunt Katie and Uncle Daryl provide sterling models of both the writing and sporting life. I owe George, *il padrino*, my vocation and much else besides—to say more would be fulsome. I said I was lucky. How lucky? I even have fantastic in-laws. Susan, Helen, Don, Gretchen, Lisa and Jeff, Heather and Dan and the kids— all provided encouragement and support during the saga.

A complete roster of friends and allies who played some moral-support or object-example role, witting or not, in this book's creation would kill an unconscionable number of trees or innocent pixels. In Portland: Dan E. (of Moscow and Mumblage infamy), Margaret and Janiac; DR; Audrey, Luke, Theo and Alex; Brooke, Lenore and Jeremy, my Shoe Boat captain; Amelia; the Graham clan; the greater Missoula exile colony (Oro y Plata!); and many others. In Montana: Courtney; Jason; Leif and Katie; Erika and Dave; Lagan; Andy S.; the whole rock scene circa 1993–1999; the Missoula literary community (McNamers, Di Salvatore, Montana MFA, Crumley [RIP], the bookstores, etc.) then and always; and many others. Beyond: Tina; the Granite State Connection; and many others.

Christina and Cash are the joys of my life. I can't thank them enough, ever.

Zach Dundas grew up in Missoula, Montana, and graduated from the University of Montana School of Journalism. He worked as a reporter and editor at the *Missoula Independent* and Portland's *Willamette Week*. His writing has appeared in *Good, Monocle, Maxim*, the *San Francisco Chronicle, Portland Monthly*, and elsewhere. He lives in Portland, Oregon, with his wife and their son.